BECOMING FROZEN

MEMOIR OF A FIRST YEAR IN ALASKA

By Jill Homer

Arctic Glass Press

www.arcticglasspress.com

2240 Homestead Court, No. 307,
Los Altos, California, 94024

Distributed in the United States by Arctic Glass Press, www.arcticglasspress.com

Editor: Tonya Simpson
Cover Design: Jill Homer
Interior Design: Jill Homer
Interior Photos: Jill Homer

Cover: Ice coats the shore of the Cook Inlet near Anchorage, Alaska. Photo by David Shaw, Wild Imagination Photography.

Back Cover: Bike commuting home from work. Photo by Jill Homer.

ISBN 978-0692496329

This is a work of narrative nonfiction. Dialogue and events herein have been recounted to the best of the author's memory.

Contents

Alaska, Again

So this is my new journal about moving to Homer, Alaska — a place where it snows in October, where moose traipse through my backyard, and where everyone can spell my last name but if you can't spell "Xtratuf," well, so help you God.

This is the obligatory first entry where I have to explain to people that I live in Alaska. I lived for a while in Idaho Falls, Idaho — home of potatoes and the self-proclaimed "northern" Mormons, and life was good. But after a brutal hot summer and several months of distant coercion from Geoff, I somehow was talked into moving to Alaska — home of grizzly bears and the self-proclaimed "northern" Libertarians. And life's still good. I guess it's possible to be happy anywhere — just as long as those studded mountain bike tires and stack of DVDs arrive soon.

We arrived, on a windy day in mid-September, at the far edge of the world. Three thousand miles, a similar number of days of adulthood, and every decision I'd ever made all came to an abrupt point on a roadside pullout overlooking the ocean — the final mile of the North American highway system.

"We made it!" I announced as I walked across the parking lot. The pavement abruptly ended at a sheer bluff that dropped directly into the sea, several hundred feet below a crumbling ledge. Winds stirred up a cloud of sand that rained into the roiling surf. I turned to my boyfriend, Geoff, and shouted over the gusts. "Even the beach is intense in Alaska!"

I was too enamored with the dramatic cut of the coastline to acknowledge that this country had already been claimed by countless halibut fishermen, artists and photo-snapping retirees in RVs. Wind whipped my hair into a frenzy as I stood on the cusp of the cliff, surveying my new kingdom. Far below, a promenade of white waves rippled across Cook Inlet. To the east, a narrow spit of land lolled like a tongue into the calmer blue waters of Kachemak Bay. To the south, a cone-shaped volcano appeared as a menacing silhouette. A ring of snowcapped mountains wrapped around the horizon like a fortress, encapsulating this place as the final bastion of civilization. Homer, Alaska. The End of the Road.

"Wow, this is where we live!" I yelled as Geoff sprinted around my sagging '96 Geo Prism to tie down a tangle of flapping straps on top of the car.

"Are you going to help me?" he called back.

"Sure," I muttered, turning away from new discoveries to refasten the canvas carrier for what must have been the forty-seventh time. Only a few more miles remained in our thirty-two-hundred-mile journey from Idaho to the last town on the Rand McNally map. Why not let the straps fly free?

But I couldn't complain because the contents of my entire life, not Geoff's, were stashed away in the red sedan. And it was my career, not Geoff's, that brought us to this isolated community of three thousand people at the tip of the Kenai Peninsula. Although Alaska had been Geoff's dream, Homer was my decision. I quietly believed it was our last best hope — a place to rebuild our lives beyond the trajectory of past missteps.

I already felt like a rugged Alaskan, but from a local point of view, I was still an obvious outsider. I was twenty-six years old with dirty blonde hair, freckles, hints of a tan, a Bad Religion T-Shirt, and black leather shoes that were far too shiny for this muddy town. Geoff was twenty-nine and looked more like an Alaskan with a hippie vibe: Long auburn hair, a trim beard, cargo pants and flannel. He had the muscled, slender body of a runner — although at the time, his passions were whitewater rafting and technical mountain biking. A free-ranging soul who refused to be tied down, Geoff had spent the past few months rambling around the Last Frontier while I worked late nights as a copy editor at a newspaper in Idaho Falls, Idaho. My most recent passions included riding my road bike for long distances alone, and staying up until dawn at riotous parties with my co-workers.

Geoff's and my relationship had spent the past year on the rocks, twisted around four years' worth of unbounded adventures and subsequently incompatible attempts at domestic partnership. I'd come to believe that our shared passion for the outdoors might be the only thread still holding us together, which is why I moved from Utah to Idaho one year earlier. Living in separate states only served to slow the unraveling of our relationship rather than sever it entirely. I still traveled to Utah every weekend, holding onto the strands of a fun but ultimately unsatisfying weekend relationship. Then, just before summer came, Geoff announced he was traveling to Alaska for three months, and had no plans to return in the fall. August rolled around, and I was still working up the courage to make the split official when Geoff showed up at my doorstep in Idaho. I hadn't expected to see him — he'd flown all the way from Alaska just to talk with me. We went camping in the Salt River Mountains of Wyoming and let soul-rending scenery open an honest discussion about our fractured love.

After that weekend, Geoff remained in Idaho with me for a few more nights. He raved about his life in the North as the hot sun cast Idaho Falls in unfavorable light.

"Don't you think you should just come to Alaska with me?" Geoff suggested nonchalantly, as though he were asking me out to dinner. Wildfire smoke filled the August air, and I'd arrived at the conclusion that I had little to lose. Geoff sat next to me at a computer in the public library as I scrolled through journalism jobs in the northern state. At the time there was only one listing for which I was qualified — an arts reporter, page designer and copy editor (all one position) at a small weekly newspaper, the Homer Tribune.

"Homer?" Geoff said with an air of strong disapproval. "I mean, it's okay, but it's really touristy. Remember that night we spent on the Homer Spit?"

I did. It was two years earlier, on the Fourth of July. Geoff, two other friends, and I were traveling dirt-bag style across Alaska during a summer-long road trip. We just happened to end up in Homer on the most popular day of the year for tourists. Tents were crammed stake-to-stake on a narrow strip of sand between Homer Spit Road and the sea, which was the only place available for visitor camping. Fireworks exploded and children screamed into the dusky hours of morning. The four of us huddled together in a single small tent — because the campground charged by the tent — and didn't sleep at all. We fled town early the next morning without even bothering to explore the community beyond the crowded spit. Still, the four of us felt confident in our assessment that Homer was the worst town in all of Alaska.

"It's probably better than we remember," I said. "Plus, it's really the only good job on here. I can't move to Alaska without a job."

I typed in my basic information and attached a resume to the e-mail. Within an hour, I received a call from the Tribune's editor, who conducted an interview on the spot. She sent me a job offer the following day. I put in my two-week notice at the Idaho Falls Post-Register, and then broke the news to my parents in Utah.

"It's a long story but I decided I'm going to move with Geoff to Alaska," I blurted into the phone. "Um, in about two weeks." The call did not go over well.

Just two weeks earlier, I celebrated my twenty-sixth birthday with friends in Idaho and toasted my freedom with new certainty that Geoff and I were done for good. That was August 20. By September 5, I had quit my job, broken an apartment lease, packed up or sold all of my belongings, and committed to live in a region three-thousand miles away from anything familiar, in a town I remembered with strong disdain, with a man who continued to make no promises about the future. Somewhere in the stratosphere of renewed optimism, this plan was completely reasonable. At the very least, change was moving too quickly for logic to intervene.

✳ ✳ ✳ ✳ ✳

After Geoff was satisfied with the latest strap configurations, we started up the Prism's overworked engine. The car made its final descent of the journey with two bicycles swaying on the roof rack and stray canvas straps still flapping in the breeze. Cassette tapes, Subway wrappers and potato chip crumbs were strewn about the floor, and the contents of my whole existence — clothing, dishes, camping gear and a few small appliances — were crammed in the trunk and back seat. We had been driving almost nonstop for five days, relying on books on tape and obscure Canadian radio stations to avoid more difficult conversations, including most of the specifics about building a life in Alaska. Only when we discussed Hillary Clinton's autobiography, or laughed at "Car Talk," did I feel glimmers of hope that I wasn't sitting next to a stranger. We had spent the better part of a year living apart, and in many ways we needed to re-acquaint ourselves.

All through Canada we slept in our tent, and I'd wake up shivering and drenched in sweat. I told family and friends that my current lack of commitments and the promise of great adventure were the impetus for moving north.

But these assertions were largely a veil for the less glamorous truth. My love for Geoff meant a lot to me, and this was the last chance for our sputtering four-year relationship. Admitting this, even quietly to myself, only perpetuated the well-worn cliché of a hapless woman following a man to the Last Frontier. So I stuck to my adventure story.

We pulled the car into a parking lot on the Homer Spit, at the same horrible campground we fled two years earlier. It was the only place we could conceive as a starting point. A few tattered tents were scattered along the beach, adorned with hallmarks of long-term residency such as makeshift driftwood tables and tarps flapping in the wind. Fishing boats bobbed in a harbor across the road. The boardwalk was quiet; the shops were shuttered. Just a few days earlier, I was still wilting through an unseasonably hot summer in Idaho. Here, a brisk wind tore along the coastline, carrying a wintry bite. Summer was already over, and most of the tourists had gone home.

"I don't really want to camp here again," Geoff announced, and I agreed the beach looked more like a homeless encampment than a campground. "Let's go find a phone book."

At the town's first (and possibly only) gas station, Geoff sifted through the phone book for campground listings while I walked inside the convenience store to buy a newspaper. The printing quality of the Homer Tribune was colorful and clear, but the shape of the newspaper — tabloid, which is about half the size of a regular newspaper — caught me off guard. I skimmed the articles with trepidation — I was scheduled to report to the office the following morning. Remembering this obligation made me feel queasy, so I flipped to the classified ads.

"Check this out," I said as I walked outside to meet Geoff, who had just used the pay phone to contact a private campground owner. "There's a rental ad for a cabin in town. It's two-thousand square feet on two acres of land for just eight hundred a month. It says there's another tenant in the basement, but it sounds like a really good deal."

Geoff squinted at the text. "Diamond Ridge? Where's that?"

I shrugged. "I don't know. The address is in Homer. How far away could it be?"

I took Geoff's place at the pay phone and called the number listed in the ad. A woman named Robin answered, sounding harried and more than a little distracted. "Of course, in Homer," she replied after I'd told her our entire story and finally read the newspaper ad verbatim. "You'll have to forgive me. We haven't had a call on the house in days. In fact, I just dropped the price from nine hundred. We live in Hawaii, so I'm not there, but I'll give you the address. Check it out and if you're interested, call back and I'll have someone come up with a key and show it to you."

Even with Robin's instructions and directions from convenience store clerk, it still took us forty-five minutes to find the house. We drove up a steep, switch-backing road that led to a ridge twelve-hundred feet above the coast. From there, a narrow gravel road passed wooded properties and rustic homes. Every structure had a haphazard look to it, as though the money ran out before construction was finished. Some cabins were wrapped in Tyveck insulation; others were accessorized with plywood outbuildings or mismatched additions. Some of the dwellings were outright strange — there was a bright red barn, a two-story structure with an uneven hexagonal shape, a cabin with a roof covered in sod and grass, and several yurts.

"Guess Homer doesn't have much in the way of building codes," I said as scanned the side streets. We drove down several cul-de-sacs that ended in empty lots filled with stacks of downed trees and broken appliances. Finally, we found the one we were looking for — Trail Court. The fittingly named road cut a narrow passage through alder branches and spruce trees. Geoff feathered the steering wheel to keep the car's bald tires from veering into muddy ruts. We passed a small clearing surrounded by a wire fence. On one side, a shaggy horse munched on grass. On the other, a moose lifted her head from a grove of fireweed stalks and blinked.

"Look," I whispered, afraid any sudden movement might scare the moose into darting in front of the car. "Look!"

"It's just a moose," Geoff said dismissively. "There are a lot of those around here. They're like squirrels."

"But this one is practically in the front yard," I said. "What if we're just taking out the trash someday and she decides to stomp us?"

"That's unlikely," Geoff said. "These are suburban moose. They don't care."

Diamond Ridge was unlike any suburb I had ever seen. Around the corner from the horse pasture, Trail Court dead-ended at a pyramid-shaped cabin. It was massive for an A-frame, at least three stories high, with the upper section painted brick red and the lower a yellowing shade of white. It had its own plywood outbuilding and a seemingly inoperable outhouse leaning against two spruce trees. The yard was a sea of white fuzz — fireweed stalks that had gone to seed.

No one answered the door at the lower level apartment, and the front door was locked. We circled around the porch and peered into the landscape windows. The entire first level was a single large room, with a set of stairs in the center that seemed to lead to a loft. The interior was lined in thick wooden beams and a finished pinewood floor. The walls were painted rust orange. There was a small kitchen in one corner and a door to what I presumed was a bathroom in another. These were the only features that gave it away as a home; otherwise, it looked like the empty lobby of a ski lodge, with a high ceiling and a grand view of the Kenai Mountains to the west.

"It's perfect," I gasped, almost beside myself with excitement. In a tourism-focused community like Homer, I would have expected to pay eight hundred dollars a month for a grimy studio apartment in a bad part of town. But here was two-thousand square feet of secluded cabin located on two acres of land surrounded by miles of open space, and it was affordable on a journalist's salary.

"Let's do it," Geoff agreed. "We should call that landlady now, before someone else comes to look at it."

Diamond Ridge had no reception for our out-of-state cell phones, so we got back in the car and raced seven miles back to the gas station pay phone. I breathlessly counted fourteen rings before a harried voice finally answered, "This is Robin."

"Robin, this is Jill. We just called about your cabin in Homer. Yeah, we want to move in. How do we apply?"

"Did Jen show you inside?" Robin asked, referring to the woman who lived in the basement.

"No, no one was home," I said. "We looked in through the window. We like it. That's enough for us."

Robin was silent for several seconds, clearly mulling the situation as my anxiety spiked. "Well great," she said. "Sounds good to me. I have a friend in town who's holding onto the keys. I'll have her drop them off at your office tomorrow. Where did you say you worked?"

"Um, Homer Tribune," I said. "But I don't know where exactly it is. I still need to look up the address. I, um, I haven't started work yet. I actually start tomorrow."

"Okay," Robin said. "I'll let her know. She'll have a lease you can sign too. It's a year lease. I'm looking for someone who wants to stay through the winter. Eight hundred dollars a month."

"Do you want us to fill out an application? Or background checks?"

Robin laughed. "Oh, no. That won't be necessary. You can move in anytime."

Geoff shook his head as I hung up the phone. Based on my side of the conversation, he thought she turned us down.

"She pretty much just said we could move in, like tomorrow."

"Wow. Really? That's trusting."

"I guess in Alaska they have less reason to be suspicious of people," I said. "I didn't even prove to her that I have a job."

"Works for us," Geoff said. "Where do we sign the lease?"

One of her friends is going to bring it to my office tomorrow, along with the keys.

"So what should we do about tonight?"

"I don't know. Did you find a campground?"

"Who needs a campground? We have a house. Let's go back up there and see if Jen is home. Maybe she'll let us in. If not, we can camp in the yard."

I felt dubious about squatting at the cabin without legal documents, but the gray sky threatened rain and a roof was an inviting prospect. Back on Trail Court, we hadn't even emerged from my car when I noticed a man with a long brown beard walking down the driveway.

"You two checking out Robin's place?" he asked as he approached us. The man was wearing a white T-shirt with orange vinyl rain pants draped loosely around his waist by black suspenders, and brown rubber boots. His hair was thin and stringy, his beard unruly, and he smiled in an exaggerated way that was both disarming and suspicious.

"Actually, we checked it out earlier," Geoff said. "We just talked to Robin. We're moving in tomorrow."

"Oh, so you're the new neighbors," the man grinned wider. "I live next door. Name's Mike."

"The place with the horse?" I asked. Mike nodded.

"What do you do?" Geoff asked.

"I'm an oyster farmer in Halibut Cove, across the Bay," Mike said. "You folks new to town?"

"Actually, we just got here today," I said. "We're moving from Idaho ... well, he was in Utah."

"Utah, huh?" Mike said. "You got work?"

"I'm starting work tomorrow at the Homer Tribune, one of the weekly newspapers in town," I said. "I'm an editor, and reporter, too."

"Tribune, yeah," Mike said. "I advertise with them." He turned to Geoff. "How about you?"

"I sell stuff on eBay, bike racks, bike parts and other stuff," Geoff said. "I'm thinking about looking for a side job in construction or something."

Mike broke out his manic smile again. "Tell you what, I have a job for you! Ever work on an oyster farm?"

Geoff laughed. "Um, no. How do you farm oysters?"

"Tell you what, it's easy," Mike said. "Just put the spat on a rope, drop it in from the boat, come back, pull up the rope, and there you have it. I could use some help on my boat, cleaning gear and other stuff."

"Do you go out for a few days at a time?" Geoff asked.

"Hell, no. I come back every night to see my wife. I like a warm bed. So do you want the job?"

Geoff shrugged. "Sure. Why not?"

"Great," Mike said. "I'm going back out again on Wednesday, early. 'Bout four o'clock. I'll come get you. Wear something warm. You two staying here now?"

"Not until tomorrow," I said. "Robin's friend is coming to drop off the keys at my office. We just wanted to check it out one more time."

"So where are you staying tonight?" Mike asked.

Geoff and I both shrugged.

"Tell you what, you don't need a key. I was in there last month helping with the remodel, and I'm pretty sure you can get in through that window," Mike said, pointing to a kitchen window that was fifteen feet off the ground. "Let me go get my ladder. I'll be right back."

As Mike jogged down the driveway, I nudged Geoff. "Do you really think it's a good idea to break into the house?" I whispered. "I mean, we technically haven't rented the place yet."

"Yeah, but we're as good as renters," Geoff said. "The landlady already said we could have the place."

"We haven't signed anything and we don't have any keys. A verbal agreement isn't going to cut it if the police show up."

"Who's going to call them? Mike?"

"True. Probably not him," I said. "That guy is pretty weird. He doesn't even know you and he offered you a job. We could be anyone, and he's helping us break into his neighbor's house. Are you going to take him up on the job offer?"

Geoff shrugged again. "Why not? I'll go out with him once. Even if he never pays me, it sounds pretty fun, going out on a boat and pulling up oyster pots."

I agreed. "I'm jealous, actually. I'd pay to do that."

Mike returned with a fifteen-foot ladder and directed us to the side of the house.

"You'll have to knock out the screen, but you should be able to slide in right there. I know it's high, but this is the only window that opens above the basement."

The "basement" was actually just the lowest level of the cabin, with the separate apartment that was hidden by the front and back balconies. It also didn't seem to contain any windows at all, as opposed to the upper level with its landscape windows that filled two walls.

"Looks tight," I said as Mike propped the ladder against the house, lending perspective to the small window.

"I'll check it out," Geoff said. He climbed to the top rung of the ladder, pried open the sliding glass, and tapped on the screen until it fell to the floor. He reached inside for some sort of handhold and wedged himself through the narrow gap. Three or four anxious minutes passed before he greeted Mike and me at the front door.

"It's nice in here," he said. "There's lot of space. The loft is smaller than I expected but there's still plenty of room for a bedroom. But check it out, this place is awesome."

Mike followed me inside and stood at the doorway as I surveyed the room. The top edge of the ceiling towered at least twenty feet over my head, and even in the waning daylight, the tall windows filled the room with light. Large trees surrounded the cabin, and the wooded back yard seemed to stretch all the way to the distant mountains. I had spent my adulthood living in small apartments, or crammed into a house with as many as nine other college students. I assumed I would have to work hard in cramped offices for years before I could branch out to a place of my own, without roommates or the ever-present noise of the city. Then Alaska abruptly landed in my path and offered this dream on a silver platter. At age twenty-six, I'd achieved the ultimate dirtbag dream: Inexpensive living, open space, plenty of outdoor activities nearby, and no crowds.

After Mike left, Geoff and I pulled a few bins from my car and spread our sleeping bags on the wood floor of the loft. "So what do you think?" I asked Geoff.

"This is great," Geoff said. "I'm glad we jumped on it. I really doubt we'd find anything better."

"What about Homer?" I asked. "Do you think you'll like it here?"

"Sure," Geoff said. "I mean, the mountains are a little far away, hard to reach from here at least. And it will probably be crazy touristy in the summer. We're far from Anchorage, too, and it's kind of going to suck to drive for five hours just to go to the airport. But yeah, I like the house. I like that guy Mike. I'm sure we'll meet other interesting people. It's definitely going to be a cool place to live."

I smiled as we laid down. "Yeah, it's going to be an adventure." How far the adventure would take me from the world I knew, I couldn't yet tell. But it already felt like a lifetime.

Homer Bound

September 12, 2005

This is Giant Iron Pterodactyl Man; I think of him as GITMo. He guards the trailhead for Homestead, an amazingly scenic cross-country trail system that begins just half a mile from my house. I walked by this rusty statue at least five times before I first noticed it. Is that a testament to GITMo's flawless integration into his environment, or a telling symptom of already spending too much time in Homer? I suspect it might be the latter. Alaska attracts some strange people; strange people build strange things. It doesn't take long before the topless mermaid statues and ten-foot burning baskets blend in like Starbucks in Seattle.

I've been thinking lately about how different this place is from the place I grew up. It's not just GITMo and the topless mermaid. It's not just the art patrons showing up at a $75-a-ticket gala in evening gowns and rubber boots, or the environmental art that appears on a nearly daily basis somewhere along the Spit. It's not what Homer is ... but what it refuses to be.

I come from the perspective of Everytown, U.S.A., growing up in a sea of suburban housing peppered with strip malls and parking lots. And now I live in a seaside community in rural Alaska, in a town that has been in a three-year fight to keep Fred Meyer away. We have exactly two chain stores — Safeway and McDonalds, if you don't count an Arby's in a gas station — in a retail community of more than 5,000 people. And, if I'm not mistaken, those stores came in fighting for their spot, too. Part of me believes this is great. That this is the way America used to be — locals dominating the local market. Buy Alaska! Feed your neighbor! It's the American Dream. But a large part of me is nostalgic for the K-marts and tract housing of my youth. Sometimes, it's not about what you love, but about what you know.

✳ ✳ ✳ ✳ ✳

The Homer Tribune was located in the lower level of a small shopping center, below an organic food co-op and next door to the Homer Department of Motor Vehicles. The architectural style of the strip mall — with teal awnings and wood paneling that had been painted chocolate brown and brick red — was distinctly from the 1970s. This decade also apparently saw the most recent renovation of the building. Awnings sagged and paint was faded and cracked. Outside, a three-foot cement barricade featured a whimsical mural of seine fishermen netting dozens of brightly colored fish.

The Tribune office itself was a minimal storefront with a single glass door and two small windows. The interior wasn't finished. Rough cement slabs formed the walls and a thin strip of detached brown carpet covered part of the concrete floor. A few cubical walls separated reporters' desks from the rest of the high-ceilinged room, but for the most part it was a drafty, open floor plan. It wasn't a newsroom; it was a news warehouse.

The receptionist stood up from her door-side desk and led me to a cluster of tables wedged into a corner five feet away. The tables were strewn with papers and five-year-old iMacs, and were occupied by the Homer Tribune news staff: one editor, one reporter, and one sports guy. All three swiveled their chairs and turned to face me at the same time.

They were younger than I expected — but then again, small-town weekly newspapers tend to employ fresh-out-of-college journalists with brighter ambitions and fewer demands. These newspapers especially needed employees who thought twelve dollars an hour with no overtime and no benefits was a perfectly reasonable wage.

A thirty-something man with a short brown beard and a surly look on his face pursed his lips in a half-smile. "That has to be the sports guy," I thought. An attractive man with curly blond hair who was younger than me — early twenties — grinned through a set of perfect teeth. "Reporter," I silently assessed. A woman with long strawberry auburn hair, freckles and expressive blue eyes blurted out, "Finally, you're here!" — as though I had taken three years to reach Homer rather than three weeks.

"Hi Carey," I said, nodding. "We made it, barely," I said.

The woman stood up and reached out to hug me in the casual way one might greet an old friend. "We've been crazy this week and now we're way behind. We publish the paper on Tuesdays and there's still a lot to do. You know Quark right?" she said, referring to the Tribune's page design software.

I nodded.

"Good, I need you to start putting together some pages. I'll show you the folders where I put the edited stories. You can browse one of last week's papers to get the gist of the design."

She plopped me down in a dusty swivel chair next to an iMac and scrolled through the various file folders on the screen, describing each one with almost frantic urgency. I watched with a terrified sort of bemusement. So much for a training period or easing into the work. Life happens fast in Alaska.

"Let me know if you have any questions," she concluded. "But give me about an hour, I'm trying to finish up an editorial."

I nodded weakly.

"Oh, and I should tell you while I remember. Don't make any plans for Wednesday night. I need you to go to a gallery opening. Watercolor painter. I'm busy, and galleries are your beat as the arts reporter."

"Okay," I said slowly. "Maybe I can just ask you real quickly, to explain the overall job description, just so I know what to expect." In truth, I had asked very few questions during our phone interview three weeks earlier.

"Well, you're the page designer, like we talked about, but Sean" — she pointed to the bearded guy — "designs the sports pages, so you don't have to worry about that. And I'll help on Tuesdays when we're on deadline. I also need you to help with editing. You'll report on local artists and events — you'll see, there are a lot — and probably also write some feature stories. Oh, and on Tuesdays we'll have you update the Web site. It's not hard. Jane will show you how to do that."

"Jane?"

Carey squinted, and I realized I'd just expressed an unexpected ignorance. "The publisher. She's out right now, but she should be back this afternoon. She's looking forward to meeting you. Eventually you might need to help build ads. We have an intern right now helping with that but she's leaving to go back to school after Christmas."

"Okay," I said, drawing out the word as though it were a sentence.

"Oh, of course," Carey said as though it hit her as an afterthought, "I should introduce you to everyone. This is Layton," she said pointing to the young man. "He's our news reporter. Layton's new here as well. And Sean writes sports. He has about eight kids at home …"

"Five," Sean interrupted in a monotone voice.

"So we let him do his thing and try not to annoy him much. Dawn over there is the office manager. Julie (she pointed to a woman with glasses and a brown pony tail at the farthest end of the room) is our ad salesperson. Our intern's name is Emily; she's a graphic design student. And Jane is the owner. She's one of the more well-known entrepreneurs in town. She built the Tribune from the ground up and has kept it going for twelve years even though we're competing with a corporate-funded paper. You know about the Homer News, right?"

"I did read their Web site," I said. "And yesterday I noticed two different Homer newspapers on the newsstand. I've never seen competing community weeklies before."

"Yeah, the Homer News comes out on Thursday. We come out on Wednesday. Most people in town seem to read both newspapers so we can hold our own, but there's always healthy competition for breaking news. That's actually going to be one of your jobs with the Web site, making sure we keep it updated."

"What kind of breaking news do you have in Homer?"

"Oh, you'd be surprised," Carey said. "Plane crashes, drownings, bear maulings, unexplained shootings. This may be a small town but it's still Alaska."

"Right," I said. "Sounds exciting."

"So, where are you staying right now?" Carey asked. "You need help finding an apartment?"

"Actually, weirdly, we already found a place. We just got in pretty late yesterday afternoon but we called about a cabin we saw in the classifieds and loved it, so we agreed to rent it. In fact, that landlady's friend should be dropping off a key here anytime now."

"Whereabouts?" Carey asked.

"Up on Diamond Ridge," I said. "On the end of a road called Trail Court."

"You're joking!" Carey exclaimed. "I live on Trail Court. You must be at the place right next door. Robin's place, right? Weird, I thought she already found renters. But that's good. You'll like it there. You have a good car, right?"

"No," I said. "I have a crappy car. An old Geo Prism."

"Well, you're going to have to get something with four-wheel drive before winter," she said. "We're a thousand feet above town, so what falls as rain in Homer usually falls as snow on the ridge. There's snow from October until May. Last year we had nearly three hundred inches over the season. You can be buried to your neck in snow. Lots of shoveling. You'll need a better car."

"Noted," I said. "I brought my boyfriend with me as well. His name is Geoff. He lived in Palmer this summer and traveled all over Alaska. His car is worse than mine, a rusty '89 Honda Civic."

Carey laughed. "Well, good luck to you two. What does he do?"

"Right now, a little of everything and nothing. Sells stuff on eBay. Picks up odd jobs. He wanted to do construction here in town. Actually, the next-door neighbor Mike offered him a job as a sort of deckhand for his oyster farming boat."

Carey narrowed her eyes. "I don't really know Mike, but I'd maybe be a little cautious with him. He doesn't always strike me as genuine. But he's nice enough. He'll probably help you dig your car out of the driveway when you inevitably get stuck."

"That's good to know."

"Okay, we really need to work," Carey said. "Just let me know if you need help with something. Good luck."

I sat down and started scrolling through the bewildering maze of data. The blond reporter, Layton, wheeled his chair next to mine.

"Welcome to Homer," he grinned through his perfect set of teeth. "Home to dreamers and misfits, even by Alaska standards."

"Have you lived here long?" I asked.

"Just since May," Layton said. "I lived in Kenai for a while. I worked at the Peninsula Clarion."

"Really, the Clarion?" I said. That was the Kenai Peninsula's daily newspaper, based in the town of 8,000 that was two hours north of Homer. "It's not often that journalists move from dailies to weeklies, especially in the same region. What brought you to the Tribune?"

"I was fired," he said. "Yeah, I was stupid. I got a little drunk. I crashed my car into a ditch. It was dumb, but that's what it is."

"Oh," I said, caught off guard by the fact Layton was willing to share this information with me when we didn't even know each other.

"What brings you to Alaska?" Layton asked.

"Followed a boy," I grinned, happy to have my own embarrassing piece of personal information to share. "Yeah, my boyfriend Geoff wanted to move here, and I just thought, why not? I lived in Idaho Falls before and it wasn't exactly paradise. I'm looking forward to the great Alaska adventure."

"It is an adventure," Layton grinned again. "Have you met the Russians yet?"

"The Russians?"

"The Old Believers. They're Russian Orthodox followers who came to Alaska to escape communism in the Soviet Union. They live at the end of the road, only speak Russian and all drive huge trucks."

"I can't say I've met any Russians yet," I said. While picking up coffee at Safeway in the morning, I did see a couple who looked vaguely Amish. The man had a long beard and brimmed hat, and the woman was wearing a lacy cap and a homemade dress. They must have been Old Believers.

"Oh, you will," Layton said. "And the Kilchers, too. They're a big homesteader family in town, one of the first. They're a crazy bunch. Jewel is one of the granddaughters. She grew up here."

"The singer Jewel?"

"Yeah," Layton said. "But she snubbed Homer once a few years back and now people in town don't like her, for the most part. They think she think she's too famous to acknowledge her roots."

"Homer definitely seems like a quirky place," I said.

"You have no idea," Layton said, and wheeled his chair back to his side of the desk cluster.

After five hours of decoding the puzzle of the Homer Tribune's layout and making what Carey deemed encouraging progress, I took a lunch break. I felt too anxious to eat, but needed fresh air to calm the throbbing pulse beneath my skull. I walked along Main Street, consciously breathing as slowly as possible. The salty breeze had a hint of sweetness from the decaying leaves already lining the gutters. Between buildings I caught glimpses of Kachemak Bay, sparkling in the afternoon sunlight. The downtown area was typical of a small tourism town — seafood restaurants, sophisticated coffee shops, a tiny library, a large civic center, an organic diner called the Cosmic Kitchen, and an assortment of art galleries.

Carey told me over the phone that Homer attracted a large population of artists, and people came from all over Alaska to buy art. I liked the idea of a community that supported the dream of creating art for a living, but didn't quite believe it until I saw it for myself. In Homer, sculptors, painters, and photographers can vie for space in more than a dozen independent galleries. Journalists have two newspapers. Writers have a large library and two independent bookstores. Chefs have at least twenty restaurants that cater to tourists. Banks, law offices and corporate buildings were, by comparison, surprisingly absent from downtown Homer.

I wondered to what extent the community really fostered a creative life, and how much of it was a facade. Economists have said that one way to measure a society's wealth is how much it invests in its art. But modern American society, wealthy as it was, seemed to have little use for art. So much of what we call art has been farmed out to machines, regurgitated by entertainment capitalists, or mass-produced for the sole purpose of taking up space on walls. Even I was guilty of taking my childhood dream to create animated cartoons and write fiction, and turning it into a career that centered around basic page design, sitting through city council meetings, and writing police report roundups. And yet, creative energy still pulsed through my veins — a desire to capture the fleeting experience of life through images and stories. I had a feeling that this "Cosmic Hamlet by the Sea," as some residents called Homer, had become a refuge for people like me — people who longed to surround themselves with wilderness and art, while still clinging to the comfort and security of modern routines.

The divide between creativity and security seemed to be at the heart of Geoff's and my disconnect as well. He wanted to spend his life in motion — a kind of creative wandering — while I wanted to find a single space where I could create my best version of life. Early in our relationship, we connected through outdoor adventure — spending weekends camping in the Utah desert or hiking in the mountains. Over the next few years, our pursuits became increasingly ambitious, beginning with a road trip across North America in 2001, carrying over to a three-week rafting trip along the Green River, then growing to an entire summer traveling through Alaska, followed by a 3,200-mile bicycle tour across the United States. When we moved together through the world, our hearts synchronized effortlessly and love came naturally.

The passion we found amid the thrill of physical challenge and awe of nature didn't weather well when we returned to home routines. I insisted on pursuing my journalism career while Geoff continued to embark on adventures without me. He didn't understand my desire for domesticity and I didn't appreciate his reluctance to make commitments. Still, we both shared passions that couldn't be broken by mundane necessities, and an affection that had the power to trump individual ambitions. This move to Alaska seemed to provide an ideal compromise — a career and security for me, freedom to move and plenty of wilderness for Geoff, and the prospect of ongoing adventures for both of us, together.

✳ ✳ ✳ ✳ ✳

After Geoff picked me up that evening, we returned to our spacious cabin on Diamond Ridge. As we grabbed the last three bags that he hadn't unloaded from the car already, I felt a rush of excitement about the nesting process. That entire house was a blank canvas, and we were going to fill it with the colors of our new life.

The vacant interior seemed to grow larger every time I re-entered the room, with a peaked ceiling that was probably thirty feet high at its tallest point. It was no longer entirely empty. Next to scattered piles of my possessions, the room also was strewn with splintered lumber and panels of particle board. A blue tarp was spread across the floor, piled with two-by-fours that emitted the pungent aroma of furniture varnish.

"Um, what have you been doing?" I asked Geoff as I stepped around the boards to grab a water bottle from the refrigerator, noting Geoff also purchased milk, cheese, bread, and a five-pound bag of spinach.

"I'm making stuff," Geoff said. "I took a trip to the dump today to drop off some garbage, and they had this big stack of wood. I strapped as much as I could on the roof rack and hauled it home. I have everything I need to make a bookshelf, a couple of side tables, and maybe even a kitchen table. Tomorrow I'm going to go scavenge some more pieces to build shelves for the shed."

"Wow," I said. "That's pretty awesome. At that rate we won't even need to go garage sale hunting this weekend."

"We still need a couch," Geoff said. "Chairs, too, which I probably can't build."

"And a bed," I added, considering the prospect of spending more nights on the wood floor.

"Yeah," Geoff said. "So how did it go at work?"

"Great," I said. "They put me right to work and it was a little crazy. There are three other people in the newsroom, but everyone was so busy they hardly talked to me — even my boss, and that was mostly just to show me the gist of what needed to be done and to give me more work to do. It seems I came at a hectic time. Hopefully the job mellows out soon, but it was fun."

"Sounds stressful," Geoff said. "Did you get the key?"

"Oh yeah, one of Robin's friends dropped it off today, along with the lease. There's only one key."

"I'll get another one made, but I doubt we'll need it," Geoff said. "This doesn't really seem like the kind of neighborhood where you have to lock the doors. Plus, we don't really have anything to steal."

"The bikes," I offered.

"Yeah, but even those aren't all that nice. Do you even ride your bikes any more?"

"I sort of fell out of the habit in Idaho," I said. "But I plan to ride more here. I'm going to bike commute to work sometimes, so hopefully I can stay in shape. I looked into gyms here and they're crazy expensive. I'm going to miss that free membership I had in Idaho Falls."

"Yeah, you're not going to be able to ride your bike in the winter."

I shrugged. "Guess not. From what I hear, the snow lasts from October to May up here. Oh, get this, my editor at work is our next-door neighbor."

"That's cool," Geoff said. "We'll have to go up and say hi sometime."

Geoff had already hammered together one nightstand by the time I unpacked boxes of camping gear and clothing, and hung a slim row of T-shirts and sweaters in the closet. We cooked the last of our spaghetti for dinner and unpacked the small assortment of kitchen items — a few pots, bowls and plates, along with silverware that didn't sell during my yard sale in Idaho Falls. This weekend we would travel north to Palmer to pick up Geoff's car and the last of his belongings. We also hoped to tap a few garage sales for the cheapest versions of necessities we didn't already own. My life was on a bullet train of change, but the simplicity of its forward motion gave me some comfort. Homemade furniture, a dedicated partner, and a clear sense of purpose were all I needed to be happy. And I felt happy, possibly happier than I had ever been.

Transitions

September 20, 2005

My friend Monika in Ann Arbor, Michigan, sent me this picture today. She took this photo of Geoff and me in late August in the Salt River Range of western Wyoming. Several old friends converged from our various corners of the country (me, Idaho; Geoff, Alaska; Monika, New York; and Chris, Utah) in this remote forest along the Grays River to camp, hike and reminisce about life before dispersal.

I enjoyed seeing the photo because it was taken just a few days before I received a job offer from Homer, Alaska. At the time I was heavily conflicted about the prospect of moving to Alaska. It was a vague plan Geoff had for a while. But after he left in the early summer, I grew more comfortable with my life in Idaho, and more leery of the unknown north. Employment was scarce, distances extreme and, if I suddenly found myself single, as my ex-boss in Idaho put it, "The odds are good, but the goods are odd."

After the trip ended, Monika moved from New York to Michigan; Chris took a different job in Utah; and Geoff set down the final ultimatum — he was going back to Alaska, with or without me. That same day, I got the e-mail from my current employer — a job offer.

"So how do you feel about living in a town called Homer?" the e-mail began.

And my first thought was: Fine, really.

Two weeks later, I returned from my last spin class, finished my last midnight shift at the copy desk, and hit Interstate 15. I had been so conflicted, but somehow this transition fell so perfectly into place that it was like merging onto a winding interchange, only to look over at the end and find you're still parallel with the highway. Something like that ... but I think, now that I look at this photo, maybe I knew that all along.

✳ ✳ ✳ ✳ ✳

I started bestowing names on the neighborhood moose that lurked near the roadside as I pedaled my bike down Diamond Ridge Road. There was "Fed Moose," a young male with knob antlers who would walk toward me every time I stopped to take his picture. "Buck" was a big old bull who would rush off the road and hide behind alder branches, as though twigs could mask his hulking body. "Bessie" was a cow moose with a sub-adult calf that was nearly her size. "Andy" was what I called the teenager because I didn't know its gender. There were always groups of moose out on the muskeg that kept more natural distances from people, and a few more that had the gall to saunter down the paved streets of downtown Homer.

Moose weren't the only large wild animals to utilize the same spaces as Homer's human residents. One afternoon in late September, Geoff saw a young grizzly bear crossing our back yard, close enough that he could see its blond fur rippling as it ran. When I expressed trepidation about leaving the house with a grizzly nearby, he said, "I wouldn't worry. It was a small bear."

Another nonhuman subculture was the congregation of bald eagles along the Homer Spit, a five-mile-long sandy tongue that juts out from the mainland. Although eagles are abundant along Alaska's coastline, they were especially drawn to the beachside home of a Homer resident named Jean Keene. Jean was a petite, 81-year-old woman with wild red curls, wire-rimmed glasses as large and round as her head, and an obsession with eagles. A former rodeo rider and professional cattle driver, she traveled all over the United States and eventually found her way to Alaska. She drove her motorhome to the End of the Road, parked at the Homer Spit Campground, and never left. While working for a seafood processing plant, Jean started saving fish scraps to throw to eagles on the beach. Word apparently got out. Soon dozens of eagles were congregating on the Spit, and then hundreds. The scraps weren't enough to feed all of them, so Jean started buying whole chum salmon from the processing plant. When she could no longer afford it, she requested donations from tourists. Even as the hobby took a toll on her health and still-active employment at the plant, the octogenarian worked tirelessly to feed them all. Locals called her "The Eagle Lady" — an Alaskan version of a crazy cat lady.

Photographers delighted in ready-made access to wild eagles, but locals soon grew weary of crowds of habituated raptors that stole fillets from halibut processors, screeched through the morning, and defecated on roofs and cars. Jean was a controversial figure in Homer, but harsh critics and even a few federal laws weren't enough to sway her from the daily feedings. I enjoyed watching eagles fight over shredded salmon carcasses and swoop in from flag poles to snatch fish out of the surf. Still, even I found their presence vaguely unsettling. It just wasn't natural for dozens of large birds of prey to crowd together on rooftops like they were chickadees. Often, a dozen white heads would turn in unison as I passed by their perch on buildings that were shuttered for the winter. This time of year, the Homer Spit was eerily reminiscent of an Alfred Hitchcock film.

It didn't help that a number of creepy characters populated the spit. Besides Jean, there was a transient population of vagabonds and homeless people that locals referred to as "spit rats." Other semi-permanent residents included a group of anywhere from one to five men — it was always hard to determine the actual number of live-ins — who occupied a derelict ship that was beached a half mile north of the harbor. Complete with broken masts and life rafts hanging from the bow, the wooden ship was draped in ragged curtains and littered with trash. Surrounding the ship were several smaller beached fishing boats, as well as scrap wood sheds. Someone had erected a life-size Styrofoam castle tower — a prop from a past production of the local theater. We called this place "the pirate ship." I often spotted men milling around outside, carrying garbage bags and sometimes, if it was raining, wearing garbage bags. I had no idea what the men did for a living, or why they resided in a leaky old boat. From the outside, their makeshift shelter had a creative if creepy aesthetic, as though it were deliberately designed to evoke a broken seafaring dream. How else could one explain the frayed ropes strung across the masts, or the hundreds of colorful floats strewn about the property? I was intrigued by the structure, but feared its occupants and never lingered long enough to explore.

There was also the Salty Dawg, a seedy bar that had become a popular tourist attraction. The single-room log cabin was one of the first buildings in Homer, dating back to 1897. The structure served as everything from a post office to a railroad station to a school house. A local businessman purchased it in the 1950s and began operating the cabin as a bar, moving it from the mainland to the Homer Spit shortly after the 1964 earthquake. He erected a fake lighthouse next to the cabin to hide a water tank, thereby creating one of the most recognizable buildings in Alaska. I walked inside only once, just long enough to take in the musty atmosphere and observe brown water dripping from a few of the hundreds of dollar bills stapled to the walls and ceiling. The bartender just grimaced and I ducked out before he could bark at me to order something or leave.

The Homer Spit had its ritzy side, too. There was the Land's End resort, where Geoff and I once devoured eighty-dollar, five-course meals on the Homer Tribune's dime. The Spit was home to most of Homer's halibut fishing outfitters, a few art galleries and restaurants, and the Pier One community theater — a bright red building that was a favorite perch of Jean's eagles and also host to quality plays in the summer. During the summer, the Spit was constantly bustling with tourists who visited a number of art galleries, restaurants, and fishing outfitters along the boardwalk. But by late September, harbor dwellers, land pirates and long-term tent campers took over as the prominent population.

After two weeks residency I'd become a near-full-time bike commuter. I often took the long way home from the office by veering onto the paved bike path along the Homer Spit and pedaling ten miles to the end and back. A stiff breeze consistently blew from the west, and seagulls hovered almost motionless in the wind. I liked to stop at the farthest point on the beach and look across the bay to the Kenai Mountains. A salty film covered my lips, but there was always a sweetness to the air. Pedaling out the Spit was my way of relaxing after work. Wind and waves roared with a soothing intensity, and I understood why self-help gurus used ocean soundtracks on meditation tapes. As I pedaled away, I'd concentrate on the rhythm of my bicycle, emptying my thoughts to the soothing hum of tires on pavement.

My new job was proving to be consistently stressful — the deadline pressure of publication day was crushing, and my list of duties seemed to compound almost daily. It wasn't unusual to attend a gallery opening or play production late into the evening, then wake up early the next morning to piece together layouts, edit Carey's and Layton's reports, write my own articles, "put the paper to bed," update the Web site and online classifieds section, and submit my feature proposals for the following week. The publisher, Jane, put me on ad design duty and had me teach the intern, Emily, how to use the company's software even though I was the newest person on staff. Carey was sympathetic but had a massive workload of her own. Jane's authoritarian management style had her assigning blame for mistakes rather than rewarding success, and all of us walked that tenuous tightrope between camaraderie and hostility.

Tuesday at noon was our cutthroat deadline, and the newsroom staff reserved Tuesday afternoons for a complaint session over margaritas at Don Jose's, the local Mexican restaurant. Sean, who was usually polite and reserved at the office, let his rants flow free after a few ounces of tequila. At the center of his tirade was something we all agreed on — we were working to the point of indentured servitude for pauper wages. Jane's often unrealistic demands only were achievable because we all feared the consequences when we failed to meet expectations.

Still, we didn't exactly have a say in the matter as long as we wanted to remain in Homer and work as journalists, which all of us did. I especially enjoyed interviewing painters and nibbling on exotic appetizers at art galleries. Long hours for low pay seemed to be the price I paid for the privilege of living in this beautiful place. There were many reasons why it was worth it, and I often voiced this opinion to my disgruntled co-workers over baskets of chips and salsa. Carey laughed and said my youthful idealism would eventually be crushed by cold reality.

"That, and you have yet to make it through an Alaskan winter," she added. "Just wait."

I wanted to point out to Carey that she wasn't much older than me — early thirties, when I was twenty-six. But she did have a young son, a mortgage on her Trail Court home, a husband who fought wildfires in the summer, and more than a decade of Alaska residency behind her. She grew up in a small fishing village in Nova Scotia, and came to Alaska when she was still a teenager. Carey was full of entertaining stories about waiting tables at crowded restaurants in Anchorage and chasing moose out of her garden with a shovel. She had earned her cynicism, although she appeared to truly love her adopted home and remained an advocate for all things Alaska. She encouraged me to purchase a pair of cross country skis and take the time to explore the trails around town.

"Otherwise," she said, "the long, dark winters will drive you nuts."

Margarita Tuesdays usually wrapped up early enough for me to squeeze in a ride out the Homer Spit before making the slow climb up West Hill. The road switchbacked steeply up a bluff, with open views to the south. When I climbed high enough, the roiling whitecaps of Kachemak Bay flattened out and the water took on the appearance of silver glass — a mirror that seemed to reflect the universe just beyond a thin film of atmosphere.

Across the hillside, autumn was emerging. Birch trees erupted into a blaze of gold, with bark as white and delicate as paper. The last cotton puffs had blown away from fireweed stalks, which had become withered and brown. Another stocky plant, cow parsnip, had faded from vibrant green to a sinewy beige that looked as though it might disintegrate if I touched it. The spruce were more timeless, with twisted branches that held strong through all of the wind and snow that punctuated their long, hard lifetimes. A few of the suburban moose were always nearby to greet me along the ride home, which was six miles long with twelve hundred feet of elevation gain. The commute from the office usually took about forty-five minutes, and an hour-forty-five if I tacked on a jaunt out Homer Spit Road.

"I thought I was going to lose all this fitness when we moved here, but this bike commuting is a tough workout," I announced to Geoff after I wheeled my mountain bike through the door.

"No kidding," Geoff said. "I rode into town yesterday to pick up groceries. Made the mistake of buying a gallon of milk. I thought my back was going to give out on that hill."

After two weeks in Homer, Geoff had developed a steady routine of managing his home business during weekdays — surfing eBay, placing orders, packaging his wares, and responding to customers. Twice a week, he drove into town to process packages at the post office and shop for groceries and supplies. He mostly dealt in bicycle racks and bicycles, buying the whole product and breaking it down into pieces so he could sell the parts individually. Even with Alaska's higher shipping charges, he was still able to bring in enough profit to cover half our expenses, if only just. The oyster boat job with our next-door neighbor never panned out. Mike never picked Geoff up for work as he'd promised, and conveniently ducked into his house the couple of times we had seen him since. For all of the friendliness he displayed the first day we met, Mike was equally reclusive every day thereafter. We didn't know whether Mike was avoiding us because he couldn't keep his promise to Geoff, or just strange. Either way, Geoff wasn't too miffed about it. We figured insincere job offers were just another quirky custom in Alaska.

Because Geoff had free time at home and apparently an unlimited supply of scrap wood, our handmade junkyard furniture stash grew at an impressive rate. He built towel racks for the bathroom, a large bookshelf and three small ones, a side table, a desk for his computer, and a full-sized kitchen table, with each board sanded and polished to a bright sheen. Diamond Ridge had no garbage pick-up service, so Geoff made regular trips to the dump to drop off trash and recyclables, and then scavenge reusables. He often returned with lumber or wooden crates, and what he couldn't use as building material, he chopped up and stacked in the backyard for future camp firewood. He found an unmarred set of plastic deck chairs, so they took up position on our back porch. We had to prop the chairs against the railing to keep the wind from blowing them away. I'd occasionally spend Sunday mornings lounging on the porch, drinking coffee until my fingers were numb from cold.

We also were becoming regulars at the Salvation Army thrift store, where I made a handful of contributions to our nesting routine. My treasures included a rotary dial phone that was at least forty years old, an espresso machine, and a juicer. The espresso machine was one of my winter survival tactics, and Geoff vowed to make economical use of the juicer even though strawberries were shriveled and oranges cost upwards of four dollars a pound in Homer. I also scored a television stand for two dollars. It had one of those fake wood veneers from the 1970s, so I peeled off the plastic paneling, sanded the surface, and refinished it with a can of rust orange paint that I found in the shed. It was the same color as the walls, so it blended perfectly into the decor. Because we had a television stand, I figured we might as well get a television, which I found for five dollars at the thrift store.

We purchased a relatively nice couch, with only slightly pilled, cream upholstery and an oak frame, at a local garage sale. The hardware store provided a beige carpet for the corner of the cabin we designated as the living room. But we struggled to find a bed. None of the local garage sales had mattresses, and any that were listed in the classifieds were snatched up before we even had a chance to call. For weeks, we slept on inflatable camping pads covered with sheets and a down comforter — until my cat clawed a number of holes into my air mattress. After that, my side of the bed was a pile of blankets.

Finally, we saw a listing for a queen-sized mattress and box springs in Ninilchik, a Native village thirty-seven miles north of Homer. We were so desperate for a bed that we made the hourlong drive, even after the homeowner told us he wouldn't make any promises about holding the bed. "I already had six calls, ya better hurry," he grunted into the phone.

In Ninilchik, a surly man with long, stringy hair and a white tank top led us into his cavern of a home, which was clogged from floor to ceiling with an unbelievable amount of clutter. The bed itself was covered in sheets and buried beneath a stack of boxes, books and newspapers that towered over our heads. The owner didn't even bother to remove the trash after we said on the phone we were on our way. There was one uncovered corner, and I peeled back the sheet covering the bed with the same trepidation one might feel when pulling a cloak off a dead body. The mattress itself was an older model, but the fabric was clean and looked brand new. This bed had possibly never been slept in before, as the dust on the boxes indicated a long career as a storage platform. The house reeked of cigarette smoke, but our need for a real bed was urgent, and we had driven nearly an hour just to look at it. Geoff suggested the trip back to Homer on top of my car might air it out at least a little. We strapped the mattress and box springs on the Prism's roof rack with nylon cords.

When we arrived at home, the initial shock of that unrighteously messy house had faded, and we caught our first full whiff of the hoarder's bed. It smelled as though someone had thrown it on top of the smoke stack of a slaughter house and left it there for years. We sprayed two bottles of air freshener into the fabric and left it on the front porch to air out for nearly a week. There was little improvement. We attempted to sleep in it one night, and the experience was horrifying. During the few hours I actually did sleep, the smell of scorched pig carcasses crept into my dreams. The next morning, I listed the mattress as a free item in the Tribune classifieds, warning that it had come from the house of a smoker. Someone else took it off our hands that same day. A week later, Geoff discovered another bed set in the classifieds. It cost a hundred and fifty dollars that we were more than happy to spend. Years later, the distinct aroma of the Ninilchik bed still penetrated my memory, haunting me in moments of sickness and pain.

Geoff cooked nearly every night. Because he enjoyed cooking, he often served up elaborate spreads of salad, bread, and homemade chili, or Thai curry and rice, or on a really good day, Indian lentils, saag paneer with homemade cheese, naan and pakoras. Indian food was Geoff's specialty, and I believed it tasted as delicious as anything I had ever been served at a restaurant. I had spent the past year in Idaho locked into a structured weight loss plan, working out at the gym five days a week and limiting my calories in an effort to lose the thirty pounds I had packed on after Geoff and I returned from our cross-country bike trip. But in Homer, where the September air already held a stiff chill, and riding a mountain bike uphill every day was truly exhausting, I felt justified in devouring a half dozen of Geoff's fried vegetable dumplings. Each bite evoked bliss — another savory reminder of the partnership Geoff and I were building.

I was in awe of the way our lives moved so flawlessly through the transitions, as though the path had been set for us all along. Sure, there were a few bumps — my stressful job, the approaching winter and the unknowns that came with it, Geoff's lack of full-time work, and the fact that our combined incomes still barely covered our expenses. As night settled in, and I once again found myself lingering over a long e-mail to the family and friends I left behind, I still questioned whether moving to Alaska was the right decision. But in the mornings, when the sun rose over the distant mountains and cast warm light across our spacious back yard, I knew I was home.

Into Winter

October 9, 2005

I'm just thawing my face after a brisk (to say the least) 25-mile bike ride. Every time I go riding, I think "this is the last one of the season." On Tuesday I skidded out on a patch of black ice and hit the pavement. Today I rode down the ridge, into town and out to the end of the spit through a fierce west wind. I was getting sprayed by surf from the other side of the road. When I got home my toes were numb and my outdoor thermometer read 12.8 degrees. I think this may be my last ride of the season.

Everyone in town says it's unseasonably cold. The pictures I posted today are from our trip to Crescent Lake last weekend. Driving there was downright brutal. We stopped at a gas station shortly after sunrise (about 9:30 a.m., as this was still one day before the clocks set back) to get some coffee. The thermometer on the door registered vaguely in the single digits and every branch and blade of grass along the highway was coated in thick frost. I was anticipating a painful death by frostbite, but once we got out of the car and hoisted our backpacks, the whitewashed landscape seemed beautiful and benign.

We hiked in about seven miles to a little cabin on the lake. We spent the first couple of hours there gathering wood in an area picked pretty clean. There was a lot of hauling and cutting with a small saw, but at least the effort kept us warm for a while. We stoked our small stove and set out in a rowboat on the lake – still not frozen over, but just barely. In the space of 40 minutes we caught a couple of big grayling. But because we couldn't bear the thought of cleaning fish in ice water, we threw them back and had burritos for dinner.

When we returned the next day there was a fresh half-inch of snow that had been wiped nearly clean from Geoff's car. On closer inspection we saw distinct paw prints in the mud on the side of the car, and the roof was dented in. Footprints in the parking lot indicated that a fairly large black bear had plopped itself right on top of Geoff's little Civic while we were gone. It's a wonder nothing caved in. I remember that this kind of bear behavior is pretty common at the Mount Whitney trailhead in California. There, the black bears will smash in your rear windshield if they see so much as a plastic bag in the back seat. Then, when you get back from your hike, you have no food, a broken window, and a $100 fine from the forest service for tempting the bears. I think, in Alaska, the bears are still the ones who get in trouble.

✳ ✳ ✳ ✳ ✳

The first snow came on October 9, not even a full month after we moved to Homer. The previous day, the Tribune's graphic design intern, Emily, invited Geoff and me to join her on a sea kayaking outing in Kachemak Bay. She arranged to meet at the harbor at nine, but the sky was still black when our alarm clock woke us up at 7:45. I leaned against the loft railing and scanned the landscape windows for hints of sunrise — a morning routine I cultivated as daylight diminished in significant increments. The upper windows were so fogged that I couldn't see anything, so I descended the cold stairs barefoot and went to the back porch. Amid the shock of cold air and delay in focusing sleepy eyes, I stepped directly into a snow drift.

I recoiled and rubbed my face. A thick layer of fluff carpeted the back yard, adding startling contrast to the dark morning. The graying landscape of autumn transitioned overnight into winter.

"Snow!" I called out to Geoff. "It snowed last night!"

"Awesome," Geoff said. He ran downstairs to join me at the door. "Wow, there must be at least five inches. We don't even have a shovel yet."

"Bummer," I said. "Guess this means we're not going sea kayaking today."

"Why not? Did Emily call?"

"No, but I mean, it snowed," I said. "Snow and sea kayaking don't usually go together."

"It's no big deal," Geoff said. "We already knew it was going to be cold. It probably only rained in town. I think we should still go."

"But what will we wear?" I asked. "Cold rain and sitting in a boat ... I don't know."

"We're not going swimming," Geoff said. "Wear a coat and gloves. Dress like you would if you were going for a bike ride."

"I hope we don't go swimming," I muttered under my breath. Accidentally rolling a kayak into the frigid waters of Kachemak Bay seemed to be one sure way to die quickly. I had a phobia of water — cultivated over several years of whitewater rafting mishaps and overly ambitious canoe trips with Geoff — that I was loathe to admit. Sea kayaking was supposed to be fun. Sea kayaking was an Alaska tradition. Real Alaskans were hardcore enough to go sea kayaking in the winter. I pulled the box labeled "winter clothes" out of the closet and began sifting through my gear.

I settled on my snowboarding uniform — snow pants, a fleece pullover, a Burton shell, ski mittens, a fleece hat, hiking boots and a thick pair of cotton socks. Neither the snow pants nor the shell were waterproof, but they were the best I had. Geoff had a pair of neoprene gloves left over from his rafting days, but otherwise his gear wasn't much better than mine.

As we eased Geoff's Civic down the road into town, gentle snow intensified to sleet, and then pounding rain. Emily met us at the dock wearing a lot more neoprene, and a professional-looking kayaking jacket with tight cuffs and an attached skirt to drape over the kayak's opening. We helped her unload the boat from the roof of her Subaru Outback. It was a tandem sea kayak with three seats and a wide wooden base. "I figured the tandem was better than individual boats," Emily said. "These are almost impossible to tip."

Wind-driven rain battered my hands as I removed my mittens to put on a life jacket. Geoff was right that it wasn't snowing at sea level, but cold rain was even worse. We dropped the boat into the harbor, which was roiling with gray seawater. Bile gurgled in my gut. I scanned Emily's face for any hint of concern, but she seemed supremely unworried about the weather. Emily grew up in Anchor Point — a community just outside of Homer — and had lived her entire life in this region. Emily was a "real Alaskan," so I figured she knew what she was doing.

Emily was also only eighteen years old, with a round pixie face and brown hair that she occasionally wore in a Tinker Bell bun. Her voice was gruff and she often spoke in terse sentences through a half-smile. Emily was the only employee at the Homer Tribune who seemed untroubled by the pressure. She invited us to a few social gatherings and Geoff immediately took a liking to her because she was easy-going and adventurous. In Salt Lake City, Geoff lived in a communal setting with anywhere from six to nine other people, and was constantly surrounded by his friends. After he left to spend the summer in Alaska, he traveled with friends and stayed in friends' homes. Then we moved to Homer, and abruptly it was just Geoff and me, alone most of the time. I understood his desire to branch out and meet new people, even if it meant the occasional Sunday morning outing into terrifyingly cold waters.

Emily positioned Geoff in front and me in the middle so she could sit in the back and steer the heavy boat with an external rudder. She instructed us to simply paddle straight on alternating sides of the boat to propel it forward. We launched in the harbor and started plying our way through a narrow alley separating skyscraper-like ships. I had only visited the small harbor on the Homer Spit, which housed private fishing boats and other small crafts. The main port, by contrast, was populated by hulking barges coated in rust and grime. I thought nervously about what might happen if any of these building-sized ships fired up its engines and pulled into our path.

But at least the water in the harbor was relatively calm, and my Burton shell seemed to do an okay job of blocking the rain that was pelting my back. Waves rippled beneath the kayak with a soothing rhythm. Geoff turned his head and grinned. Maybe sea kayaking in October wasn't so bad.

When we arrived at the edge of the breakwater, Emily steered the boat toward an open entrance.

"Isn't the sea kind of rough out there right now?" I asked.

"Should be fine," she said. "We won't venture too far out."

Geoff responded by paddling faster. We cleared the harbor walls, where the surf picked up velocity in sync with a strengthening west wind. The kayak bucked and bobbed, and Geoff responded by ferrying his paddle in attempts to turn the bow. From his river rafting experience, he knew to point the nose of the boat directly into a wave to avoid flipping.

"Just paddle straight!" Emily shouted. "I've got the rudder."

We slammed into waves as seawater erupted over our heads, soaking all of us. Cold wind needled through my saturated clothing, and I could feel my fingers going numb. The kayak continued to rock violently, injecting an intense nausea.

"I'm feeling seasick," I lied. What I was feeling was terrified.

"Paddle!" Emily screamed, just as the kayak lurched sideways toward the jagged pillars of an old dock. We'd drifted close enough that I could see individual barnacles clinging to the weathered wood. The boat plunged over a car-sized wave, launching another wet explosion. I clenched my fists and eyes, bracing for the underwater dive I was certain we were all going to take. But true to Emily's promises, the bow shot out of the hole like a whale, and the kayak righted itself.

"Okay, that was a big wave," Emily giggled. "We should get away from the dock." Shivering rocked my core and my hands went limp. I couldn't grip my paddle, so I just held it at my side. Even fear had lost its edge, numbed by either ice water or resignation. I stared blankly through a curtain of rain toward the liquid gray horizon. Emily steered the boat farther from the harbor as Geoff contributed exuberant forward strokes. Neither of them said anything about the fact I wasn't paddling.

Although the wind still howled, the rough water took on a more predictable flow once we cleared the dock. Finally, my shivering abated enough to at least put my paddle in the water and give an appearance of effort. Emily chatted amicably as she steered the boat to a satisfactory distance, and then arced back toward land.

The breakwater walls appeared much closer than they were, and minutes passed slowly as we forced our cold arms through the motions. Rain turned to sleet, and then clumpy flakes of snow. Geoff was visibly shivering by the time we returned to the harbor.

"Probably the last time this year we'll be able to go kayaking," Emily observed as we hoisted the boat back onto her car. "Good we got out today."

Geoff's car stalled out in the snow on the way home. Several more inches of powder had accumulated on Diamond Ridge, burying the tire ruts that we'd been able to follow during the drive into town. All we could do was put the car in reverse and slide backwards half a mile back to the pavement. We drove twelve miles around the Sterling Highway to try the other end of Diamond Ridge Road, where we were again thwarted, so we returned to town to purchase snow chains and a shovel. The sun was already low on the horizon after a long day out, and my fingers and toes were still numb.

"I always forget about my fear of water," I said to Geoff as we walked into the hardware store. "That was really harrowing for me. But you and Emily seemed to be having fun."

"I was cold, especially toward the end," Geoff said. "But, yeah, it was definitely fun. I missed this. It was similar to whitewater canoeing, but I would have liked to paddle my own boat. We need to look into getting some sea kayaks before next spring."

"Sure," I agreed, without admitting that I didn't plan to ever again venture into Kachemak Bay on any craft that wasn't a large fishing boat with a motor. Even during the summer, water temperatures never registered higher than fifty degrees, and submersion could trigger hypothermia in minutes. Our near-plunge near the dock pilings reminded me that all it took was a single rogue wave to shift a situation from fun to deadly. Winter activities were bound to present dangerous situations, but at least on land, chances of surviving the cold were marginally better.

✳ ✳ ✳ ✳ ✳

Over the next few weekends, Geoff and I directed the entirety of our incomes into battling the onslaught of winter. We acquired chains and studded tires for each of our cars, extra blankets for the bed, an electric heater for Geoff's desk, and an outdoor thermometer. Geoff purchased a used chainsaw to cut down a few of the dead trees on the property, then sectioned them into logs to sell to others as firewood.

Our cabin didn't have a wood stove, and Robin wouldn't permit us to get one, claiming she didn't have fire insurance. The only heating source was a Monitor heater that guzzled diesel fuel. We purchased a hundred gallons to store in a drum on our porch. The diesel delivery guy surveyed the size of our cabin and told us that amount of fuel would never get us through the winter. But at three dollars a gallon, even a hundred was a stretch for us in late October.

"We'll be comfortable enough at sixty degrees," Geoff told me. "Buy some more sweaters."

Autumn snow continued to fall but often lingered for only a day or two before melting. The month was gray with frequent rain, adding an especially dark tint to the diminishing daylight. By Halloween, the ground was covered in white crust that appeared to be settling in for the season. Neighborhood children surprised us when they donned Arctic coats and hiked long distances at fifteen degrees to trick-or-treat.

The holiday weekend brought an opportunity to hike into a backcountry cabin near the northern edge of the peninsula. Light snow fell as we packed up Geoff's Civic with all of the camping gear we owned. He pointed to a pile of eight summer tires that we had recently removed from our cars, now covered in several inches of fresh powder.

"You're probably not going to see those again until spring," he said.

Geoff stopped to buy fuel in Anchor Point. A sign on the door advertised free coffee, so I exited the car as well. Outside air caused me to gasp involuntarily. The temperature felt ten degrees colder than it had on Diamond Ridge, probably due to an inversion trapping cold air at this low elevation. A thermometer outside the door confirmed my suspicions.

"It's only eight degrees out," I hissed at Geoff as I ducked back into the car with my Styrofoam cup of lukewarm sludge.

"I'm not surprised," Geoff said. "It definitely feels cold."

I nodded toward the frost-covered landscape. A chain-link fence, needles on trees, and alder branches looked as though they'd been dipped in blue frosting. "Are we really thinking about camping in this?"

"We'll be fine," Geoff said. "We have tons of gear, and it's not like we're sleeping in a tent. Those cabins have stoves and an ax to cut wood. And anyway, it's only like seven miles from the road. If we have any issues we'll just leave."

"Seven miles," I said. "Right. A quick little jaunt."

Similar to our sea kayaking excursion a few weeks earlier, I was anticipating some sort of painful cold-related death. This time my focus was frostbite. But again, the promise of adventure trumped fear's empty threats. I swallowed my trepidation with a large helping of pride — the "I'm going to prove I can be Alaskan by going camping in the winter" sort of pride.

We organized our gear at the trailhead and hoisted backpacks that together weighed as much as a third person. I strapped snowshoes onto my hiking boots and took labored steps across the highway. The backpack pinched my shoulders and its weight nearly buckled my knees. The snowshoes felt more like anchors than walking aids. Despite the single-digit temperatures, sweat started to trickle down my back. I was wearing enough layers to sleep outside in Antarctica — probably too many for a hike. But I preferred to take my chances with overheating in the micro-climate of my body heat, rather than solidifying in a vast freezer.

Light snow continued to fall as we marched up steep switchbacks. The narrow snowshoe trail was covered in six inches of fresh powder. Geoff broke trail several yards ahead as I continued to struggle with my heavy pack and altered sense of balance. I stomped along like a Yeti, breathing loudly and exhaling thick clouds of vapor as I punched giant tracks in the snow.

My overstuffed backpack swayed from side to side, knocking powder from alder branches. The landscape, by contrast, was eerily still. Only the hiss of falling snow interrupted a primordial silence. Blurred figures of mountains and trees, stripped of all color, flickered between the flakes. Everything had the delicate look of a silent movie, archived for so long that the black-and-white film was fading around the edges. It was beautiful and benign. I wondered why I had been so fearful.

Geoff reached the cabin — a single-room log structure near the shore of Crescent Lake — just after one in the afternoon. I was at that point nearly half a mile behind him, nursing my sore knees and back, and vowing that I would never, ever gain sixty pounds. By the time I reached the cabin, Geoff was nowhere to be seen, but his backpack was propped inside and snowshoe tracks into the forest indicated he had gone looking for firewood.

I dropped my pack and surveyed the area. Crescent Lake was rimmed by a wall of steep mountains above the U-shaped valley. A cloud ceiling obscured the peaks, so it appeared as though bald slopes dropped out of nothing. The valley floor was dotted with scattered spruce and birch trees, which faded out altogether just a few hundred feet higher. The lake hadn't frozen yet; the surface was as flat and calm as a mirror, casting a reflection so clear that I could see the subtle definition of clouds in the water. Except for a blaze orange sign warning of recent bear sightings in the vicinity, color remained nonexistent.

A chill settled in as I unpacked my belongings onto the wooden bunk bed. When shivering commenced I stripped down to my underwear so I could change into a dry base layer and fleece jacket. Geoff returned with a modest stack of wood. "The pickings are kinda slim out there," he said. "Seems this place has been worked over by people before us. And it's hard to find dead wood because everything is covered in snow."

"Great," I said. "My sleeping bag is only rated to twenty degrees. Just great."

"We'll find enough to get through the night," Geoff said. "We just have to spend a little more time looking."

I pulled on the rest of my layers and returned outside to help him gather branches and other scraps. We eventually used the ax to chop down a dead birch tree and sawed the branches off, then dragged the trunk to the front of the cabin in case we needed to chop that to pieces as well.

Because we needed to conserve firewood, we decided to spend the rest of the

daylight hours exploring Crescent Lake. The cabin rental included a small aluminum boat and oars, which were probably intended for summer use. But only
a thin layer of ice rimmed the shore, and the water was calm enough for boating.
Geoff even brought his fishing pole in hopes the lake was open.

We donned sun-faded life jackets over our winter coats and pushed the boat
from its winter storage area in the woods to a small wooden dock. A shallow
film of steam wafted across the surface of the lake, as though the water were
hot instead of cold. Geoff arranged his fishing gear as I rowed. He chose a silver
spinner for his lure. The metal chunk disrupted the glassy calm of the lake with
every plop, but by the fourth cast he had a bite. He reeled in a ten-inch grayling
— large by grayling standards. Geoff held the dorsal-finned fish delicately in his
mittens as he removed the hook.

"Are we going to eat that for dinner?" I asked.

Geoff considered it for a moment. "It would be tasty, but I don't want to
have to clean it with my bare hands in this water." He reached back into the
steam and let the grayling slip through his grasp. I watched the fish dart toward
freedom as Geoff continued casting his line.

Sunlight escaped through the clouds in the late afternoon, just in time to
cast its last gold rays on the water before disappearing behind the mountains.
We pulled the boat back on shore and walked through crunchy snow toward the
cabin. I noticed that marbles of ice had formed on my coat and pants. The palms
of my hands tingled from removing my mittens to grasp the searing metal edge
of the boat. Still, unlike the first encounter at the Anchor Point gas station, this
cold no longer felt like an impenetrable wall. It had become more like a room,
encompassing me as my body adjusted accordingly.

Once I'd reached equilibrium, the icy breeze lost its sting, and chills gave
way to internal warmth. This was a new revelation — that I could not only
survive an entire day outside when the temperature was near zero, but I could
be comfortable. My veins pulsed with life even as the landscape lay dormant in
the quiescence of winter.

"Like the grayling," I thought. "Soon Crescent Lake will be frozen over, and
the water below will be cold enough to stop my warm-blooded heart in minutes,
but that grayling will keep on swimming toward spring." I smiled with appreciation for that spunky little fish. I was glad Geoff let it live.

Darkness returned by six in the evening. We stoked our small fire, warmed
tortillas and rehydrated pinto beans on top of the iron stove. Geoff sautéed
carrots, green peppers and onions on his camp stove, adding pinches of salt,
cayenne pepper and curry powder — a gourmet chef even in the woods. I lit a
few tea candles that I found in a cupboard. The dull yellow light and flickering
shadows gave the room a soothing ambiance. Even though we were miles from

a familiar space and modern comforts, I couldn't remember the last time I felt so cozy or secure.

"Wouldn't it be awesome if we could live like this all the time?" Geoff mused. "If we had some property by a lake where we could build a cabin, chop wood, catch fish and live off the land?"

"Yeah," I said. "It would be a really great life. But I wonder if it would get boring sometimes too. Always having only the same mountains to hike, the same trails to walk, the same lake to fish."

"If you were really trying to live off the land, you wouldn't be bored. You'd be too busy trying to survive," Geoff said.

"This is probably true," I said. "I think that's why I prefer to live the dream in smaller doses. True back-to-nature living would be extremely difficult, probably in ways you wouldn't even anticipate. I mean, just think about how much time we'd have to spend chopping down trees and gathering wood if we wanted to stay warm all winter. Or how many grayling we'd have to catch to equal the calories in these burritos."

"Yeah," Geoff said. "But at least it would all be real, valid work. Work that had some kind of tangible meaning to our lives — more than selling stuff to make money to buy more stuff."

I wanted to counter that my work already had meaning. Serving as a political watchdog and disseminating information to the public was important. But I remembered with amusement that the last article I wrote had been about a Homer resident who collected every single issue of National Geographic that had ever been printed, filed away in rows upon rows of shelves. That, besides being an entertaining but otherwise unimportant fluff piece, was also a perfect example of amassing stuff for the sake of stuff.

"True," I said. "But if you want to live in the modern world, you don't really get much of a choice. Either you participate in society, or you have to leave it completely behind. And there's not a whole lot of room left in this world for people who choose to leave."

"There's still a lot of room left in Alaska," Geoff said. "I can't wait for next summer."

Geoff had grand plans for the warm months, when he planned to put his eBay business on hiatus and spend weeks exploring the Kenai Mountains, floating the Yukon River, and embarking on an expedition across the Brooks Range in Alaska's far north.

I nodded. "Hopefully we'll have a chance to do some exploring." And by that, I meant that I hoped we'd find a happy compromise between Geoff's long-distance ambitions and my weekend warrior limitations. Adventure, comfort and a functioning role in society — these were all pieces of my personal happiness puzzle that still seemed impossible to fit together. But I remained hopeful that Alaska would provide an answer.

'Til November

November 3, 2005

It's mid-November, and the weather reflects it. A steady drizzle of rain hits the snow like acid, pooling in pockmarks and emerging in gray streams of slush on the city streets. Evening approaches and everything is gray, monotone, shadowless, as you're driving toward the spit with a camera that has only one shot left on it. You're heading due south on the narrow strip of land, so you scarcely notice sunlight slipping below the clouds and emerging through a thin sliver of clear sky to the west.

You don't have time to notice because the change is instantaneous anyway — as sudden as a camera flash, the distant shoreline erupts in a magnetic shade of turquoise you never even imagined existed in nature. It startles you so much that you pull over that second, like one of those tourists who just spotted the backside of a bear, and you get out of your car, and take that one picture. Then, when you look at the image reflected on the tiny camera screen, washed of all its color and surprise, it almost breaks your heart, but not quite.

✳ ✳ ✳ ✳ ✳

" So what brought you here?" the raspy-voiced man said into the phone, turning the questioning toward me. I had been interviewing a local author for an article, and so far he was even more entertaining than I expected.

He arrived in Alaska in the late 1940s and lived on a homestead, hauling in halibut and shooting black bears for years before Alaska became a state. He mused about an old railroad of which I had never seen any remnants, and remembered the 1964 earthquake as "the day the spit sank most of the way into the bay." He turned to writing when state and federal bureaucracy made it more difficult to glean a living from the land, and specialized in books that showcased the awe and terror of life in Alaska. He'd had some success as an author, and combined with enviable old-timer Alaskan credibility, was an instant hero to me.

"To Homer?" I replied.

"To Alaska. What brought you to Alaska?"

I wasn't sure how to answer that question. There was a lot the author knew about Homer that I did not, and I felt a need apologize for my status as an extreme newcomer. In Alaska, prolonged residency is more respected than wealth. If you haven't yet even survived a full winter, you might as well hold up a cardboard sign that says "Cheechako: Yes. Contempt: Noted." But this old-timer seemed friendly enough.

"I don't know," I said. "To live in Alaska, I guess."

"Is that right?"

I drew a breath. It didn't sound right, but it was the best vocalization of the truth that I had. Yes, I was here to pursue a relationship, and yes, I was actively searching. For what? It was difficult to define. But in two months, Alaska had taken on an appeal wholly separate from Geoff, my job, adventure prospects, or any single entity that drew me here initially. The attraction was almost chemical, manifested by the way my pulse fluttered every time I glanced toward the bay on my way home from work, or the way my heart raced as I pedaled beside towering hemlock trees and imagined lurking mysteries. Similar to making eye contact with a handsome stranger on the other side of a bar, I didn't yet understand why Alaska's rugged beauty and mysterious character tugged so firmly at my heart. I only knew that I wanted Alaska, and wanted to be with Alaska, in any way I could.

"Yeah, a lot more coming up here from Outside these days," the old-timer continued without waiting for me to expand my explanation. "Just trying to get away from something they left behind."

"I suppose so," I trailed off, and let a few seconds of silence bring the conversation back to the author and his books. After we hung up, I leaned against my desk and considered the old-timer's question. Was I running away from something? That was often the excuse non-Alaskans presented when they tried to comprehend why anyone would choose to reside in the Far North, displaced from more civilized society, and barely scraping a living from the harsh landscape. Anyone who wasn't native to Alaska had to be hiding something, or perhaps just couldn't find a way to fit in anywhere else. Why else would anyone willfully choose to live in the ice and snow?

I believed this was an unfair generalization. Even the old-timer had moved here from somewhere else, back when Alaska really was a frontier, for his own reasons. We all have to be outsiders somewhere, at some point. I viewed myself as running toward the future, not away from the past. But the author's question left me searching. Something about his assumption rang true.

It's true I'd grown weary of the person I'd become in Idaho. That version of myself worked as a copy editor at a daily newspaper, laying out pages and checking grammar and spelling rather than writing or planning the stories herself. The job was neither stressful nor intellectually stimulating. She went out with her co-workers nearly every weeknight, often lingering late into the night at bars or house parties thrown by strangers. She slept through the morning hours and then hit the gym for a half hour every day before going into work at two in the afternoon. She fretted over her eating habits and carefully measured portions of rice and vegetables at home, while regularly going out to binge on big meals at restaurants with her friends. She started making more time for spin classes and strength training, and began to lose weight. The gym made weight loss easy, and that ease soon overshadowed her desire to seek beauty and adventure in the outdoors. She rarely rode her bicycle; she stopped going hiking. She used her weekends to drive three hours south to Salt Lake City to visit Geoff. Sometimes they would go camping in the desert and it would be like old times. Other weekends, they would sit on the couch, chatting away idle hours with Geoff's roommates.

Then summer came, and Geoff went to Alaska. The person — the person I'd been just four months earlier — still traveled to Salt Lake every weekend to visit her family and hang out with friends at the house Geoff no longer occupied. Now all they did was chat away idle hours. They never went camping. She was growing tired of the couch. Back in Idaho, she continued to party with her co-workers. Although she had all but shunned alcohol before she moved to Idaho Falls, there drinking had become a nightly activity. She guzzled cocktails, danced at clubs, and played poker until dawn. She only occasionally talked on the phone with Geoff. As their long-distance relationship slipped into limbo, she flirted with strangers and started casually dating a co-worker.

Then, on an unseasonably cool morning in early August, she woke up dazed on the linoleum of her own kitchen floor. She had no idea how she got home, why she was on the floor, or where she had been for most of the night. The following day, she was so sick with alcohol poisoning that she could scarcely lift herself out of bed, and had to use her kitchen trash can as a vomit container. She called in sick to the newspaper, knowing her co-workers understood exactly why she couldn't work that day. The shame was so deep that she couldn't ask them what she desperately wanted to know: What happened? Where was I all night? Who drove me home? For her, it was all a flicker of half-memories and dark space, and she was terrified of unknowns that were now in her past. This incident was a harsh wake-up call, and she quit drinking cold turkey. She began to reassess this unwanted version of herself and her life.

Two weeks later, Geoff showed up at the door, holding the promise of change, of new life, of Alaska. I had no desire to go back to any time before that moment. I never wanted to be that version of myself again.

✳ ✳ ✳ ✳ ✳

"Were you happy in Utah?" I asked Geoff one evening as he served up another elaborate dinner spread. He set a pot of chili on the table and looked at me.

"Well, yeah," he said. "We knew some great people there. And I already miss the desert. It doesn't matter where I am, the desert is still my favorite place."

It occurred to me that I too might begin to feel homesick for the desert. I grew up with its sculpted canyons in my backyard. My family hauled my two younger sisters and me along on weekend camping trips in Zion National Park or Moab. We weren't the kind of family who went sightseeing in our car. From a young age I hiked with my parents, sometimes veering off trail to play on rolling mounds of sandstone. Even during my surliest teenage years, I could stand beneath the canopy of Delicate Arch and lose myself to the vastness of time. The desert had a way of reducing my human problems to shadows, flickering and fading on walls of ancient rock. I loved sandstone arches for the way they framed the landscape, refocusing miles of incomprehensible geology.

Alaska, conversely, offered no well-defined edges. Alaska was simply a human title for an incomprehensible amount of space — from the frozen tundra of the northwest to the moss-carpeted rain forests of the southeast. When I thought about the Aleutian volcanoes, the wind-battered villages of the Yukon Delta, and the snowbound peaks of Denali, I felt regret for all of the spaces I was never going to know. At least in the desert I could look through the eyelet of an arch and convince myself that I almost understood the beauty of the world. Rivers sectioned the Colorado Plateau into explorable pieces. Canyon walls housed an intimate world of colorful rock and cottonwood trees. I learned to recognize sedimentary layers and could discern their geological era. I often picked up shards of sandstone and pictured the floor of a primordial sea. I liked imagining the contrast between a teeming coral reef and the parched conglomeration of minerals it had become. Plant biodiversity was minimal in the desert; it didn't take me long to learn names and uses for many of the prominent flowers and brush. This knowledge allowed me to believe I understood the desert. Alaska, indefinable as it was, offered no such assurances.

"So why did you decide to leave Utah?" I asked Geoff. "What was it about Alaska that drew you away?"

"I've traveled up here so many times and every time it just feels right, like it's the place I want to be," Geoff said. "I could spend my whole life here and not even do a fraction of the things I want to do. So far it's been fun, don't you think?"

"Well, yeah. I love it here. But I wondered if you missed everyone there. Chris, Bryan, Jen ... pretty much all of our friends still live in Utah."

"Of course I do," Geoff said. "But we can always go back. For now, I'm really enjoying myself — working, traveling, skiing. It's a good balance." He paused. "And I am really glad you decided to move here, too. I wasn't stoked about Homer at first, but it's growing on me."

I nodded. "It's strange how this place seems to fit me so well. Maybe not strange, seeing as it's Homer," I said, and cracked a grin at my bad pun. "But I still feel like an outsider here. Like I'm still searching for my place."

"Well, would you ever go back to Idaho?" Geoff asked. "Were you happy there?"

I raised my eyes to meet his. "No, I wasn't. I was just thinking about that today. I wasn't happy at all." I paused. "I mean, you know I moved there because I was having a difficult time in Utah. I didn't like working full-time and living with all those people like we were still freshmen in college, setting couches on fire in the back yard for fun. But when I moved to Idaho it was even worse. I was alone out there even when I wasn't. I missed you. You didn't really seem to care." I shrugged and scanned Geoff's expression for hints of remorse.

"I did care," Geoff countered in a wounded tone. "You seemed so dead-set on leaving and I didn't know what to do. I wasn't going to move to Idaho."

"I know that," I said. "But I told you even before I took a new job that I was willing to get our own place in Salt Lake. You didn't even seem remotely interested in that. You thought it was great living with all your friends and paying a hundred-twenty-five a month for rent."

"There was no reason to pay more," Geoff said, clearly frustrated. "It was an ideal situation. You were the one who wanted to leave."

"We shared a house with six other people!" I said, unintentionally raising my voice. "They threw obnoxious parties every weekend and we all squabbled like children over the dishes and stolen food and other stupid crap. I was getting too old for that."

"But you weren't too old," Geoff said. "You were what — twenty four? See, this is the main issue. You're always too focused on the future to just live in the moment."

I leaned back in my chair as Geoff began dishing up chili. "Maybe," I said. "I only knew that I felt like I was suffocating. I was losing my mind."

"I know," Geoff said.

"But having my own space didn't end up working either. In Idaho, the suffocation only got worse. I guess I just needed space to figure out that's not what I wanted. I'm grateful I came here. I really am. I'm sorry if you felt like maybe I never appreciated living with you just because it didn't work out the first time."

Geoff and I had rehashed this before — the reasons why I moved away from Salt Lake. We spent comparatively little time discussing the discontinuity in our relationship. Even as Geoff tried to talk me into following him to Alaska, the fact that we had been effectively separated for nine months only rarely came up in conversation. I think we were both reluctant to call it what it was — a breakup — because we were both afraid of what it might mean to not have the other person in our lives. We had been friends first, and ending our relationship would dually fracture what for both of us had been an empowering friendship. Geoff taught me to trust myself, to take chances, to be brave. I fostered his compassion and desire to explore. But these individual advancements didn't trump the devotion we felt for each other. Our love was subtle but sincere.

After dinner, Geoff decided he wanted to go cross-country skiing by moonlight. He had been going out for snowshoe hikes or ski explorations almost daily since the snow started to accumulate on the ground. He stomped his own trail from our backyard, descending a steep embankment into the creek drainage, where he weaved through alder branches and spruce trees until he reached the Homestead Trail. Snowfall regularly obliterated his tracks, so he'd go out the next day to cut the trail again. Geoff was proud of his work and vowed to put his own trail system in place by the middle of winter — trails that could potentially take us from our cabin to all of the hidden pockets of Homer's backcountry.

I liked the idea of having trails out our back door, but had yet to explore any of Geoff's routes myself. I reasoned that I was always working during the day, and still felt reluctant about going out at night when moose lurked behind alders and I might stumble into the winter den of the resident grizzly bear family. Geoff did most of his workouts during the daylight hours, and preferred to spend his evenings unwinding with a New Yorker magazine and a mug of mint tea. I was still riding my bike to work, but the buildup of ice and snow was becoming too precarious even for my knobby mountain bike tires. Late sunrises and early sunsets meant even my bike commutes required riding with a weak headlamp in the dark.

I was looking into the expensive proposition of a gym membership so I could at least stay active through months of shorter days and cold weather. I also was awaiting a pair of used cross-country skis I'd purchased on eBay. Until they arrived, my only means of snow travel was a clunky pair of snowshoes, which punched holes into smooth ski trails. That night, citing exhaustion that was likely more emotional than physical, I declined Geoff's invitation to join him on a moonlight outing.

"Are you sure?" he asked. "There probably won't be any other skiers on the trails this time of night. I doubt anyone will care that you're on snowshoes anyway."

"No, I really am pretty tired," I said. "Plus, I need to e-mail my parents. It's been a while since I wrote home."

I stood at the landscape windows and watched Geoff's headlamp beam disappear into the purple shadows of the forest, then climbed the creaky stairs and sat down at his aging Hewlett Packard computer. The hand-built desk was strewn with cardboard boxes, paper, and tape. Piles of load bars, rack towers, trays, and bicycle components were neatly stacked in the corner of the loft. I glanced at a notepad scribbled with indecipherable handwriting — Geoff's version of accounting — and felt a rush of affection. For whatever Geoff and I had been, and whatever our future would be, I knew that I loved him in that moment, and that was enough. The future was an illusion anyway. The past was locked in memory. This desk, built of junkyard lumber and covered in the debris of Geoff's livelihood, was all I had in the immediate present. It was all that I needed.

I fired off an e-mail to my mother and started on my regular "newsletter" to friends who were now scattered all over the country. Because it was difficult to write them all individually, I had developed a habit of sending mass-e-mails to everyone I knew. Instead of rambling on about a bland list of news items, I spent quite a bit of time crafting stories that emphasized the more unique sides of our life in Alaska — such as the grizzly bear in our backyard or the October snow. I attached digital images of our snow-blanketed cabin with the Kenai Mountains in the background, sunset over Kachemak Bay, and moose grazing on fireweed stalks. My intention was to spark maximum envy in hopes of enticing a few friends to visit. But these e-mails also indulged the cathartic pleasure I derived from telling stories. When one of my friends made an off-handed joke about clogging up her inbox, I began to wonder if I should just expand this satisfying hobby to a wider audience rather than continue to burden my friends.

I was already an avid journal keeper, with notebooks about my life stretching all the way back to the third grade. But it's difficult to devote the mental energy to descriptive writing if you don't think anyone is ever going to read it, and I soon fell into the trap of journal entries that said little more than "Today sucked. It was boring. Nothing happened."

During Geoff's and my road trip across Alaska and cross-country bike tour, I updated a Web site that gained a small following. But hosting the site was expensive and I soon resented paying twenty dollars a month to maintain an old trip journal that even Geoff only occasionally browsed. I took it down and returned to my paper journals. In the next two years, personal Web site opportunities advanced to the point where anyone could launch their own blog, complete with image hosting, free of cost. For several weeks I toyed with the idea of starting a blog about life in Homer.

"If everyone is so annoyed by me clogging up their inbox, they can go online to see Alaska awesomeness," I thought. I Googled the word "blog" and scanned hosting services. It seemed simple enough. I pondered a name for my blog and immediately thought about a pop song that helped inspire my move to Alaska, "Grey Ice Water" by Modest Mouse. The lyrics included a long refrain about life "On the Arctic Blast." I checked the Web address "arcticblast," which was taken. I remembered when I first heard the song, I thought the lyric was "On the Arctic Glass." The phrase always brought to mind sheets of blue ice floating in the open sea, and this tranquil image still appeared every time I heard the song, even after I learned the truth. "Arctic Glass" was a beautiful description for Alaska, and for a blog.

After I secured my Web address, I drew the blog's header title from another Modest Mouse lyric from "Grey Ice Water." It was a simple phrase to describe a blog penned by a newcomer in the northern state — "Up in Alaska."

"You got a job, up in Alaska. It's easy to save what the cannery pays cause there ain't nowhere to spend it," I sang to myself, grinning as I hit the necessary buttons to secure my tiny space in the World Wide Web.

I gazed at the blue template that was to become my outlet for storytelling and a record of my life in Alaska. It was simple and blank but glowing with potential. I felt the sense of opening to the first page of an epic novel, about a hero who embarks on a life-altering adventure. "So this is my new online journal about moving to Homer, Alaska …" I typed.

Learning to Ski

November 17, 2005

So I took the new cross country skis out for a little slide today. It was my second time ever — the first being at least four years ago. That was an experience that left both my ego and my knees so bruised that I put the memory out of my mind to the point of repression. But I remembered today as I snapped into my brand new bindings and started to slide forward ... wait ... I've been here before. It was the kind of thing that comes flooding back in a moment of silent dread ... Remembering the borrowed boots that were too small, the pair of battered skis with too much wax, and the small misstep that sent me careening into a creek.

But it's funny how much you can learn about something in the space of four years, even when you haven't revisited it once. Since that humbling first experience, I learned to downhill ski, took up bicycling for the first time since I was a child, learned to ride with sixty pounds of weight dangling from the frame, began riding in mud and gravel and even snow. My balance has improved; I'm a little stronger and a little less afraid of eating snow (tastes much better than sand, you know). So when I started sliding out of control today, I just pulled the other foot forward, and kept going for three miles.

❋ ❋ ❋ ❋ ❋

Cycling proved to be a difficult habit to quit. I was determined to improve my fitness and maintain the weight loss I worked so hard for in Idaho, but the difficulties of winter in Alaska were discouraging. Geoff had recently added weight lifting to his exercise routine. Two nights a week, he drove into town work out in the student weight room at Homer High School, which opened to the public on weeknights after five. I joined him a few times, but cardio options were limited to two ancient treadmills. The weight machines made unnerving noises, the benches were worn, the free weights were coated in a slimy film, and the entire place smelled as though someone had murdered a dozen high school wrestlers, doused the bodies in ammonia, wrapped them in rubber mats, and stored them beneath the floorboards for the past decade.

"How can you spend a whole ninety minutes here?" I asked one evening after the fragrance became too much to bear.

Geoff just shrugged. "It's cheap," he said.

As I awaited mail delivery of my cross-country skis, I discovered another community gym that allowed patrons to pay per visit rather than purchase a membership. The former residential house had been converted to a physical therapy office. A single large room held all of the exercise and weight machines, and there was another small yoga room. The gym even had an on-site trainer, a small but muscular man with a bushy mustache and wavy hair that hung most of the way down his back. He was perpetually enthusiastic and aggressively helpful, commenting on my body position or electronic settings every time I set myself up on the spin bike or elliptical machines. I preferred privacy while sweating — hard to find in that small space — so I often buried my nose in fitness magazines.

As I flipped through the glossy pages and read trite declarations of well-being, it occurred to me that I was reverting back to old habits. My gym routine in Idaho Falls was a major part of my identity, and yet it became just another method to mindlessly pass the time. I would escape into television screens and magazines while I ran on treadmills, then submit to the commands of my spin class or body pump instructors without giving any thought to how these movements actually made me feel. I enjoyed the physiological benefits — fat loss, muscle growth, and surges of energy and endorphins. But there was no connection between my mind and my body. I conducted myself like a hamster on a wheel, carelessly spinning circles with a vague hope of future benefit. My mindset during these sessions felt manufactured, full of derivative mantras, pulsing beats, and pop music. I understood the benefits of healthy activity, but emotionally, it was difficult to discern how my daily visit to Apple Fitness differed from my nightly retreat into alcohol and superficial human connections. Either way, I was tuning out.

Even here, three thousand miles away in Alaska, I could still find a climate-controlled gym, an elliptical machine and a convenient fitness routine. And here the magazines still told me this is everything I should want — "Get Killer Abs in Six Weeks" … "Lose 40 Pounds by Christmas" … "Make the Perfect Cocktail." I always believed the magazines, because why shouldn't I? My friends went to the gym, showed off their biceps, chatted about protein sources, and got wasted at parties. Magazines and media reinforced these activities as habits of successful people — get a good body, get some more friends, get a good man, and get some money. Only then will you be on the path to happiness. I liked to think of myself as immune to popular culture, and yet here I was, pursuing these things because I didn't know what else to pursue. Even as I fantasized about a tight butt and six-pack abs, I could still see these desires for what they were — glossy images on paper, lacking depth and substance. I looked down at my white cotton T-shirt, saturated in sweat and nearly translucent. Were six-pack abs even what I wanted out of life? I highly doubted that.

"It's not nearly as bad as the high school, but it's still kind of depressing to work out at a gym," I told Geoff after I returned from my first visit.

"Oh, I agree," he said. "But it's good for variety and it's convenient, too. How much does that gym cost?"

"They have these ten-visit punch passes," I said. "Sixty dollars for ten."

Geoff shook his head. "That's pretty steep."

"Yeah, but I figure I won't go there all that often. Hopefully those skis come soon and I can start going out with you some evenings. Also, I've been thinking more about riding my bike."

"All winter?"

"Yeah," I said. "I was reading online about these mountain bike tires with carbide studs, that have good traction on ice. When the weather's not too bad, I could go out and ride on the roads, even if they're packed with snow."

"Studded bike tires, huh?" Geoff said. "Where did you find out about those?"

"People talked about them on my blog," I said.

"Up in Alaska" had been up and running for just over a week, and it already acquired a small readership. Some readers even left comments at the end of posts. I wasn't sure how random strangers were stumbling across my blog already, but their advice was useful.

"A lot seem to live in Alaska — Anchorage mostly — and the other day one sent me a link to these tires," I said. "They're made by Kenda. Kind of expensive, sixty-five dollars each. But if I could ride my bike all winter long, it would be worth it."

"A hundred thirty for two? That's expensive for tires, but it's a good idea," Geoff said. "Maybe once I get my ski trail in place we can pack it down and widen it to singletrack for the bikes. Now that would be fun, riding snow singletrack."

"Exactly," I said. "That might be doable."

The following day was Tuesday, deadline day. At 5:30 a.m., I stepped out of my cabin to a blast of single-digit cold and a foot of new snow.

"Oh no," I groaned. Geoff had recently contracted the services of a snowplow driver to clear our driveway after every snowstorm, but he rarely showed up before nine in the morning. On Tuesdays I was supposed to arrive at the office by six, and my only means of transportation — bike or car — were blocked by deep powder. Driving the Prism out of the driveway was going to be next to impossible unless I spent the next two hours shoveling. Walking six miles was also impractical under my time constraints. I looked at my mountain bike — a three-year-old Gary Fisher Sugar, built for riding rocks and dirt — and sighed.

"Worth a try."

Without waking up Geoff to warn him of my plan — to save myself embarrassment just in case it backfired spectacularly — I pulled on an extra pair of cotton socks, changed into a thick pair of hiking boots, and pulled ski pants and my Burton shell over my work attire. I put on a pair of mittens, a fleece balaclava, and for good measure, goggles. Now I was ready to bike commute in the snow.

I shoved my mountain bike down the porch steps, and the wheels promptly sank to their hubs in snow. The small handlebar headlight and blinking red taillight cast jarring reflections on the white surface. A half mile from our cabin, Trail Court intersected with the main corridor of Diamond Ridge. That road hadn't been plowed yet, either, but enough trucks had driven down the center to cut smooth ruts into the uneven surface. I wheeled my bike into one of the ruts and began coasting down the hill. Every time I turned the crank, the pedals skimmed against the hard-packed walls of the rut and the front wheel started to shimmy. But by simply coasting, I could make forward progress through the snow. I smiled as though I'd just discovered a new method of motion, like learning to fly.

As the descent became steeper, the front wheel jumped out of the rut and sliced through the deep snow. After negotiating the icy rut, plowing through powder felt weightless. I wondered if this is what Alpine skiers felt as they carved turns in a white cloud. Still, the mountain bike was hardly an alpine skier, and after a few seconds I began swerving wildly out of control. The bike tipped over and hurled my body into a snow bank, where I landed in a soft pillow of powder. With snow packed into my collar and pant legs, I laughed and stood up. That didn't hurt at all. The rest of Diamond Ridge passed with more of the same — flying, swerving, launching, laughing. However, when I reached the intersection of West Hill Road, the pavement was recently plowed and icy. Fear returned.

"I need studded tires for this," I thought. West Hill Road was covered in thick, black ice that had been scraped clean of forgiving snow. On top of that, the road lost a thousand feet of elevation in just over two miles — a considerably steep descent that was frightening enough when it was dry. I walked my bike to the edge and pushed the tires over the surface as a test. The front wheel slid out almost immediately and I nearly lost my footing trying to right the bike.

"Oh, it's impossible," I grumbled. I looked back toward Diamond Ridge. I was only a couple miles from my house, and could walk or attempt to ride the bike back. But my car was still buried in snow, as was Geoff's, and short of shoveling for hours, there was little he could do to help me.

The only solution I could see was to hike two miles down the slippery road while cars streamed past in the dark. I wheeled my bike onto the shoulder of the road and waded through knee-deep snow drifts left behind by the plows. I had walked only about fifty feet when the first truck to pass pulled over.

"You need a ride?" asked a gruff-looking man with an unwieldy ginger beard. In any other part of the world I would have been frightened of him and his intentions. But this was Homer, Alaska, the epitome of small-town values, where everyone not only knew each other but unconditionally helped each other. A few weeks earlier, when I asked Carey why Homer residents were so extremely helpful, she told me, "It's really like this everywhere in Alaska. I think it's because everything is so dangerous here. In a place like Ohio, if you see someone stranded on the side of the road, you're inclined to keep going because chances are they'll be fine. But in Alaska, leaving someone stranded could mean leaving them to die. And no matter how self-involved we are, all of us are hard-wired to try and save somebody who's in trouble." I had no doubt that the red-bearded stranger's intentions were purely altruistic. After all, I was a solo woman walking a bicycle in knee-deep snow at 5 a.m. It should have seemed obvious that my pathetic life was in need of saving.

"I'm going to work," I said. "My car was stuck. I thought I could use my bike, but it's too icy."

"No problem!" he bellowed. "I'm on my way to the harbor. Fishing for winter kings, should be a good day for it. Throw the bike in the back and I'll take you to town."

As the truck screamed down the icy road at butt-clenching speeds, the red-bearded man expounded on the fine art of fishing for salmon in the winter. He spoke rapidly while waving a hand that I wished would stay on the wheel, pausing only long enough to ask me, "Where was it you said you were going?" I pointed him to the office of the Homer Tribune, thanked him, and moved the bike from the truck to the streetlight where I always locked it.

"Did you bike here?" Carey exclaimed as I brushed snow off my ski pants and stepped inside. She had a horrified look on her face.

"Kind of," I said. "My car was buried so I didn't really have a choice. I made it to the bottom of Diamond Ridge, and then it was too icy to ride. Luckily, this nice fisherman took pity on me and gave me a lift the rest of the way in his truck."

"Oh!" Carey said, laughing. "If you ever need a ride to work, just call me. You know I live right next door."

"I know," I said. "I got a late start and you were probably already gone. I could see your tracks on Trail Court. Anyway, sorry I'm late."

"You really need to get a better car," Carey said.

"I know that," I said. "Tell that to Jane. I'm not exactly raking in the dough right now."

"True," Carey said. "But seriously, a Subaru is a good investment."

"I'm thinking about getting some studded tires for my bike," I said. "They would have really helped me out this morning. My problem wasn't the snow, it was the ice."

Carey shook her head. "West Hill on a bike in the winter is a death wish. I don't want to have to write your obituary."

"I can see the headline," I laughed. "Crazy cheechako on bike mowed down by truck driven by real Alaskan. Driver sues for damages."

"Exactly," Carey said. "I don't want to be the one responsible for that headline. Until you get a truck, or at least a Subaru, call me for a ride when the weather's bad."

After we put the weekly paper to bed and the crew had finished up their Tuesday margaritas, Carey asked me if I needed a ride home.

"I don't know," I said. "The weather has cleared up, and I still have about, what, one and a half hours of daylight? Might actually be a nice afternoon for a ride."

"Are you serious?" Carey said as I grabbed the last tortilla chip, mouthing the words "bike fuel." "Fine, it's your funeral."

Most of the morning's ice had melted in the afternoon sun, even though the temperature remained a few degrees below freezing. Gray goo covered the road, and a steady spray of slush coated my mittens and face as I pedaled down the road. Sweat pooled beneath my sweater and trickled down my back. Even though the same layers had barely blocked the chill during the morning hours, they were too much in the relative heat of the day. I was learning valuable lessons about the effect of physical effort on body temperature, and the importance of layering.

I stopped to remove my balaclava and unzip my coat. I didn't take it off for fear of ruining my clothes in the slush shower. This proved to be a poor strategy, as most of the slush spray erupted from the front, and my sweater was soon soaked anyway. A cold wind needled through my wet clothing. Instead of stopping again, I just pedaled harder. On the switchbacks of West Hill, I studied the road for patches of black ice and stole brief glances toward Kachemak Bay. The surface reflection appeared especially shimmery that afternoon, as a snow-covered shoreline intensified the contrast. Fresh snow clung to the tiniest surfaces of spruce needles and chain-link fences, adding an ethereal dimension to their ordinary shapes.

At the intersection of Diamond Ridge, I saw that the gravel road had been plowed and was now covered in an inch of packed snow. But to the right, Skyline Drive was still covered in deep powder broken only by vehicle ruts. I still had daylight to spare, so I decided to practice the technique of riding uphill through snow.

I steered into the fresh powder first and immediately stalled. Instead of hopping off the bike, I pedaled harder. The rear tire spun in place as gravity began to pull me sideways. I leaned into the handlebars, furrowing my brow in determination. The crank resisted even my hardest strokes, and the bike balked and stalled as though I were pedaling through quicksand. I avoided tipping over, but forward motion happened at a rate slower than crawling. I knew logically that adding studded tires would do nothing to alleviate the resistance of deep snow. Yet, this whole winter biking thing no longer seemed impossible.

At the top of the hill I turned around and let gravity carry me back on a cloud of powder. As I carved downhill, I passed a couple on cross-country skis. They looked up in surprise as I pried my clenched fingers from the handlebars for a split-second mitten wave. The sun had settled behind the trees, casting pink light across the frosted forest. By adding a simple white veneer, winter had painted a scene that was almost impossibly beautiful. The silence and serenity of the landscape was so absorbing that I became almost completely lost in it, until the skiers jolted my mind back to the human world. I gathered the skiers hadn't seen anybody else on Skyline Drive that afternoon, as I had not. We were among the few who ventured beyond our heated buildings and vehicles to immerse ourselves in beauty. Even though I was a weirdo on a bicycle, the skiers seemed to appreciate our solidarity, and waved back. Or maybe they were just being friendly.

Geoff came down the stairs as I wheeled my slush-coated bike into the cabin. "So you rode to work today? How did it go?"

"Not all that bad," I said. "I ended up hitching a ride on the way to work because there was so much ice on West Hill. But I was able to ride all the way home. I even took a short detour to check out Skyline Drive. It's hard but possible to ride a bike through fresh snow. If I get studded tires, I can't really see any problem with riding all winter long."

"Were you cold?"

"Not really," I said. "I over-dressed if anything, although I probably would have gotten pretty cold if I actually had to ride down West Hill in the morning. Plus, I got soaked riding home and was starting to feel cold as the sun went down. But all in all, it wasn't a bad experiment in winter bike commuting. I think it went well."

"And guess what, your skis came!" Geoff said. "I had to wait until the plow guy came at noon to go to the post office, but I went to drop of some packages and your skis were there. I was going to see if you wanted to head out after dinner. Just a short ski; I'll show you some basics."

I looked down at my coat and mittens. I didn't have any other winter clothing that wasn't soaked in slush. "I'm really pretty exhausted from all this biking today," I admitted. "And I was hoping to have some time to write a blog post tonight. But, really, thanks for picking up my skis. Maybe I can join you tomorrow."

"Are you sure?" Geoff said. "It's a nice night."

"Really," I said. "I still have bad associations from trying to ski with Monika like four years ago. I'll need more mental stamina for my first time in Alaska."

Geoff shrugged. "Okay. I kept it simple tonight, just vegetarian tacos, and I made some salsa. If you don't want to come, I'll probably head out for a couple of hours."

"Great," I said.

As Geoff finished cooking dinner, I scanned the planks that he had already removed from the box. They were an older pair of Salomon skis, navy blue, with clunky-looking bindings. To me, they seemed a difficult piece of gear to connect with, almost oppressive in their anchor-like attachment to feet and legs. Memories of my first experience cross country skiing in Utah were still tinged with fear. I remembered the way they always pulled me toward places I didn't want to go. I had to side-step up every hill because I kept sliding backwards. And then, when we were only a few hundred yards from the trailhead, I accidentally careened down a gully and fell face-first into an icy creek. Skis were a difficult piece of gear to control. They didn't have the all-terrain utility or brakes of a bicycle, and yet most people accepted that skis were the only way to travel in the winter.

Still, options were never a bad thing. Anything was preferable to spending every single day languishing in the hot and humid gym, toiling without engagement and traveling nowhere. Why I hadn't figured this out when I lived in a more temperate climate, I'll never know. But I did now know the subtle beauty of bike tracks in the snow, and I knew the awe of a winter sunset. I sensed a deeper understanding written in the frozen landscape, and I wasn't about to go back to the gym.

Susitna Dreams

November 28, 2005

Scenic drive back down the Peninsula today. A rather rough freeze has transformed the Turnagain Arm into boulders of ice. I looked out at the tortured seascape and thought of Death Valley — a beautiful desolation born of heat, not ice.

We stopped at a bike shop in Anchorage and bought studded tires for our mountain bikes. And it looks like we'll have snow cover to practice on for a long time now. We returned home to nearly two feet of new powder on everything. We spent a better part of the clear and cold evening stamping through thigh-deep snow to find the snowshoe trail we've been working on.

Anyway, Geoff and I were so giddy at the prospect of extending the cycling season indefinitely that we picked up a brochure for the Susitna 100 and began planning our training regimen. We thought we were all bad because we even had thoughts of participating in a winter bike race that crosses snow-covered tundra during the deep freeze of subarctic night. But then we discovered the prohibitive entrance fee, regulating the races to those who have, well, a little bit more than blind gumption and gear. But if anyone out there — anyone at all — feels inspired to sponsor us in our efforts as virgin ice bikers tackling a decidedly hardcore bike race in the frozen north, we will proudly display your logo and our gratitude on this blog for as long as it takes. I'm not joking. Really. Why are you laughing?

✳ ✳ ✳ ✳ ✳

It didn't take me long to locate the mystery bus, which turned out to be deliberately not secretive, adorned as it was in blinking Christmas lights and destination placard that read "Visa Quest." The glittering vehicle was parked next to the Beluga Lake Lodge, a floatplane-themed bar at the edge of town. Muffled melodies from banjos and fiddles carried through the otherwise still air. I shouldered the Tribune's clunky digital camera and hiked through knee-deep snow toward the log building.

Two younger men stood on the front porch. One was my height with a buzz cut and a goofy grin. The other was tall with a broad chin, wavy blond hair and blue eyes, and so attractive that I instantly felt weak-kneed and embarrassed. Both men wore the ever-present Homer uniform: Tan Carhartt pants, Xtratuf rubber boots, and flannel lumberjack shirts. Neither was wearing a coat or a hat despite the fact that it was about zero degrees outside. I, on the other hand, was bundled in full snow gear just so I could take a few photos of this supposedly unofficial, underground bluegrass concert. Carey assigned this mission to hunt for a secret bus that was reported to have rolled into town earlier in the day. In Alaska, old-time and bluegrass music is a big deal, and this event — an annual gathering of musicians at an undisclosed destination — included all the big names on Alaska's scene. It wasn't exactly undercover reporting, but the secretive nature made me feel like a real journalist. The attractive blond flashed a toothy grin as I approached the door.

"Um, is this Visa Quest?" I asked.

"Sure is," the man with the buzz cut said.

"And it's open to the public, right?"

"Yeah," the attractive guy said. "What's with the camera?"

"Oh, this," I said sheepishly. My cheeks suddenly felt flushed. "I'm going to take some pictures for the Homer Tribune. Hope that's okay."

"Don't see why not," the other man said. He had a strange inflection in his voice, almost like a southern drawl, although he seemed distinctly Alaskan. "So do you want an interview? I'm Nikos Kilcher. This is my cousin, Eivan."

My flushed cheeks became hot. "Oh, so you're the Kilchers! I've heard so much about you."

"Yeah? Well, we're all over the place," Nikos said.

"That's what I hear," I said. "Do you know my co-worker, Layton?"

"Layton?" Eivan interjected. "Of course." His grin grew wider.

"So you guys hang out with Layton?"

"Yeah," Nikos said. "He's cool."

"I'm guessing he's here as well, huh?" I said. "I'm mostly here to shoot photos. Are you guys performing tonight?"

"We play some," Nikos said. "Eivan is a fire spinner. Were you at Burning Basket on the Equinox? Eivan was the one twirling the fire baton."

"That was you?" I said to Eivan, feeling my face glowing like the sun. "I was there. That was a really incredible performance."

"Thanks," Eivan said as he pursed his lips to more of a shy smile.

"How long have you guys lived in Homer?"

"Our whole lives!" Nikos practically shouted. "The homestead is out East End Road. There are some good mountain biking trails. You should drop by sometime."

My heart raced. I hoped Nikos' gorgeous, unattainable cousin would think my face was red from the cold, not raging attraction. Of course I had no intention of leaving Geoff to pursue the shallow excitement that was fluttering in my chest, but it was fun to experience these sensations all the same. It had been a while since I had developed a real crush.

"Sounds very beautiful," I said. "I'll have to check it out sometime."

"We're mostly around in the winter," Eivan said. "In the summer I travel all over the state for an independent film company. We go to Kodiak and the Aleutians, and shoot documentaries."

Oh, be still my heart.

"That sounds awesome," I said. "That must be a really great job."

"It's fantastic," Eivan said.

"So, are you going to meet the elders?" Nikos interjected.

"The elders?"

"The elders of Visa Quest. Don't you know about the elders?"

I did know about the elders. I had interviewed one of them a few days ago, when rumors erupted that Visa Quest would return to Homer. There were a lot of secret-society codes surrounding the event, but I managed to find the name of a guy who lived in Juneau and was said to be the main organizer. He told me it originated about a decade ago, when he and two friends in Fairbanks decided the Far North was too cold, and they wanted to travel to Homer for a fair-weather jam session. They called it "Visa Quest" because the trip apparently inspired abundant credit card use.

Since then, Visa Quest had grown to an annual tradition involving a reunion of old friends, a beer-fueled bus trip from Talkeetna, a few hundred participants, and dozens of musicians awaiting their turn on a stage that purported to make room for everyone. From an outsiders' view, Visa Quest was just a large party with bluegrass music. Insiders, however, treated it as a mythical journey, an annual quest for enlightenment through old-timey music and copious amounts of whiskey. The event wasn't advertised. The elder I interviewed wouldn't even disclose where they planned to play, but he did tell me to find the bus and come inside.

"Oh, of course, the Visa Quest elders," I said. "I talked to one of them already, the one who lives in Juneau. Can't remember his name right now. Anyway, they seem like interesting guys."

"You should go in," Nikos said. "I think he'll be playing soon."

I purposely avoided eye contact with Eivan as I shuffled through the door. The temperature instantly shot up at least eighty degrees as I squeezed into a tight crowd of dancing fans. There must have been two hundred people in the bar, and I was baffled by how so many knew about Visa Quest when I was a journalist and had to jump through a dozen hoops just to get there. I supposed you had to be one of those "real Alaskans."

I unzipped my outer layers and pushed my way through the roiling mass to the front of the stage, which was simply a carpet laid out on the wood floor. The crowd was characteristically eclectic, featuring everyone from aging hippies to black-leather-clad teenagers to a man wearing a medieval jester costume and guiding a similarly dressed wooden puppet across the floor. Nearly everyone was twirling to the melody of a frantic fiddle player and clapping along with the drummer's erratic beats.

I raised the camera and began shooting portraits. In my opinion, the music was the least interesting aspect of Visa Quest. The rampant popularity of old-time music in Alaska was confusing, given the geographic distance — four thousand miles — from the American South, and the fact that many of the themes — farming, 1930s nostalgia, Appalachia — had little to do with the culture of the Far North. I was admittedly not a fan of the music; I found fiddle and banjo harmonies to be fun in small doses but grating after five minutes. I couldn't get past the notion that the music all sounded the same and the lyrics had no relevance to modern life. But Alaskans love their old-time, and the music does bring together the most interesting people.

As I held my camera over the swirling mass, I caught a glimpse of Ivan's blond mane a head above the crowd. He turned and smiled at me, or at least at my camera. I blushed again and looked away. What was wrong with me? I didn't think harmless flirtations were particularly bad, but I did wonder what it was about Eivan that ignited this rush of hormones. Amid the loud music and sweat-soaked dancers, I felt like a teenager again, floating through an electric storm of music and motion, with the thrilling sense that anything could happen, and might.

Still, I was older now, and becoming more content by the day about my simple life with Geoff. I wondered if, on some primal level, Eivan represented a wistfulness for the youth I was leaving behind. But as I continued to steal glimpses of his flannel shirt in the crowd, I realized that one of the reasons Ivan was so attractive was because he was a Kilcher. He was handsome, but my interest hadn't been fully sparked until I learned his family status. The Kilchers were the locally famous progeny of Yule Kilcher, a farmer and statesman who immigrated from Switzerland to Homer in 1940. He built a homestead that is an ancient relic by Alaska standards, and raised eight children, who in turn raised numerous grandchildren and great-grandchildren. One of those grandchildren was Jewel Kilcher, who, after growing up on a six-hundred-acre Alaska homestead without running water or electricity, went on to sell millions of records and become a folk superstar. As far as I could tell, Nikos and Eivan were probably Jewel's cousins. But beyond that, they were part of the storied dream of starting a new life in the Great Land. Yule came to Alaska with nothing, hauled fish out of the sea, constructed a home, got involved in politics, contributed widely to the budding culture of the state, and built an empire that now spanned four generations. His grandchildren were the reflection of that pioneering spirit.

So I didn't necessarily harbor a crush on Eivan himself, but more on the idea of Eivan — the freedom and opportunity of Alaska. Maybe someday I would travel the Alaska wilderness, and be paid to work on nature documentaries in beautiful landscapes. For now, I was paid to lurk at bluegrass concerts and shoot newspaper photographs of quirky Alaskans. Still, it was an engaging assignment. Why would I want more?

❋ ❋ ❋ ❋ ❋

Thanksgiving was my first major holiday away from home. In my twenty-six years, there had never been a late November that didn't involve a crowd
of extended family members wedged into my grandparents' small house, my
mother's pies, or my grandmother strong-arming every child into a draw-out
speech about thankfulness over a table full of rapidly cooling turkey and stuffing. I didn't anticipate longing for these family gatherings, but as the holiday
approached, I felt tinges of a cultural crisis. Why acknowledge holidays at all
when everything they represent is so far away? How much value does beauty
and adventure have without the people I love? What is more important, a sense
of place or a sense of belonging? Despite brave intentions, homesickness crept
into the cracks.

Geoff's and my best friends in Alaska lived two hundred and fifty miles north
of Homer, in the Matanuska River Valley. Craig and Amity were old friends,
part of the "D Street" clan from the communal house in Salt Lake City. The couple moved to Alaska a year before Geoff and me, after Craig graduated from law
school and landed a clerkship at the courthouse in Palmer. They loved Alaska so
much they decided to stay. Craig found a job with the state attorney general, and
Amity worked part-time at a bookstore in town. The distance was far enough
that we only had visited once since we moved to Alaska, so we made plans to
spend Thanksgiving together.

Amity went back to Utah for the holidays, so Craig took on the bulk of the
cooking. An admitted anti-gourmet, he served up several dishes that were mainly variations on potatoes and dairy fat. Geoff provided stuffed mushrooms and
salad, and I purchased rolls, soda and pumpkin pie at the grocery store. Craig
also invited two other couples who contributed a turkey breast and booze, which
Craig, a Mormon, didn't condone but also didn't forbid.

As the seven of us sat down to a spread of foil-wrapped food, I couldn't
help but smile at the strange family we had compiled for the holiday. There
was Libby, another young lawyer, and her boyfriend, Geoff, a Jewish couple
from New York City; Zion and Nevhis, other recent law school graduates from
New England; Craig, the temporary bachelor; and Geoff and me, whose families
lived in upstate New York and suburban Salt Lake. These divergent paths managed to meet on an ice-coated gravel road that dead-ended in a veritable wall of
the Chugach Mountains, branching out toward the wilderness. We compared
Craig's side dishes and discussed major league baseball as a blizzard ranged on
the other side of the kitchen window.

On Friday morning, Craig guided Libby, me and the two Geoffs to his favorite ski trail. It was morning in the Alaskan sense of morning, which on weekends
begins bleary-eyed and saturated in coffee well after the 10:30 a.m. sunrise. If
an Alaskan asks you to meet them for breakfast in the morning, they most likely

mean sometime around noon. In the Matanuska Valley, Craig told us, the winter sun never quite rose over Pioneer Peak, so the region was perpetually bathed in shadow if not darkness. As we drove toward the Crevasse Moraine trailhead, the streets were as dark and quiet as the pre-dawn hours of more civilized latitudes. It was 12:30 in the afternoon. The temperature was one below zero.

My "new" cross-country skis were both split down the center, a major flaw I failed to notice before it was too late to return them. On top of that, my ski boots were European size 44, which apparently translated to four sizes too large. The tips of the skis curled up and frequently caught low-lying branches. No matter what I tried, I moved like a lame duck on roller skates every time I used them. I awkwardly shuffled after the group until we reached the first hill along the otherwise pancake flat shoreline of the river. Crevasse Moraine was the lumpy bed of a disappearing glacier. For millennia, the land had been crushed and compacted under the considerable heft of its occupant. A rapidly warming climate sent the river of ice recoiling back into the mountains, and the land sprang back up like a rebounding mattress.

This ripple of earth was adorned with a young forest of skinny birch trees and alders coated in frost. With my focus all directed toward keeping my skis on the ground, it was difficult to discern the lines between trees and the trail. As I stopped to gather my bearings, I noticed a strange configuration of brown ornaments perched near the tops of the tallest trees. I squinted until I could see black eyes staring right at me, attached to camouflaged white heads. Bald eagles. There were at least a dozen occupying one tree — yet another Alfred Hitchcock scene that sent shivers down my spine.

"The city dump is next door," Craig said by way of explanation. I nodded. Of course. The only reason eagles ever gather in such large numbers is for garbage and handouts. A person could venture through wilderness for weeks and never see an eagle. But here, dozens had congregated beside a mountain of trash, contaminated with bothersome people and diesel fumes. Eagles were like people in that way — we all tended to gravitate toward places that were easy if uninspiring, comfortable and annoying at the same time.

I waddled up another hill and strained to make an A-formation with my skis. The tips crossed as I careened down the slope, knocking fresh snow and frost off branches along the way. I managed to keep myself upright until the bottom of the hill, when the skis ripped apart like the dangling pieces of a broken pencil. I tipped and tumbled to a stop in a cloud of powder.

My friends were too far ahead to witness the crash. The snow settled, and for a few stunned seconds, all was quiet. Lying on my back, I watched my breath curl into ribbons of frost around my hair. When I blinked, my eyelashes froze together. I reached into my pocket and fished out my digital camera for a self-portrait. The image on the screen showed an enchanted version of myself: a bright red face brushed with snow, a black hood bedazzled in frost, and glittering white hair and eyelashes. I was not one for make-up, but found this frosted makeover enchanting. Subzero air and frozen respiration painted a raw, intense kind of glamor on my face. I felt beautiful.

I reattached my skis and scooted along my friends' tracks. I ran to make up lost time, awkwardly lifting the ski anchors and clunking them back down until all of the glitter fell from my face. Geoff looked back as I ran up beside him.

"Jill, you're walking on your skis again," he said.

"I know that," I said. "Shuffling was too slow. I couldn't keep up."

Geoff laughed. "We've gone over this. You need to kick and glide." He launched into an exaggerated shuffling motion, supposedly to show me what he meant.

"I see what you're doing," I said, and mimicked him by dragging my feet over the snow. "I just don't see how it's different than what I'm doing."

Geoff continued to make attempts to teach me proper cross-country skiing technique, eventually throwing his arms up in exasperation. I purposely fell fifty meters behind, so I could continue to run in my skis. I was still keeping a similar speed, and judging my the volume of frozen sweat clinging to my hair and skin versus my friends, I was getting the better workout anyway. After ninety minutes, the sweaty effort left us all chilled, so we opted to take a short-cut back to the car. We agreed it was a solid workout anyway, enough to justify a feast of Craig's starchy leftovers, cold turkey, and more pumpkin pie.

✳ ✳ ✳ ✳ ✳

While driving back to Homer, Geoff and I stopped at REI in Anchorage to purchase studded mountain bike tires. I was excited for an opportunity to commute down West Hill Road without killing myself, and Geoff figured he'd join my weekend rides. We picked up four tires, tubes, and extra chain lube for the slush and snow. As we browsed the bike section of the store, I noticed one of the strangest looking bicycles I had ever seen, hanging from rafters in the ceiling. The grape-purple frame had grotesquely wide tires, large enough to fit a motorcycle, which made it look like a bicycle with an unfortunate case of elephantiasis. It looked like a mountain bike, and yet it had no suspension. I was mesmerized.

"Check it out," I pointed the hanging bike to Geoff. "Weird bike, huh?"

"Yeah, that's one of those snow bikes," Geoff said. "See?" he pointed to the decal on the frame. "That's the Surly Pugsley."

"Snow bike," I repeated. "But why doesn't it have studded tires?"

Geoff shrugged. "Guess you don't need them if you're just riding on snow-mobile trails, not icy roads. The wide tires help you float on top of the snow. Sort of like wide skis."

I craned my neck until it hurt, examining the shiny components and chevron tire tread. I had read about fat-tire bikes on Internet forums, but I'd not yet taken the time to research options. Although independent frame builders had designed custom fat bikes since the 1990s, the Surly Pugsley was the first mass-marketed fat bike, and it just came out that year. "This is exactly what I need," I thought. Then I caught a glimpse of the price tag. Eighteen hundred dollars. Nope.

As we checked out the tires and supplies that were already stretching our budget, I picked up a brochure that was sitting next to the register. The cover featured an illustration of a person riding a bike through the snow, next to a skier with a backpack and a hiker dragging some sort of sled. Above the log was the title, "Susitna 100: A Race Across Frozen Alaska."

"Check this out," I said to Geoff.

"Oh yeah, I've read about that race," Geoff said. "People ride their bikes a hundred miles in the winter on the dogsled trail. I think it's called Iditarod, er, Iditabike. Something like that."

"Susitna 100 is the name of the race," I said. "Really interesting."

I continued to flip through the brochure as Geoff drove along the frozen contours of the Turnagain Arm on Alaska Highway One. "You know, this race is open to everyone," I said. "It's in February, so we still have three months to train for it. Maybe we could sign up."

"What, are you crazy?" Geoff said, laughing. "A hundred miles in the winter on a bike? Are you serious?"

"I don't know," I said. "It would be like a winter camping trip, but … longer. It would be kinda fun."

Geoff smirked. "Fun. That's probably what I'd call it, too. How much does it cost?"

I nervously turned the brochure over. "Well, it's two hundred and twenty five dollars."

"What? For one race? You've got to be kidding."

"But get this," I said. "They give out gear, have good checkpoints, food, safety patrols."

"Maybe it sounds cool," Geoff said. "But that is a lot of money. I don't really get why you would want to do it. Have you ever even entered a race before? It's going to hurt, a lot. And you're going to have to train for it."

"That's the point," I said. "I could use a goal for this winter. I mean, yeah,

I've never really been in any kind of race before. But I don't see how training for this race will be all that different from when I was preparing for our bike tours."

"What? It will be completely different," Geoff said. "For starters, you're going to have to ride a lot longer, every day, in the cold, in the dark. You're going to have to learn how to manage things like nutrition and pacing. You're going to need to get the right gear, too."

"I have these," I said, pointing to the studded tires in the back seat. "It's a start."

Geoff laughed. "You're crazy." I could understand his reservations. Geoff knew all about the difficulty of racing. He had been a star on his high school cross-country team, and ran for the single year he spent at Syracuse University. He placed well in all of his races, but burned out on the schedules and training. Racing burn-out was the main reason he dropped out of college. I, on the other hand, was on my high school debate team, and that was close as I ever came to competitive sports.

Still, Geoff and I shared a similar adult athletic pedigree. We had all of the same hobbies, and did a fair percentage of our hiking, cycling, rowing and skiing together. We were well-matched on our cross-country bike tour, and I could usually keep pace with him on backpacking trips. I had my gym phase and Geoff dabbled in snowshoe racing and the occasional relay or ten-kilometer running race. Geoff was certainly the more natural and talented athlete, but when it came to motivation and drive, I thought we were similarly matched.

"Look," I said. "They have a ski division and a running division. You could ski instead of bike. They also have a smaller race, only fifty kilometers. It's called the Little Su 50K."

"A 50K, huh?" Geoff said, suddenly perked up. "That at least sounds more enjoyable."

"Yeah," I said. "That would be more realistic." But in my mind, some strange urge was still pulling me toward the hundred miler. If you're going to be ridiculous, I thought quietly, why not be completely ridiculous?

"How would we pay the entry fee?" Geoff said. "It's not like we're going to find sponsors."

"I'll think of something," I said. "Something will work out."

Revisited

December 1, 2005

I spent an hour grinding away on my bike trainer to-day, staring at a fuzzy television program I couldn't hear anyway and thinking about how I'd really like to attempt the Susitna 100. Geoff is still talking about doing the Little Su 50K ... he thinks he may even run it ... but I don't know. If we're going to all that effort, why not go all the way? I know, I know. I've already had the "crazy" talk with Geoff. And I know I'll need to acquire some more gear and a little good 'ol Alaskan toughness and all of that. But still, I want to do it. Why, you ask? Well, why cross the country on a bicycle? To see if I can.

I still have that other aforementioned problem of pay-ing the entry fee. I came up with an idea while riding the trainer that may seem more crazy than wanting to do this race in the first place. In charity rides, people usually put some sort of monetary value on their miles and collect pledges. So here's what I resolve to do: I set up a little donation box in the sidebar of this blog. For every dollar, I'll ride one icy mile on my mountain bike before Dec. 31 (the payment due date). Even if I have to ride in the middle of the night in a blizzard to meet my goal, I figure that will do more to help me get ready for this race than anything. I'll keep a log of the rides and their sponsors on this blog, and offer regular updates of my progress. And, if I come woefully short of the entrance fee or if another unforeseen circumstance keeps me out of the race, I'll donate any funds raised to a worthy charity such as the Lance Armstrong Foundation. Is that too crazy of an idea? (Keep in mind I just thought of it a couple of hours ago while I was sweating buckets on my living room rug.) I don't know, but I thought it might be worth a dollar or two to some out there just to read about the horrors of headwinds at -5 degrees.

✳ ✳ ✳ ✳ ✳

The sun finally rolled over the Kenai Mountains at 10 a.m., setting the horizon ablaze — a bright inferno without a hint of heat. Kachemak Bay glittered as I turned to pedal up the final small hill to my office. At the front door, I had to squint against a blinding reflection of crimson light as I removed my mittens and fumbled with the keys.

"It's already open," Dawn said after I shuffled inside, bundled in my snow jacket and pants, three fleece jackets, three pairs of cotton socks, one pair of long johns, and a ratty pair of jeans and a T-shirt. I no longer bothered to don more appropriate business clothing at the office, because it was rare for me to remove more than the outermost layer of my bike commuter moonsuit. I even wore ski hats indoors. This morning was no exception; the indoor temperature barely registered as warmer than the subzero air outside. The inside window glass was caked in frost, which explained the blinding reflection, and wisps of condensed breath curled over my face as I turned on my computer.

"Ugh, doesn't Jane ever turn on the heat?" I complained as I stashed my bike mittens in the drawer and pulled on wool gloves. The thick material was not conducive to typing, but it was still superior to the alternative — completely numb fingers.

"No," Carey said without looking up from her screen. "I did warn you about this."

"And she won't let us buy space heaters, why?"

"Because those use a lot of electricity, too," Carey said. She was wearing a bulky wool sweater and knit hat. "You know, if you didn't ride your bike in the morning, you wouldn't be so cold when you came to work."

"Not really," I said. "I dress warm enough, and I work up heat when I pedal. I shiver a lot more when I drive my car. Six miles is not enough for the Geo's heater to kick in at all."

"Working out is part of the problem," Carey said. "You sweat, which makes you wet, which makes you colder."

"Not on my way to work, I don't sweat," I said. "It's all downhill. I have to wear five layers just to keep the wind out. My fingers freeze every time. Still, between keeping our home thermostat at sixty and then freezing here, any time I spend riding my bike outside is the warmest I'll feel all day. Well, that and hot showers. I do look forward to showers."

Carey laughed as I convulsed with shivers, a symptom of my body readjusting its core temperature. Since the first of December, the cement box that housed the Homer Tribune had slipped into a state of perpetual refrigeration. Even Sean, who claimed a preference for wearing shorts throughout the subarctic winter, started donning a hoodie at his desk. And at home, Geoff analyzed the Monitor stove's fuel consumption and deemed sixty degrees as the best setting for the heater while we were home. This temperature setting wasn't too bad if we stood right next to the stove, but the outer corners of our spacious cabin often cooled to ice-forming temperatures by morning.

Even my daily shower was pathetic. Our small water heater dredged up pungent sulfur water from the well, then pumped it upstairs through mineral-encrusted pipes until the water pressure was reduced to a trickle. I stood under the faucet for as long as the warm water reserves would allow — ten minutes or so — straining to absorb a whole day's worth of heat. This feeling dissipated quickly during dinner, so afterward I would wrap one of our Afghan blankets — gifts from Geoff's grandma — around my shoulders like a shawl when I moved about the house. I wore gloves to write blog posts, and put on thick fleece leggings and two long-sleeved shirts to go to bed.

The Monitor stove was set to automatically turn down to fifty degrees at 10 p.m. By 11 p.m., a cave of cold air would coax us into bed whether we were sleepy or not. The mattress was lined in cotton sheets, a thin down comforter that I brought from Idaho, and a cheap cotton quilt that Geoff and I purchased at Fred Meyer. I usually threw one or more of the Afghans on top, and pulled on a thick pair of wool socks before crawling between the sheets. Geoff and I always started the night embraced in a tight cuddle, shivering slightly as we generated a small bubble of body heat. These embraces were emotionally satisfying, and allowed us both to drift into happy oblivion, where we would remain unconscious through all of the best hours of warmth, only to awake to inky darkness and ice buildup in the inside of every window.

It's cold in Alaska — a fact that all Alaskans talk about, complain about, and brag about. But I'm not sure most urban Alaskans understand, really understand, the true depth of the cold here. They move from their heated homes into heated vehicles on their way to heated buildings such as offices and gyms. They buy remote vehicle ignition starters, pull up to roadside coffee stands, and generally gripe about short walks across grocery store parking lots. Relatively few are active outdoors in the winter, and those who are tend to favor groomed park trails, close to heated eateries, which only border the vast tracts of wilderness just beyond city limits. I also was too inexperienced to understand what it was really like to live a frontier lifestyle in Alaska, but these struggles with the cold indoors were just enough to let me envision almost unimaginable hardships.

Because I could understand how life could be so much more unforgiving, I found it amusing that many outsiders viewed my lifestyle as an unimaginable hardship. Since I started keeping a blog about my life in Alaska, several people whom I had never met left comments to offer condolences or advice. At first I was confused about how strangers found my blog, but gradually I began to click through their Internet links and read their stories. In just a month I was drawn into a large virtual community of eclectic individuals. There was a middle-aged woman and avid skier in Minnesota who urged me not to give up on the winter sport that I referred to as "death planks." There was the journalist in Fairbanks who recommended cold-weather gear and gave me tips for entering Alaska Press Club contests. There were several cyclists from Anchorage who shared my snow biking enthusiasm. There was the commuter advocate in Washington, D.C., who wrote quirky prose in the comments, the Florida mountain biker with a dry sense of humor, the Norwegian woman who claimed not to even care about cycling but loved my photographs, and at least a dozen others who engraved their voices into my ongoing narrative. All of them offered enthusiastic encouragement for my Susitna 100 ambitions, and even pledged financial support when I published a proposal to ride one mile for each dollar donated. These contributions, however, rarely came without caveats. The first ten dollars, from a woman named Tracey in Iowa, arrived under the heading "For Pain and Suffering."

The thermometer read eleven degrees at 9:30 a.m. when Geoff and I set out for our daily dose of "pain and suffering." He came up with the innovative idea to cut off the top of old wool beanies to pull over our faces and necks. Diamond Ridge hadn't seen new snow in nearly a week, and traffic had polished the packed snow on the road to a hard sheen. Our studded tires crackled like soda pop as we rolled down the hill, fearlessly accelerating against brain-searing blasts of wind.

"Ugh, ice cream headache," I groaned as we applied brakes and actually managed to stop at the street intersection. "But, wow, what a rush, riding right on top of the ice. I love studded tires."

We pedaled up Skyline Ridge just as a shock of scarlet light erupted over the Kenai Mountains, reflecting across Kachemak Bay more than a thousand feet below. Fingers of golden light stretched across the snow-covered bluff next to the road, again with a richness of color that doesn't register during the high-angled sunlight of summer.

"Pain and suffering," I called out to Geoff. "Ha!" If only Tracey in Iowa could be here with us, riding an ice bike along this ridge, with the frost-coated forest painted by a late morning sunrise, I thought. She would understand what we sought was the opposite of pain and suffering. Everything here was color, light, and bursts of energy that resonated as joy in our minds. With simple adjustments in attitude, bodies were quick to adapt. Eleven degrees didn't feel so cold anymore. The long darkness didn't feel like such an hindrance. People are products of their landscape. Given enough time and experience, even the most extraordinary conditions become ordinary.

Still, Tracey obviously saw something unique in the act of riding a bicycle in Alaska in December, and admired it enough to send me ten dollars. More contributions continued to trickle through the extraordinarily diverse net of the World Wide Web. The skier from Minnesota expressed anticipation for a future Susitna 100 race report, even if my version didn't involve any death planks. John in Maine said winter was cold where he lived, too, so he could sure as hell cough up a few bucks to ensure I buy better clothing than what I was using. People who weren't strangers also intervened. Monika, one of our friends from the D Street crew who now lived in Michigan, simply responded with a valid but misinformed question — "What has Geoff put you up to now?" Chris, who had helped comfort me on more than one occasion of adventure-induced panic, followed his donation with a personal e-mail along the lines of "I don't have a clue what prompted this, but I don't want you to die."

In the hidden context of strangers' and friends' messages, I sensed a widening split between my past self — the person my friends knew and the person I understood myself to be — and my future self — the person the readers of my blog envisioned and the person I wanted to become. The person Chris and Monika knew was a lover of adventure but often hobbled by doubt and timidity. She viewed her body as necessary but not her first priority — it was more important that her mind reach heights of awareness amid natural landscapes even if her body was weak and struggling. Nutrition, gear and training were distant afterthoughts. She had no patience for the discipline and dedication of an athlete. Training was only as good as her resolve to get something done, and she rarely paid attention to the nuances of preparedness. She wore jeans and Sketchers on twelve-hour canyoneering adventures. She was terrified of moving water and exposure, clung precipitously to ledges while her friends dove from cliffs, and expanded her risk acceptance in the smallest increments possible.

Geoff knew this person from the beginning, and he had regularly been the witness to moments I finally released my grip on the ledge and let my body plunge into the waters of chance. He contributed with gentle urgings to let go, and also by teaching me how to navigate these new depths once I arrived. Geoff's influence was the main reason I had expanded my horizons to the farthest corners of my psychological safety net, but the Susitna 100 constituted a blind leap off the edge. Even Geoff didn't approve, although he remained supportive.

Now I had an assortment of strangers around the world who knew me not as a timid non-athlete or dabbler in outdoor sports, but as a fierce and dedicated winter cyclist. For someone who had always been a follower in a decidedly more experienced group of friends, it was surprising to receive e-mails from people across the globe who regarded me as some kind of expert. They said my blog inspired them to venture outside during the winter months, or try ice biking, or simply get over their motivational hump and go to the gym. "If you can ride a bike outside in Alaska all winter long," one woman wrote, "I can certainly spend an hour on the treadmill."

I often sat at my home computer, bundled in cheap fleece jackets and flannel pajama bottoms, bemusedly pondering my new identity. "If only they knew," I would smile to myself. From the narrow window of my blog, these strangers couldn't see the fifth-grader who was laughed off the softball field after she threw a pitch that failed to reach the plate. They didn't know the sophomore who failed to make the generous cut for her high school's cross-country team because she didn't crack ten minutes for a mile run. They couldn't know the seventeen-year-old who was still incapable of serving a volleyball over the net. I had spent my entire childhood being so distressingly bad at competitive sports that I hid the entire notion of athletics behind a curtain of resentment. I couldn't even watch Olympic events without feeling mildly disgusted. "Jocks," I would shake my head in derision. "A life of rigid training for the superficial goal of physical perfection. What do they know of the beauty of the world or discovery of their true selves?"

The culture that heralded athletic excellence only served to drive me further away from anything resembling a competitive effort. For too long I had compared throwing a baseball with climbing a mountain, convinced I must be equally bad at both. The fact that I loved to climb mountains was something I viewed as a fluke, a diversion from my natural path. "I was built to become an accountant, or maybe a librarian," I would joke with my friends as I flung my awkward limbs up a rocky slope. Like many young women, I had a negative body image, but this had more to do with my abilities than my looks. If asked to describe myself, the first words that came to mind were slow, clumsy, and average. For physical attributes, I thought of my tree-trunk legs, too-large butt, and flimsy upper body. Still, I always believed that the strength and beauty of the body were only a superficial shadow of the strength and beauty of the mind. I needed discovery of the outdoors to expand my mind. I needed my body to get there.

A dismissive attitude about competitive sports persisted, but I couldn't help but draw satisfaction from the ways in which my body was becoming stronger. My legs developed new definition where muscles bulged against my skin. My collar bone and shoulder blades became more pointed. Fat was beginning to melt from my torso. My heart beat stronger and my lungs drew cold air with an intensity that could have crushed the gasping breaths of my youth. Fitness settled over me like armor, protecting my mind from its own uncertainties and fears. In turn, my mind perpetuated a heroic story about becoming the endurance athlete my blog readers thought me to be. So I pushed my body harder.

This satisfaction was what kept me pedaling after I was too exhausted to find motivation in the scenery. Geoff talked me into installing an odometer on my bike. I'd long resisted the mile counter, and preferred to move unencumbered without the tyranny of numbers to bog down my perception of flight. But I agreed that I needed to track speed and time in order to improve. It didn't take long for the numbers to start taunting me. If I averaged seven miles per hour on the climb up West Hill Road, I was driven to push it to eight. If my fastest speed was thirty-two miles per hour down East Hill Road, I wanted to gun for thirty-five. If I completed the Kachemak Drive loop in three hours and six minutes, it became necessary to cut that to less than three. Even as my lungs seared in the cold wind and legs burned with lactic acid, my mind targeted those numbers as a source of motivation.

Geoff turned around from the "pain and suffering" when he felt like it, about eight miles from our cabin. I continued along Skyline and up the ice-coated gravel of Ohlson Mountain Road. As I climbed, my arteries pumped warm blood beneath chilled skin, and my mind cycled through a whirlwind of emotions and ideas: elation ... what Geoff and I would do with the upcoming weekend ... fatigue ... the article I needed to finish that afternoon ... gratitude ... the weirdly personal conversation I had with the clerk at Ulmer's Hardware Store yesterday ... hunger. For all of the benefits of my new training habits, it was the unhindered flow of thoughts and emotions that I valued the most. In the midst of hard effort, both were often shallow and fleeting. But there was a deeper sense that these flickers of memories and biological urges were collectively meaningful. They fell like raindrops from the clouds of my subconscious, polishing the granite walls of my identity into something beautiful.

I pedaled until my odometer clicked to fifteen miles — which meant that to make it to the office by noon, I'd have to exceed my pedaling average by two miles per hour. I looked away from the numbers because, in that moment, they were an unwanted distraction. The sun lifted over the jagged mountains, casting a white glare across Kachemak Bay. It was going to be a cold, blinding descent, and I wished I could suffer it over and over for the rest of the day, watching the sun crawl along the bottom of the southern horizon and fade too quickly from view.

December Treatment

December 9, 2005

Today was all about color, sugar and speed. I love it. While the good folks down in Austin, Texas, are digging out of an ice storm, I'm pacing trucks on my road bike — in Alaska, in December. Sometimes, life turns upside down and smiles at you.

No one at the office wanted to work today. The publisher announced yesterday that we were having a pot luck and *no one* was allowed to bring anything but desserts. Even the girl who brought in Fuji apples the size of small pumpkins was frowned upon. So we stuffed our faces with cookies, brownies, pistachio pie — then, bloated and reeling from sugar shock, we pulled out all the Christmas decorations and started throwing tinsel everywhere. At about 1:30 p.m. I looked outside and could see a hint of sun showing through the rain clouds. And I knew a rare window had opened.

I arrived home at 2 p.m., unhooked my road bike from the trainer I thought it would sit upon for at least three more months, walked it along the precarious ice sheet that my driveway has become, and went for a ride — a fast ride. After a month on the mountain bike slogging through the snow, I was coasting along pavement and sucking in warm breeze like it was suddenly spring. Everywhere colors emerged that have spent so long buried in hoarfrost: deep greens and yellows reflecting off what was left of the snow, blue and orange in the sky. The headwind out of the west was fierce but I rode as hard as I could, and felt like I was flying.

Geoff joined me for what turned out to be the last half of my ride: down the Spit and around Kachemak Drive, for 17 miles. By the time we returned, just after 4 p.m., the sun was long gone. The clearing sky signaled the cold will return. Alas, it's December, and there's nothing that will stop it. But for a small window within winter's icy grip, I had a 32-mile road ride on a 40-degree afternoon and almost believed it was spring.

✳ ✳ ✳ ✳ ✳

Winter's long nights closed in like a curtain. By mid-December, the sun snoozed until well after 10 a.m., only to roll lazily just above the crest of the mountains before sinking back into darkness by 4 p.m. It reminded me of a shy cat, absent most of the time, occasionally peeking around the corners of doorways, and obstinately withholding affection. Even during daytime, sunlight was often dull and shrouded by gray clouds.

The cement walls that surrounded my workspace effectively blocked what little daylight remained. There was one window at the front of the building, and the blinds were always drawn to "protect newsroom privacy." (According to Jane, there were plenty of people in town with guns who did not want their names in the paper. At least with the blinds down they wouldn't know where to aim.) Slits of sunlight sometimes escaped, drawing sad yellow lines across the floor. Still,

I liked to watch sunbeams creep along the carpet. Sometimes I held my sweater-covered arms in their path, as though these dim rays could somehow provide the ultraviolet boost I craved.

Carey made her annual escape to Hawaii and left me in charge of overseeing production of the Homer Tribune for two full weeks. Layton, Sean, Emily, and I were already operating on a tight margin of productivity. The holiday season meant more print ads, which in turn increased the number of newspaper pages, and thus increased the amount of space that the newsroom needed to fill with content. The additional duties tipped my workload from barely manageable to crushing. By the third day following our captain's departure, it felt like the four of us were crowded against one side of a ship, rowing in circles, as Jane stood at the stern beating a drum and barking orders. My newfound fitness could not prevent me from withering under the pressure.

On deadline day, I slumped out of bed at an unconscionable hour to ride my bike to work. I barely had time to use the bathroom during these two weeks, but if my job was going to force me to sit in a frigid office all day long, I was at least going to squeeze in a workout during the commute. It was 5 a.m. when I stepped out of my cold and dark cabin into the colder, darker morning. The sun wouldn't come up for five more hours. A thin veil of moonlit clouds was strung across the sky. I pulled on my face mask and watched my own breath curl into silver wisps. A recent snap of subzero weather had broken; it was cold outside, but not deathly cold. Probably somewhere in the range of twenty degrees.

I switched on my headlight and pedaled up the driveway. A "sizzling bacon" sound crackled from the bike's studded tires, amplified by the morning's otherwise complete silence. I rode past darkened windows and frost-coated cars, enjoying the distinction of being the only object in motion. Years earlier, when I was a student at the University of Utah, I worked part-time as a bagel baker. My shift started at 4 a.m. On the rare weekend morning that I actually went to bed before I had to be up again, I relished the sensation of arising to an abandoned world. My neighborhood was comprised of students and young families, and was characteristically chaotic during the day. The early-morning absence of activity gave it an apocalyptic atmosphere. The air was always cool, even in the summer, and I could drive through stop lights without worrying about consequences. If I felt so inclined, I thought, I could take off all my clothes and run naked through the streets, or climb a street lamp, or paint illustrations on the sidewalks. Who would stop me? At 4 a.m., the world belonged solely to me, and I imagined living as the last human on Earth. This sensation always filled me with guilty intrigue.

In Alaska, amid the persistent darkness and cold of December, these hours became even more lonely. Alaskans tended to go into semi-hibernation in the winter, moving through the frozen world only long enough to complete the necessary functions of their lives. Sure, there were still gallery openings, basketball games, movies, and plays during the winter. People still went to work and occasionally, if the weather was nice, ventured outside to ski or push children around in sleds. But even the mid-afternoon hours were quiet during the winter, and the morning hours were downright ghostly.

What would it really mean to be the last person alive? What would I do? Would I continue to pedal my bike along the deserted streets, searching for other people, scraps of food and some sense of continued purpose? If civilization came to a catastrophic end, most who remained would probably hunker down, build up protective fortresses, hoard provisions. Not me; I'd wander. As long as I stayed on the move, I would never have to feel alone, because I could always cling to hope that I'd eventually find something … anything. With a bicycle I could move freely. I wouldn't have to worry about fuel, or the inevitable deterioration of roads and buildings. I wouldn't be encumbered by technologies that no longer served a purpose. I would eat berries from the ground, drink water from the streams, and scavenge bike parts and food in the ruins of civilization. I would never stop riding, never stop searching.

I smiled at the idea of a bicycle lifting me from the crushing loneliness of being the last person alive. What would a ride be like in that world? I imagined rolling past crumbling buildings and abandoned cars, along streets thick with ice and snow. As I visualized this apocalyptic world, I pedaled past an abandoned cabin with a toppled roof, a storage shack constructed of crumpled aluminum sheets, and two 1960s-era trucks half-buried in snow drifts. A thin husky darted across the road, stopping briefly to face my headlight with luminescent yellow eyes. A moose and her nearly full-grown calf also turned their glowing eyes on me. My imagination was only reflecting the very real destitution that was my Alaska neighborhood before dawn.

The Tribune office was similarly dark and destitute first thing in the morning. I groped around for the light switch. Florescent bulbs flickered with a hypnotic hum. I took off my mittens and balaclava, and pulled on typing gloves and a hat. Now I was outfitted for the arduous expedition of deadline day.

First on the agenda was finishing the weekly calendar, as well as writing a preview of Homer High School's production of The Nutcracker. The previous night, I went to a rehearsal and interviewed the teenage star and her teacher on the set. A cluster of kindergartners dressed in mouse costumes swarmed around us as the girl rattled off a rapid-fire description of the plot, as though I'd never before heard of The Nutcracker. Her teacher gushed about how amazing this year's production would be, the best ever. I nodded and recorded the obvious sound bites, but kept my focus on the girl, whose wide eyes darted rapidly around the room as she faced me with a fixed smile.

"Poor girl," I thought. "She probably puts in hours every night rehearsing for this play, and wondering whether the time and stress is really worth a couple of bullet points on her college applications. Meanwhile, her school is charging fifteen dollars a ticket and funneling the proceeds into the general budget, where they'll go toward new uniforms for the football team."

Still, I couldn't blame her for pursing time-consuming extracurricular activities. I had after-school jobs during high school, and now I had little to show for the income I earned as a youth: photographs of a car I discarded years ago, a snowboard that collected dust in my closet, and a few great memories of concerts I otherwise wouldn't have been able to afford. I too had a knack for overextending myself, trying so many different avenues of education that I never excelled at any one thing, and working in fast food for five dollars an hour. At least this ambitious young actress was helping create something meaningful, something that had value to her community — even if fifteen dollars was pretty steep for a seat at a high school play.

I just wondered whether she understood that she had so many years of this ahead of her —years where responsibilities trapped her behind the curtain of life's proverbial stage. That all of her hard work would simply fade into the selective pages of memory. That even as her blood, sweat and tears poured into the audiences' consciousness, they'd still be distracted with the detritus of their own lives. Ultimately, this was another thing to be forgotten. And despite her hard work and best intentions, the future was always uncertain. She might think she had it all figured out — sprinting through college, racking up good grades, being offered good jobs, getting accepted to law school. And after all that, she might just reject this path entirely, and instead travel for a while, move somewhere far away, take a low-paying newspaper job, buy a bicycle …

But of course I couldn't include any of these wild speculations in my article, so instead I quoted the gushing teacher and wrote about the "fun" costumes and "colorful" set. Sean and Emily shuffled into the office just after 8 a.m., and without more than a few words joined me in a keyboard-tapping frenzy. Layton showed up at 9:25 with a case of bed head, oblivious to my icy glare.

"You would not believe what happened at city council meeting," he said. "Not sure I can fit it into my story, though. Kind of off-topic, but hilarious."

"Are you serious?" I growled. "You haven't written your city council story yet? Layton, it's 9:30. I was planning to put it on the front page. I need to have everything out by noon."

"Don't worry, I'll have it for you," he grinned.

"It's not like city council is a breaking story," I said. "Why didn't you write it last night?"

"I was … busy," Layton said sheepishly. Sean turned to me with a raised eyebrow and a knowing smirk.

"Whatever," I said. "I need it by 11 at the latest. Seriously, if 11 comes and you're still writing, I'm killing the story. I'll wedge my Nutcracker fluff piece in that spot if I have to."

"Okay, okay, no worries," he said. "I'll get it done."

Being the default boss was worse than being a real boss. I had twice the responsibilities and none of the power. Even as I fumed about Layton's tardiness, Sean turned to me and said, "I need to finish writing my column. Do you mind editing the basketball story for me?"

"Yeah, yeah, I guess," I said. "But don't expect anything thorough. I still have to edit all of Layton's stuff, plug in the ads and then write an editorial. What message are we going for this week? That it's the most wonderful time of the year?"

Sean laughed. "Hardly," he said. "But that will work if you desperately need a topic. Write about how important it is to give, not receive." Again, he said this with a knowing smirk.

I sighed, because I knew I would likely pick this easy "opinion" because it wouldn't inspire any wrath from Jane, or take up more time that I did not have. A newspaper editorial was a great platform, and there was so much I had to say. I could write about the city's lack of a recycling program, or its push to fund tourism infrastructure while locals drove on potholed streets and went to decaying schools. I could write about residents' efforts to keep a big box store, Fred Meyer, out of the community, or about the large numbers of residents who drove to Kenai, eighty miles north, to shop at Wal-mart on a regular basis. I could write about highway crews' lazy snow-removal tactics, pushing snow and ice onto the sidewalks and forcing schoolchildren and pedestrians to walk on the street. I could even write about this supposed hilarious incident that happened at the city council meeting if Layton ever revealed it to me. This was community news after all, and the opinion page was meant to be the home of thoughtful commentary on local happenings.

But instead, I was going to write some pallid piece about holiday cheer. I had temporary control of a newspaper, and yet I lacked the courage to create anything of value. It was the worst kind of powerlessness — impotency masked as power. An image of the teenage actress's tired eyes appeared in my mind, reflecting my own frustrations.

In the midst of these typing frenzies, it was easy to imagine another kind of apocalyptic world. My co-workers' faces were frozen and featureless, locked on glowing screens. The indoor air was still and cold, and the fluorescent lights flickered dully. My blood pressure rose to a boil as I grappled with the futility of my efforts, and my mind churned frantically until every thought had been whipped to a dull mush.

Some people conduct their whole lives in these clouds of stress, until years of gray days finally erased all memories of the sun. There is relief, freedom even, when enough time had passed, and they could no longer remember the way the sunrise used to cast crimson light over the mountains. They no longer missed the sensation of cold wind on their face. These were relics of childhood.

Life does deal some stormy days, but most of us knowingly walked into the fog. We embraced it. We called it reality; we called it life. The clarity of childhood was reconstructed as naivety; tunnel-minded ambition became virtue. The most driven among us seem to be jockeying for a position near the top of the clouds — a place where we can lift our heads above the gray pall and see the sunshine again, if only for a few beautiful moments. But the sunlight was there all along. Even during the shortest days of winter, hidden by closed blinds, it was always there.

By the time I uploaded all of the finished newspaper pages to our printer, transferred the articles to the Web site, updated the classifieds and archived everything, the sun had already set for the day. We had missed our deadline by an hour, and Jane spent ten minutes lecturing me about why this wasn't acceptable. Despite the vocal beating, I clung to my conviction that I deserved a medal for assembling an entire ten-thousand-piece puzzle only one hour later than expected. Standing quietly and pretending to listen to complaints proved to be the most relaxed twenty minutes of my workday, which is really just another way of saying that the other ten and a half hours were comparatively unbearable.

Strips of red light still clung to distant mountains in the west as I pedaled home, but the sky overhead was a deep violet. I'd been at work for eleven hours, but it felt like days had passed since the morning commute. Thoughts were washed in gray; muscles were tight from stress. Anxiety still felt like sharp bits of metal in my gut. Those who don't believe office work is an endurance sport in its own right have probably never tried endurance sports.

My bike's headlight was dim from too-cold batteries. I removed the batteries and warmed them in my cupped hands until my fingers were numb, then placed them back in the compartment. The light flickered for several seconds but did cast a dull beam onto the snow.

Clouds obstructed the stars overhead, and the evening air felt considerably colder than morning. I shivered as I pedaled along Main Street, not really working up any body heat until I started climbing West Hill. Steady breathing replaced anxious thoughts, and I pedaled up the snow-covered road in a mental fog. Soon, real fog closed in around me. Familiar landmarks blurred, so I had to sharpen my focus. Swirling particles of ice reflected the beam of my headlight until I was blinded by the light, so I switched it off. The pulsing red taillight illuminated the cloud in an equally distracting way, so I killed it too. Cars would not be able to see me, but I felt confident I would see or hear them and dive off the road before anything catastrophic happened. Anyway, there didn't seem to be another soul moving through the fog. The loneliness had returned.

New hoarfrost had collected on pine boughs and alder branches. Through the fog, these silver-tinted silhouettes of trees appeared as ghosts materializing from air. Amid the featureless gray, they seemed to levitate in an expanse that contained nothing else. If my morning commute had been a glimpse of the end of the world, evening revealed the beginning — an era when the whole universe was just vapor and light.

I pedaled with growing uneasiness about the unfamiliarity of the landscape. I was less than a mile from home, but it seemed much farther than that, as though I'd jumped light years through space and time. My fingers and toes felt numb, my mind was fractured by fatigue, and I was frightened, genuinely frightened. But a deeper part of me longed to explore this uncharted galaxy.

I bypassed my driveway and climbed another mile up the road to the beginning of the Homestead Trail. The snowmobile-groomed track was coated in a thin layer of ice, which crackled and popped beneath my studded tires. The ghost trees closed in. Some were hunched like old women beneath a shawl of snow, others were draped in a silky lace of frost. The trail veered down the hill, and I accelerated until the spooky trees were nothing more to me than a blur of white. I briefly plunged beneath the cloud, caught a glimpse of the black hole that was Kachemak Bay, and climbed back into the fog.

I never bothered to switch on my headlight. Even at night, faint reflections of ambient light off the snow and fog allowed me to discern shapes and depth. Blasts of cold wind scrubbed away stress, and hard pedaling purged any lingering fatigue. The last thing to disappear was fear, released in curls of breath. I was exhilarated and emancipated — a ghost flying through a ghost world, a vapor of energy at the beginning of time. As my spirit floated free, my legs seemed to move effortlessly. I arrived at the crest of the trail with a sense that I had reached a higher state of being.

Of course, I was still human. My bones were still attached to my muscles, which were shivering in the cold. My brain was still battling fear about the dangers that lurked in the night. I still had the stressful job to return to the following day, and a partner at home who was probably worried about me. But for a few peaceful seconds, these unsettling thoughts didn't register. My body was just part of the world, which was ultimately just a conglomeration of energy — trillions upon trillions of particles floating in space. Everything I interpreted as myself was simply a reflection of particles that were forever converging and diverging.

Who I was in that moment — a cyclist in the mist — would change in an instant, and never be exactly the same again.

I stopped so I could absorb the experience. By capturing this moment in a memory, I embraced the impermanence of all things. Shortly after I started pedaling again, the trail crossed an open meadow, and the ghost trees retreated into the fog. All visual and audible stimuli disappeared into the gray infinity. After a few more minutes of seeing and hearing nothing, I noticed a small break in the clouds. Through that window I could see a tiny patch of real sky, dotted with stars and laced with a ribbon of green light.

"Northern Lights?" I wondered. It had to be. Green light on the northern horizon. Anchorage was two hundred miles away, too far to generate light pollution. What else could it be? I squinted at the sky for several more seconds until the clouds closed back together, and I was again alone in the fog.

A shiver rippled down my spine — a startling sensation amid the sensory deprivation of the fog. If those had been the Northern Lights, it was the first time I had seen them in Alaska. Even if I could never be certain, the fog break seemed significant — the point where the ghostly world of the past opened into the infinite universe of the future. And this was the kind of future that rippled with surreal green light. Alaska. Never before had I felt so certain about my place amid the vastness of the world. All of the particles that needed to collide to bring me here were astronomically unlikely, and yet here I was. Alaska — the right place at the right time.

Orphan

December 24, 2005

Here I am in Palmer, Christmas Eve, 250 miles from my bike and 3,000 miles from home. I went for a 90-minute run along the Matanuska River this morning that felt amazing. The last time I was here — Thanksgiving — I definitely was not in the kind of shape to run for 90 minutes straight. And now I am. How quickly my body has responded to relatively casual conditioning really surprised me. I felt strong, in charge. I was tearing off layers like it wasn't 8 degrees out, feeling the crisp air on actual skin, sprinting, sweating, gliding across the windswept ice.

I eventually came home because it was 11 a.m. and

the sun hadn't yet crawled above the mountains. It felt like a good idea at the time, but now it's high noon and the sun still hasn't made it up (my friend Craig informed me that this time of year, it never does); I've eaten a bowl of Special K and two salmon-shaped Christmas cookies, and all I want to do is head back out. All I can think about is taking off down the river, running harder, faster, colder, until I don't have to think anymore about how homesick I'm feeling today; about how much I miss wearing my Christmas jammies; about what I would give right now to eat an ice cream sundae while watching "Christmas Story" and playing Scrabble with my sisters. This year is my first year as an orphan. I thought I was prepared for it, but it's hard. It's harder than I thought it would be. In comparison, running is effortless.

✳ ✳ ✳ ✳ ✳

Shortly after winter set in, Geoff landed part-time work in construction. His boss said it was difficult to keep warm bodies on job sites that time of year, so a willingness to work a nail gun beneath floodlights in sub-zero darkness was all the experience he required. Geoff received ten dollars an hour under the table, and worked as many shifts as he could squeeze out of his boss — usually twenty to thirty hours a week. He purchased his own tool belt, a few rudimentary tools such as a hammer and screwdrivers, and insulated leather work gloves. His coworkers taught him the basics of framing houses and pouring cement. This contractor didn't deal in remodeling or home improvement projects — comfortable work that could be done inside heated buildings. No, they were building new homes from the ground up. Summer construction season is so short in Alaska that some contractors opt to work year-round — after all, snow and ice in December isn't more difficult to work around than snow and ice in May.

Geoff frequently returned with harrowing tales about his day. Mornings were often spent removing piles of snow dumped by overnight storms. He wielded a powerful nail gun while wearing bulky gloves, which were charred on the fingertips where he tried to warm his hands near the blue flame of a propane torch.

Metal tools became searingly cold, as did ladders. An inexperienced craftsman, he usually took off his gloves when a job demanded finer dexterity, and soon sustained frostbite blisters on his fingers. His toes were always numb, even when he ran up and down the job site to boost circulation. His boss's latest project was up on Diamond Ridge, where the weather was often extreme. Snow flurries developed into blinding blizzards before the workers could even put their tools down and seek shelter under the skeleton roof of the building. Unexpected gusts of wind sometimes toppled entire walls. Freezing rain resulted in everyone being sent home in the morning without pay.

The more brutal Geoff's working environment became, the more envious I felt. His job featured real-world excitement that my office was decidedly lacking. I pictured him straddling a scaffold high above the snow-covered ground, wearing his Carhartt jacket and wool neck warmer. I could almost hear the chorus of hammers muffled by a howling wind, men yelling over gales, frost forming on their tools. Of course it was just house construction, but during Alaska's December, even this simple work contained a beautiful element of life-and-death struggle. I couldn't explain nor admit why I'd prefer Geoff's arduous job to my own — sitting all day in the relative safety of a partially heated office — but I believed I did.

And because Geoff wasn't an official employee, his employer had no choice but to grant him a few weeks off so he could fly to upstate New York to visit his family over Christmas. I had no such luxury at the Homer Tribune, which was still falling further behind deadlines even after Carey returned from Hawaii. Jane made it clear that I couldn't take any extra time off during the holidays, and I couldn't afford a plane ticket to Utah anyway.

I anticipated a grim and lonely holiday alone. However, Geoff needed a ride to the airport in Anchorage, and the Tribune did grant two days off work. Craig's wife was still in Utah, so he proposed I come visit Palmer for his "orphan Christmas."

How I met Craig is its own funny story. During my sophomore year at the University of Utah, I decided to join the student-run environmental club, Terra Firma. Like many 19-year-olds, I was more interested in the social functions of a club than in its context — but planting trees, protesting highway projects, and camping in the desert appealed to my predominant passions at the time. Craig was the club's president. I remember walking into the crowded meeting room and developing an instant crush on him — he was tall and wiry, with chiseled facial features and a bushy beard that screamed "fun-loving dirtbag." He announced that the club needed more volunteers for a fundraiser that night, manning a concession booth during a Mannheim Steamroller concert. My hand shot up. I was so excited that I didn't even notice the shy boy with curly brunette hair across from me, raising his hand as well.

The boy's name was Mike. Craig drove both of us to the stadium in his clunky Subaru sedan. The entire drive, Mike and I were quiet while Craig regaled us with tales of derring do, such as the time he contracted hypothermia in the San Rafael Swell. At the concert, our assigned concession was the Dipping Dots cart, selling a gimmicky dessert made of globules of ice cream. Synthesized Christmas music in December isn't exactly the best venue for overpriced ice cream beads, and we didn't get much business. Craig disappeared for a while and I started chatting with Mike, who was an anthropology student from Idaho.

As these things often go, Mike turned out to be the guy who asked me out, and Mike was the one with whom I entered a serious relationship. After he graduated the following summer, Mike moved to El Salvador to volunteer with the Peace Corps. We established a long-distance relationship based entirely on hand-written letters and infrequent e-mails. As these things often go, we'd both moved on long before either of us admitted it, but I continued to grasp the fraying strands of this relationship even after Geoff entered the picture. Craig and I became good friends in the interim, but drifted apart after Craig graduated from law school, married, and moved to Alaska. Now that we were reunited in the Frozen North, I amused myself with daydreams about what all of our lives might look like if things had turned out just a little differently at that Mannheim Steamroller concert.

Six years later, Craig was still tall and thin with a bushy beard, which these days screamed "freedom-loving Alaskan" more than tree-hugging hippie. I also hadn't changed much; newspaper work allowed me to dress like a college student — albeit a northern version that incorporated six layers of fleece pullovers and hats. Watching Craig putter around his kitchen as snow swirled outside the window made me think that our lives wouldn't have turned out dramatically different in any case.

Craig planned Christmas Eve dinner for me and two law clerks from Palmer. Similar to his Thanksgiving menu, he served three different variations of Mormon funeral potatoes — a cornflake-coated, cheese-and-potato casserole that, as its name indicates, is a popular side dish for Mormons to serve at funerals — and a pre-cooked turkey breast. We dined on the carbohydrate-laden meal, and I joked that funeral potatoes would be great fuel for an endurance race.

Craig shook his head and smiled. "So are you still thinking about doing that bike race? What was it?"

"The Susitna 100," I grinned. "Sign-ups go until New Year's Eve and I'm planning to send my entry in as soon as I get home. I actually raised enough money from my blog. I put up this silly challenge that I would ride a mile for every dollar donated, and people actually contributed to my cause. I rode 289 miles but actually made nearly 400 dollars. I'm giving the extra money to the Livestrong Foundation."

"People actually paid you to ride your bike?" Craig shook his head. "That's like the ultimate grubber move."

"It was a fundraiser," I shot back. "The gimmick was riding my bike in frigid Alaska weather and blogging about it. Anyway, it was not exactly easy money."

"Is Geoff going as well?"

"Geoff is going to run the Little Su. It's a fifty-kilometer version of the same race. He thinks the hundred-mile race is crazy."

"It is," Craig said. "I never pictured you as the type for extreme sports."

"Why, because I backed out of a few of those scary canyoneering trips in Utah? Because I cried in Quandary Canyon?"

"No, it's just … you never struck me as a competitive type."

"I guess I'm not," I said. "I mean, I've never competed in any race before. Not even a 5K. The Susitna 100 will be my first race. But that's the appeal of such a huge and impossible-seeming thing — it's not a competition with other people. It's a competition with myself. I missed out on too many cool trips because I was scared. I'm getting tired of being that kind of person — one who won't take chances. I moved to Alaska; that was a big leap. This is the next."

"So you think you can finish it?" Craig asked.

"I have no idea," I said. "My longest ride so far was thirty-four miles, and it was mostly on pavement, and even that was really hard. I got home and I was wasted; spent the rest of the night curled up on the couch in a blanket, eating Fruit Loops out of the box. So three times that? On snow? Yeah, it seems impossible. That's pretty much the point."

Craig grinned. "Well, better you than me."

"That's what Geoff said, too," I said. "But thirty-one miles on foot isn't exactly going to be a pleasure cruise."

"Sure, but Geoff … well I can see him doing something like that," Craig said.

I shrugged. "Yeah, I get it. I'm not an athlete. I guess we'll see. You probably didn't think I'd ever end up in Alaska, either."

"No I did not," Craig grinned. "When Geoff was here over the summer, we thought it was over between you two."

I smiled. "It was over at the time. But life's funny like that. One day you finally embrace being single in Idaho Falls, and the next you're training to ride a bicycle a hundred miles across frozen Alaska."

✳ ✳ ✳ ✳ ✳

My gut was still heavy with funeral potatoes when I ventured out at first light, just before 10 a.m. The air was a brisk eight degrees, cold enough to bite the tips of my earlobes where they poked out of a yellow wool beanie my mother knitted for me. Strips of pink light stretched over Pioneer Peak, towering six thousand feet over my head. Stuffing myself with turkey and frozen cookie dough (Craig offered to bake the cookies, but all of us declined) left a shrill pounding in my head. I could have killed for a cup of coffee, but Craig didn't drink the stuff and Christmas Day business closures left me without other options. The streets of Palmer were empty, and the morning so quiet that I could hear the crunching steps of unseen animals walking through the snow.

It was my first Christmas Day without my family, without the rustling of wrapping paper, laughter with my sisters, and the aroma of Dad's waffles wafting through the house. I thought that at age twenty-six these traditions would be a remnant of my childhood, easy to leave behind. Instead, the thought of familiar sounds and smells still taking place some three thousand miles away made me feel even more lonely. Palmer was cold and quiet, a place where I couldn't even count on the one thing you can always count on — that the sun will come up.

I tightened the laces on the New Balance road running shoes that Geoff talked me into buying at a bargain basement outlet store three years earlier. We went for all of two runs together before the first snowfall that year. When spring came, I packed them in a box to stow away while Geoff and I joined two friends on a road trip to Alaska. I hadn't seen them since, and wasn't even sure how they managed to survive the three relocations that had happened in the interim. But when I unpacked my Geo Prism in Homer, there they were, smashed into a corner of the trunk.

"I should take up running again," I'd said to Geoff as I carried them into the cabin.

"I thought you hated running," he replied.

"I do."

But I couldn't haul my bicycle up to Palmer, and I wasn't about to permit myself five days of sloth amid this most important period of Susitna 100 training. So with my snowboarding coat and fleece pullover, liner gloves, and two pairs of cotton socks stuffed into my neglected shoes, I took off down the street at a stiff lope. This enthusiastic stride quickly deteriorated into a skittering shuffle as I slipped along ice-coated pavement. I veered into the snow bank, which only served to slow my pace even more while filling my shoes with cold powder.

"Running is crap," I thought. But at least this pathetic effort didn't hurt too badly. After one slow mile, I reached the edge of the neighborhood. Lurching like a wounded deer through shin-deep snow, I followed a narrow trail through the woods, which ended at the Matanuska River. Wind had scoured the shoreline of snow. Hoarfrost feathers coated an intricate braid of gravel and glare ice.

Unlike the skating-rink road, the river ice was rough thanks to the sand-like texture of hoarfrost. Traction set me free. I kicked up my knees and breathed in a rush of cold air as my speed soared — at least that was the sensation of accelerating from a slow shuffle to something marginally higher. Icy mist swirled around my ankles, and pink light reflected off the ribbons of ice. It was like running in the sky, like when you look out an airplane window at 30,000 feet and imagine what it would be like to traverse the carpet of clouds below.

"This is what running is about," I thought with a smile.

I could have run that way all day, until I reached the mouth of the river, where it emptied into the churning, icy waters of the Knik Arm. But after forty-five minutes, my knees ached and my fingers were numb. I'd been running so hard that sweat had already soaked the fleece pullover beneath my coat. An all-too-familiar fear of the cold clamped down, filling my mind with the same panicked conclusions: "I need to go home. I don't want to die out here."

Fear coaxed me to turn around, but I rebelled by increasing my pace to outrun the clammy chill. Despite my awkward gait, I was amazed how well my body was handling this foreign motion. Maybe all the biking I was doing really was paying dividends, by strengthening my muscles and increasing my endurance. That was the point, of course. But like the reluctantly religious trying to emulate the faithful, I wasn't ready to accept fitness until I could see proof of its existence.

When I loped back into Craig's driveway, I realized I hadn't felt lonely for ninety minutes. I didn't think about my parents and sisters back home and all the hot chocolate they were enjoying, and I didn't dwell on the uncomfortable notion that Geoff had left me alone over the holidays just because he could. Although I could appreciate that he missed his family just as much as I missed mine, he never discussed his plans with me or checked to see whether I could join him. I came home from work a few weeks prior, and he already had a plane ticket. This was the way things had always been between Geoff and me— he did whatever he wanted, and I either genuinely didn't mind, or pretended I didn't mind and quietly stewed about it. Complaining was futile; he didn't understand why I wouldn't want him to have the things he wanted. And yet, I had hoped that as we forged this new life in Alaska, some aspects of our separate-yet-together attitudes would change. That somehow our individual longings would fuse together.

I stopped short of Craig's front door to untie my laces, which had become soaked and re-frozen to a hard knot.

"At least I'll always have this," I thought.

"This" was the ability to put on a pair of shoes or mount the saddle of a bicycle and use my own body to move through the world. It was simple enough to do anywhere at any time, and yet demanding enough to clear my overcrowded head of everything save for my body's most immediate needs — energy, motion, and warmth. All I needed to do was go for a run or a ride, and for those isolated moments, every difficult emotion would dissipate. I wouldn't feel anxious about my job, stressed about my financial situation, or sad about the absence of people I love. Of course, I couldn't run away from fatigue, fear, or pain — and yet, even these feelings seemed preferable to the Christmas loneliness that started settling back in before I'd even removed my icy shoes.

Craig was awake by the time I returned to the warmth of the house. The television was tuned to a generic football game and he was eating what looked like a bowl of leftover funeral potatoes. He waved vigorously as I hobbled up the stairs with already-stiff knees. Craig wasn't quite the right person to fill the void I was feeling, but he was a friendly face and I was thrilled to see him.

"Did you go for a run?" he asked.

"A short one," I replied. "But it was nice."

✳ ✳ ✳ ✳ ✳

On New Years Eve, the Tribune assigned me coverage of the Edible Arts Extravaganza, an end-of-year gala at the Bunnell Street Gallery, which featured arty sculptures built entirely out of food. In order to blend in at the event, I dug through my closet until I found my nicest dress. It was black, sleeveless, and fell elegantly away from my hips. It wasn't exactly high fashion, but it was better than the other dressy thing I owned, which was a brown peasant skirt. Since this was Homer, the best way to complete the ensemble would have been a pair of XtraTufs. The mud-colored rubber boots are often worn at formal events as a point of quirky local fashion rather than necessity — although any Homerite will remind you that there will always be mud, everywhere, at all times. I didn't yet own this accessory footwear (almost as an act of rebellion, because XtraTufs were so ubiquitous that they qualified as trendy, and a Cheechako trying to establish her individuality as an Alaskan does not blindly embrace trends). So instead I put on a pair of black flats that were most certainly going to become swamped with slush before I entered the gallery.

I fed our cats a celebratory can of tuna-flavored Fancy Feast that I'd been promising them all week (because I'd been home alone long enough that I'd taken to talking to the cats and bribing them for affection). Outside, temperatures had recently warmed to just above freezing, and slushy puddles covered the driveway. My Geo Prism balked at repeated attempts to turn the ignition, and then the wheels spun uselessly atop a sheet of ice. I briefly considered riding my bike to the downtown gala, but I was in a dress and didn't even have XtraTufs to stave off the slush spray. Finally, after I stopped flooring the gas pedal and instead employed a light tapping technique, the sedan pried itself away from the slush bog.

The Edible Arts Extravaganza was exactly what I expected — a plastic-table display of artfully arranged foods. There was a cake shaped like the volcanoes of Cook Inlet, a sculpture of a cat made out of processed cheese, an abstract art vegetable tray, and a leaning tower of cookies. I followed the line of viewers along each table and snapped photos for the Tribune. The shutter kept sticking and I wondered if there was some way to more artfully photograph these perishable masterpieces than simply flooding them with flash. I never told the Tribune I was a photographer. In fact, before I moved to Alaska I didn't even own a camera. I purchased a two-megapixel point-and-shoot for $139 just a few months prior so I could document my life in Alaska. Since I started my blog, a desire to illustrate each post sparked a new interest in photography. But I had yet to take a photo more complicated than my bike propped against a snow bank with the sunset in the background. When it came to art photography, I had no idea how to frame still objects, and the Tribune's bulky Cannon DSLR was still foreign to me. I hoped Carey didn't expect professional images.

As the event wound down, the artists started cutting into their creations and serving little bites of art that were not only beautiful, but delicious. I was both horrified and intrigued — it seemed a shame to unceremoniously destroy what had no doubt taken hours to create, but I also hadn't realized there was going to be free food at the Edible Arts Extravaganza. I tried the volcano cake — slightly doughy and stale — and moved on to the piece I spent the most time trying to photograph well — the Sushi Gown. For this piece, the artist took the torso of a mannequin and applied pieces of nori in the shape of a hip-length, emerald gown. She took scissors to the nori to create an elegant lacy trim, and then accessorized the ensemble with sushi rolls. Sushi was my favorite food and I hadn't yet found any place to eat it in Alaska. This was the one piece of art whose demise didn't make me feel bad; I dived into the plate with shameless abandon.

After the all-I-could-eat gala, I stashed the Tribune's camera in the trunk of my car and waddled over to Duggan's Pub for a New Year's Eve concert. I had little interest in going out by myself, but it seemed a shame to spend such a celebratory holiday holed up in my cabin with my cats. I held this glimmer of hope that I'd see at least one of the six people I knew in town at Duggan's. And anyway, The Whipsaws were playing. The Whipsaws were a twangy rock band from Anchorage. They sent the Tribune a CD and press release ahead of their

New Year's concert, and Carey gave it to me to review. I'd listened to the album every day since, spinning "Ten Day Bender" on a Discman that attached to a garbled tape deck in my car. I enjoyed their gritty alternative country, and decided that, if nothing else, I'd be able to squeeze a concert review for the newspaper out of this solo outing.

Inside Duggan's the air was smoky and stale. Booming base from poorly arranged speakers was drowning out all of the melody from the Whipsaws' set, and the pub was still half empty at 10:30. I sat down at the bar to order a Diet Coke, and almost as soon as I did, my stomach started lurching. If it wasn't for speakers on full volume, everyone around me would have heard the gurgling and moaning. It was a full gastrointestinal rebellion, with sharp pains and a wide-eyed sense of urgency. Of course I instantly knew the culprit. I could only guess at how many hours or days earlier that Sushi Gown had been constructed, not to mention fermented under hot lights in a crowded room.

I slumped over the bar and rushed outside as fast as I could waddle, knowing that the situation was about to become dire and I still had to drive home. At least I brought my car. Twenty minutes later, I ran into my house and nearly tripped over one of the cats as I hit the answering machine button on my way to the bathroom. A three-hour-old message from Geoff wished me a Happy New Year and told me he'd just celebrated the East Coast occasion with his friends in upstate New York. He sounded like he was having all the fun and I was stuck in Alaska, working on New Year's Eve, and dealing with the consequences of poor food choices before the clock even struck midnight in this part of the world.

"Aw, screw him," were the only words I could form before I dived into a long and painful purging of perishable art.

Ashes to Ashes

January 11, 2006

Somewhere, hidden deep within a shroud of fog and the forgotten hours of the morning, Augustine coughed up an explosion. Unseen, unheard, almost as if it never existed — except for the five-mile-high ash cloud that is now probably drifting over Denali National Park.

The volcano began what is expected to be a series of escalating eruptions at 4:44 a.m. It was enough to raise the concern level to code red and keep people glued to their radios after raiding stores for face masks and Spam — but didn't really do much else. The ash headed north and east and pretty much away from Homer, Anchorage and any relatively populated area of Alaska. The fog stayed, blocking anxious eyes from any view of the rumbling mountain, and gripping the town in an eerie sort of silence.

My editor rushed into the office first thing this morning to update the Web site. In the great irony of weekly newspapers, our current issue — published yesterday and released two hours after the volcano blew — ran with the headline "Scientists say eruption not imminent." Our ad rep won the office poll with an exact guess of Jan. 11 — but in the great irony of advertising executives didn't even take the opportunity to gloat. We just typed quietly and waited for a glimpse of ash or a phone call from a panicked resident — anything — but all we did was wait. "Something is just off about today," my co-worker said. Maybe it was because a volcano 70 miles from here erupted. Or maybe it was because a volcano 70 miles from here erupted and nothing happened.

✳ ✳ ✳ ✳ ✳

The eruption of Mount Augustine wasn't so much a bang as a chronic cough, like a lifelong smoker casually emitting phlegmy barks at regular intervals. After its initial early-morning eruption on January 11, the volcano continued to belch ash throughout the day. A milky haze hung in the air, and a film of fine gray dust coated the snow. A local radio station broadcast warnings for residents to cover all of their electronic equipment in plastic and avoid starting their cars, because volcanic dust can clog hoses and tear apart engines from the inside.

A heavy fog draped over the neighborhood the following morning. When I walked outside to grab the copy of the New York Times that we had specially delivered every morning, it wasn't there — ash fog canceled car deliveries. But as I breathed moist air, the fog didn't seem too insidious. Shards didn't rip up my lungs, and dust didn't clog my sinuses. I hadn't been told not to come into work, so I prepped by bicycle with extra chain lube, then strapped a pair of goggles over my eyes and a scarf over my mouth for the commute into town.

I arrived at the office to find Carey balancing on a stool outside the front door, covering the entryway in duct tape. Tire tracks from her truck were visible in a thin layer of ash dusting the parking lot, which was otherwise empty.

"Um, what are you doing?" I asked as I wheeled up beside Carey.

"What are you doing?" she exclaimed as she glanced at me through the eye of her massive roll of tape. "You're riding your bike? You're not even supposed to go outside. You know this ash is just like tiny shards of glass, and it gets into your lungs when you breathe."

"I brought a scarf," I replied with mock indignation, gesturing at the fleece bunched around my neck, although I'd long since pushed it away from my face since the fabric made it too hard to breathe. "And goggles. And anyway, you didn't tell me I shouldn't come into work."

"I wouldn't tell you to ride your bike to work. Jane called and we're shutting the office down for the day. Augustine went off again this morning and it was a big one. They're expecting the ash cloud to move over Homer in less than an hour. I covered all the computers and sealed the doors. You should do the same when you get home. And for god's sake, don't ride your bike around in this. I don't want to have to put out an ad for a new arts reporter because you went out and choked on volcanic ash."

"Okay, but I still gotta ride home," I said with a shrug.

"Oh no, you can't do that. Throw your bike in the back of the truck. I'm headed home right now anyway."

Carey took the long way around Diamond Ridge in hopes of getting a better glimpse of the ash-belching island southwest of Kachemak Bay. We parked at Bay View Drive and looked toward the blurred horizon. Morning fog had cleared out, revealing the first sunny day in what felt like weeks. But a high, gritty haze obscured the winter sun, transforming it to a crimson bulb. Across the bay, we could see the indigo silhouette of Mount Augustine, with an equally opaque plume rising into the stratosphere.

"That must have been a big eruption," I said as Carey cracked open her window and pushed the big lens of the newspaper's camera through a narrow opening. She fired off a few clicks but seemed unwilling to venture outside the truck. Bright orange specks shimmered on the northern face of the mountain, and I squinted in an effort to discern whether this was lava or my imagination. Homer often felt like the end of the world, and it was eerie to witness a live volcano spewing fire and blackening the snow.

Augustine was far enough off shore that scientists assured residents there was little threat to human life outside the polluting effects of the ash cloud. Still, planes throughout Southcentral Alaska had been grounded, offices had been shuttered, and the radio repeated strict warnings to stay indoors as long as Augustine was active, which could continue for hours or weeks. The well-oiled machine of modern life still creaked to a halt amid primordial natural forces, in Alaska and everywhere else.

Carey dropped me off at the end of Trail Court. A fine layer of gray dust had already collected on the bike during the short time it sat in the back of the truck. I wheeled it toward the cabin just as Geoff emerged wearing his standard winter running outfit: a loose pair of thin polyester pants, a thin fleece jacket, light trail shoes, thin gloves, and a gray buff wrapped around his head above a curly ponytail.

"You're going running?" I asked. "You know that the volcano went off again, right? It's not safe."

"It'll be fine," Geoff said as he pulled his buff over his mouth to demonstrate his version of the same breathing mask I had constructed that morning with a scarf. "The gym isn't open so I'm going to get in my run today."

"How long?"

Geoff shrugged. "Not long. Eight or ten miles."

"What about the ash?"

"It seems to be settling," Geoff said. "The radio said that the last eruption is blowing northwest of here."

With that, he took off up the driveway, with a loud crunch of snow echoing under his feet. As he turned the corner out of sight, I considered his resolve. As soon as he committed to run the Little Su 50K, he formulated a structured training plan that appeared both effective and grueling. On days that the Homer High School gym was open to the public — Mondays, Wednesdays and Fridays — he drove the thirty-minute, round-trip commute to town to lift weights for ninety minutes. One day a week, he went to the high school track to complete speed-work intervals, even amid driving rain and white-out blizzards. Two days a week, he went for runs of various lengths on roads and trails, increasing his mileage by small increments each week. He always saved one day for fun "cross-training" activities such as skiing or biking along the Homer Spit with me, and had one day reserved for a rest day, although he often went skiing on those days as well.

His dedication reminded me of something I'd forgotten during our four years together: Geoff was an athlete. He was a talented cross-country and track runner in high school, racking up a number of state titles and wins in several distances. He earned an athletic scholarship to Syracuse University and ran cross-country while studying engineering. During his freshman year, he trained constantly but couldn't achieve the same level of success he enjoyed in high school. This only drove him to work harder, and for nine months he did little else but run, compete, and study. This only left him dejected and exhausted, and burnout raced through his nineteen-year-old body like a brush fire. He took the summer off to drive across the country in his car, and didn't enroll in any classes in the fall.

Geoff also quit the cross country team, citing injury, but later admitted his injuries were minor, and his quitting stemmed from a desire to be free from a structured and oppressive routine. He officially dropped out of school and continued to take road trips throughout America in his diesel Volkswagen Jetta.

He drove hundreds of miles each day and camped in sandy desert washes, high mountain plateaus, Midwestern corn fields, suburban culverts — really, anywhere he could bed down for the night free of charge.

For money, Geoff went into the jewelry business. His wares were handmade, started by tying hemp string to pins in his car's dashboard. Then, while balancing the steering wheel with his knee, he wove the strands together in intricate patterns. He added plastic or clay beads, and sold the finished necklaces and bracelets for a large profit at outdoor concerts and music festivals. His travels were largely dictated by bands' touring schedules, although he often found time to spend a full day hiking, or camp alone in the desert and read classic novels that he purchased at used book stores. "Nothing good has been written since 1970," Geoff explained to me once when I was rifling through his piles of dusty, dog-eared hardbacks that carried the distinct aroma of my great-grandmother's basement. He refused to retract this statement after I reminded him that most of Edward Abbey's work was published after 1970.

Geoff preferred to sell his jewelry at Rusted Root concerts. The venues were smaller, the music was more organic, and he had become friends with the band members. However, like any good businessman, he followed the money — large crowds of college students and trust fund hippies attending stadium concerts headlined by Phish and Dave Matthews. He let his auburn hair grow long and grew a bushy beard, both of which he occasionally twisted into dreadlocks. For several years he operated as a vagabond, living as though he was penniless while raking in tens of thousands of dollars in jewelry sales. He put his earnings into savings as insurance to continue his lifestyle indefinitely. He no longer had any interest in an engineering career, winning races, breaking distance records, or anything else that he pursued in his youth. He just wanted to be free.

I met Geoff in late 2000, five years after he dropped out of Syracuse University. During his traveling years, Geoff didn't involve himself in romantic relationships, and didn't make many new friends. He preferred solitude. When he did crave the company of others, he reconnected with a group of close friends from his childhood. One of these friends, Jen, had since relocated to Utah to attend the University of Utah, and had taken up residence with seven other students in a communal housing situation in Salt Lake City. This group had become my friends through Terra Firma. Although I graduated in the spring of 2000, I continued to live in Salt Lake City, work part time as a graphic designer, and show up at their house on weekends to hang out or join camping trips.

In the fall, Geoff decided he needed a few weeks of downtime, and came to Salt Lake to visit Jen. He and I first met at the Terra Firma house while playing a board game called Settlers of Catan. The housemates had recently become obsessed with this game, and invited me over to learn how to play. A wild streak of beginner's luck led to multiple wins and Geoff's first direct words to me — "You're some kind of Settlers genius." This "genius" never managed to reveal itself any further — it really was beginner's luck — but I'd managed to make a good first impression.

Our paths crossed many times in subsequent group events — at the University bowling alley, at a favorite Mexican restaurant, and on a long hike in the San Rafael Swell. But months passed with little more than brief, casual exchanges. It certainly wasn't a flash-fire romance — perhaps because we were both shy, or more likely because there wasn't initially an attraction. Geoff wasn't interested in relationships, and I was still hung up on Mike, who still hadn't returned after two years in El Salvador.

Geoff and I continued as acquaintances until Christmas Day, when I flew out to New York City for the holiday break. One a whim, two days earlier, I'd purchased a plane ticket to visit Jen in upstate New York, neglecting to look at a map and realize that New York City and Syracuse weren't exactly neighboring communities. She laughed about the misunderstanding and recruited Geoff to pick me up at the airport. It was a five-hour drive to La Guardia, one way, and my flight was more than four hours delayed. At the time Geoff barely knew me, and I didn't expect he'd wait around at the airport if he'd shown up at all. I was twenty-one years old and terrified about being all alone in Queens, and walked out of the gate nearly in tears. To my surprise, Geoff and his unruly red beard were waiting for me in the terminal, which at that point was nearly abandoned. It was two in the morning, the day after Christmas, we had five hours of driving in front of us still, and there was a blizzard on the way. We still spent the rest of the night wandering the deserted streets of Manhattan, listening to each other's stories.

Our magical holiday in New York would have made the perfect setting for a romantic comedy: hiking along the frozen waterfalls of Ithaca, playing a riotous game of Spades with his parents and siblings, ringing in the New Year at a thumping college party in Oswego. Still, even this adventure failed to bind us together immediately. Six more weeks went by before Geoff sent me an e-mail to my work address, professing that he had a crush on me. We arranged for a first date for the evening after Valentine's Day, attending a cross-dressing-themed house party with the Terra Firma crowd. "St. Hades Day" was intended to be a celebration of anti-romance, where women dressed like men, men wore prom gowns and bikinis, and we burned the relics of past relationships in a backyard bonfire. Geoff and I spent the whole party talking, and kissed for the first time while I was wearing a fake mustache, and he donned a sundress and gaudy blue eyeshadow.

The following night I took him snowboarding at Brighton Ski Area, with two discount tickets for the night session. Geoff had never ridden a snowboard before, but had recently purchased his own board in the interest of taking up the hobby. I was a terrible instructor — having taught myself the techniques, I had no idea how to explain them — and Geoff was recklessly nonchalant about careening down the slope at high speeds. Florescent lights flooded the slopes, casting ruts and other hazards in confusing shadows. On the third run, Geoff took a cartwheeling fall that resulted in a badly hurt wrist. At first he brushed off the injury, but soon pain reached the point that he could no longer tighten or loosen his bindings. Still, he downplayed the severity and told me he just want- ed to warm up at the lodge for a while. I selfishly continued for several more runs on my own, each time returning to check on him in the lodge. He insisted I should continue snowboarding. "You already paid for the tickets. One of us should enjoy this." We finally left around 8:30 p.m.

"Do you want to go camping?" Geoff asked as we drove down the canyon in his Toyota pickup. Although I offered to drive, Geoff seemed loathe to let me take the wheel of his truck, and gingerly handled the wheel with his swollen hand.

"Obviously," I replied, and we drove four more hours to Goblin Valley, in the red rock desert of Southern Utah. In the meantime, any remaining shock wore off and Geoff's wrist was enveloped in pain. We'd planned to hike into a cave amid the sandstone formations, but he could barely drive anymore. I suggested returning to Price and finding a medical clinic, but he brushed off this idea be- cause he had no health insurance. Instead we crawled into the back of his truck and started kissing. Geoff told me, "This is what I've always wanted — a truck, the desert, and a beautiful woman to share it with."

Temperatures dropped well below freezing that night, and we cuddled against each other because we had no sleeping bags. Under the cold sunlight of morn- ing, it became clear that Geoff's wrist was broken. His hand was badly swollen and bruised, and the joint itself was crooked. It looked as though each bone in his arm snapped apart and then realigned several degrees in the wrong direction. Geoff insisted he could set the bone and brace it himself, and never went to the hospital. His wrist healed crookedly, and years later still caused him pain when lifting heavy objects. But he did continue snowboarding, and he did continue to invite me on beautiful meanders through the desert. I began to realize that this was all I ever wanted — a truck, an adventure, and a man to share them with.

The significance of certain life events often don't register until much later. I'd come to think of Geoff's broken wrist as symbolic, beyond the folly of youth. The still-crooked joint reminded me of the sacrifices he made to invite me into his world, and also his stubborn refusals to acknowledge when he was in pain or needed help. Geoff loved me, of that much I was certain. But he didn't need me. In his heart he was still the same independent spirit who drifted around the continent, eyes always fixed on the horizon, anchored nowhere. I was Geoff's girlfriend of four years, but in many ways I was no different than his childhood friends who were now scattered all over the country. I was another person he could go home to, when the desire for companionship struck.

We'd been in Alaska for four months, and Geoff was already formulating new ideas for the future.

"I wonder if we should go live in New York City for a year, or maybe San Francisco," he'd tell me. "I really miss Utah sometimes," he'd muse. And sometimes he'd ask, "How would you feel about maybe hiking the Continental Divide Trail the summer after next? We could still come back to Alaska afterward, or not." Although I relished Geoff's zeal for travel and fresh opportunities, it was becoming clear that he wasn't setting the same emotional hooks into life in Homer as I was. Alaska seemed to be just another stop-over for him, a waypoint in the adventure of life.

To me, life in Homer symbolized our life together. As he spoke about moving again, I couldn't help but feel continuously unsettled about our status as a couple. One night I brought up marriage, and Geoff just laughed. "We're already together. Marriage doesn't accomplish anything," he said.

"Do you think you'll ever want kids?" I asked another time, and he shrugged.

"Probably. I'm not sure, though. I can't really say why I believe this, but I always suspected that I might not be able to have children. Not that I've been checked, but ..."

Geoff and I had never been particularly careful with birth control, so this notion that he might be infertile wasn't implausible. As for myself, as soon as I entered puberty I'd become increasingly more ambivalent about breeding. The idea of bringing demanding and dependent children into my life was more repulsive than enticing, and at age twenty-six the motherhood urge had yet to kick in. If any partner at the time told me he had no personal desire to have children, I would have embraced his decision and declared myself officially child-free. But Geoff's way of questioning his physical capability to reproduce struck me as strange, as did his ambivalence about marriage.

"Just what are Geoff and I doing?" I sometimes wondered. "Why is it that we all try so hard to adhere ourselves to one person, as though nothing ever changes?"

"It's because every time we rip ourselves apart, the scars remain," I thought. But Geoff was different — he didn't seem to regard potential emotional pain as a risk. He was willing to accept the consequences of falling in and out of love, just as he happily accepted that his wrist was permanently crooked, that it ached after long days of hammering at construction sites, and that arthritis in his later years was all but guaranteed. Wounds were never the end — he knew he could prop up the broken pieces himself and keep moving.

Geoff's cavalier attitude stretched to all aspects of life; he didn't care about the ash cloud warnings, either. The moose, wolves and rabbits could breathe this air. So could he.

I envied Geoff's disregard for danger and resolved to set out myself. I was already suited up for outdoor adventure, so I mounted my bike and followed his tracks in the snow. Each footprint was a white imprint in the dull gray surface, revealing at least a half inch of ash on top of the snow. I wrapped my fleece scarf around my face and pedaled toward the Homestead Trails, where I expected to find Geoff. But his footprints faded on the icy access road, and I lost track of his route.

"Oh well," I thought. "It's not like I can run with him while I'm riding a bike." This was just another area of our lives where Geoff's and my paths paralleled but didn't quite connect. We were two planets orbiting the same star, but sometimes it felt like we were still an unbridgeable distance apart. Geoff seemed forever resistant to gravitational forces; he could bounce into the next galaxy as easily as he could go for a run during a volcano eruption.

The sun was setting, and a billowing fog had moved back in over Kachemak Bay. Above the cloud cover, I could still see the smoking silhouette of Augustine, but soon the fog obscured that as well. I pedaled up a hillside, chased by the rising cloud. I descended into a steep gully shrouded in gray fog, then climbed onto a ridge where I saw my last gasps of clear sky. The clouds beneath me were drenched in golden sunlight. I raised my fleece-covered chin and imagined I was flying over them, utterly free.

I returned home forty minutes sooner than Geoff, whose eight-mile run had morphed into fifteen miles, all the way down the next valley along Bridge Creek and back.

"Do your lungs hurt?" I asked. I felt okay after my ride, but paranoia had resulted in a dry cough as I repeatedly cleared my throat, then consumed so much water that I could feel it sloshing around in my gut.

"No, it's fine out there," Geoff said. "There's like a centimeter of ash on the ground, and it just sticks to the snow."

"I ended up going for a ride," I said. "It was short, just a Homestead loop, but I got above the fog before the sun set."

"It was a nice afternoon," Geoff agreed. "Even better when no one's out on the roads."

I nodded. The rest of Homer was patiently waiting for a disaster that wouldn't come. Augustine would continue to belch out ash and even lava for a few more weeks, but never in the quantities feared. Geoff and I didn't lose a step of training to the ongoing ash forecast (I still tuned in every afternoon and chose to start heeding the warnings, but favorable winds kept alerts on low.)

Every time I glanced over at the steaming silhouette of the cone-shaped island, something still seemed off. It was strange that a volcano erupted, and nothing happened.

Long Ride

January 21, 2006

I have a little of that serene, drugged-out drowsiness going on right now ... long ride, big dinner, warm house, storm raging outside.

Today I set out just before sunrise with the intention of putting in an eight- to ten-hour ride that would mimic my attack of the Susitna 100. To do that, I had to ride on a lot of soft, rutted trails that are punchy and slow and there's no way around it (winter riders call this stuff "mashed potatoes" ... in my case, very lumpy mashed potatoes). I rode the ice roads, open snow (about 5 inches of powder) and on Caribou Lake itself. I also did a fair amount of pushing. Any food I ate, I ate while pushing. I kept my full stops to an absolute minimum, to keep my core temperature higher, and also because it's the way I deal with the muscle strain of long rides ... just keep moving, moving, moving, and there's less time for hurt.

✳ ✳ ✳ ✳ ✳

In marketing materials, the city of Homer often advertises itself as "The End of the Road" — but it's not. A narrow strip of pavement continues east for forty miles beyond the edge of town. This road eventually tapers into a boggy dirt track that leads to the reclusive Russian immigrant community of Voznesenka, which then tapers to ATV-trammeled mud flats at the lip of Kachemak Bay. If one were to keep walking across the tidal plain, they could access the glaciated valleys of the Kenai Mountains, then climb the towering granite peaks that appeared unobtainable from Homer's side of the bay.

It was my dream to someday cross this point of inaccessibility. Still, the end of the road — the point where East End Road curls into Basargin Road, bringing thousands of miles of the North American highway system to a splintered end — held its own mysterious allure. An overcast sky threatened snow as I drove along the icy pavement, past the fancy restaurant at the edge of town, then past the outlying estates occupied by Homer's wealthier residents. Beyond the city residential zones were the outliers — ramshackle cabins with Tyvek siding, hand-built dwellings that seemed to not only defy building codes but also a few laws of physics, and the driveways of the longtime homesteaders. Eventually there was only the occasional street intersection leading into the woods. As the road climbed several hundred feet above sheer bluffs, views opened to the far end of the bay. At that elevation, roiling whitecaps appeared as diamonds glittering in a charcoal sea.

"It's windy today," I thought.

I turned off the road just before the outskirts of Voznesenka, and parked in a small clearing alongside a half dozen trucks with empty snowmobile trailers. As soon as I stepped outside, I had to battle a surging panic. The air was a humid ten degrees — moderate cold that becomes bitter when infused with moisture and driven by a steady breeze. The sensation of transitioning from a heated interior to that kind of cold must be the number one reason why people hate winter — it sucker-punches you in the gut, saps the feeling from your extremities, and burns your lungs with ice. Most people react to this by grumbling loudly and rushing to the nearest heated interior. Here, out the End of the Road, there was no indoor escape. I took a deep breath and rushed to complete the outdoor transition before my fingers froze: removing the mountain bike from a rack on top of the car, re-attaching the front wheel and rim brake, attaching the handlebar bag full of peanut butter sandwiches and Power Bars, and changing from my tennis shoes to hiking boots and knee-high overboots. My intention was to spend the whole day in this dreadful hinterland.

A biting wind forced me to turn my face away from it at all times. This wasn't my ideal day for a long ride — if I could switch this weather for clear, subzero cold, I would. But it was exactly three weeks before the Susitna 100, and my self-generated training plan called for a peak effort on this day. Although I'd never traveled this far east from Homer, a co-worker told me about dozens of miles of trails that were maintained by the local snowmobile club, the Snomads. Traveling forty-five miles out a dead-end road was a risky trip for my Geo Prism. If it snowed more than a few inches, the city's snowplows wouldn't make it out here until Monday and I'd be stranded. Still, I wanted to prepare for the Susitna 100, and I understood that would happen only if I mimicked the conditions of the race — remote and wild.

The crackling sound of my studded tires on pavement was comforting in its familiarity, but the noise abruptly ceased as soon as I passed the Snomads' trailhead sign and crossed the backcountry threshold. Here snowmobiles traveled freely over hills and swamps, blazing their own paths across an otherwise unbroken canvas of snow. This basin was a rare geographic hiccup here on the southern coast of Alaska, at least in comparison to the volcano-dominated ranges that rise like fortresses straight out of the sea. The coastal mountains are guarded by glaciers and cliffs, inaccessible to machines and all but the most daring humans. The thumb of the Kenai Peninsula is comparatively flat, yet still nearly empty of human presence. Beside East End Road, the boreal forest stretches across the basin with very few interruptions all the way to the Sterling Highway, some fifty or sixty miles northwest. These small, rolling hills a few dozen miles from Homer were still very much a wild part of Alaska.

Cold wind licked my cheeks I mashed the pedals along the soft trail. Its surface resembled a soufflé, and turning the bike's crank was like stirring batter, with similar results. Forward motion was precipitated only by applying enough force to plow the rear tire through the trench created by the front tire. Three snowmobiles raced by in a cloud of powder, obliterating my trail-breaking trench and all other evidence of my labors.

After twenty minutes of maximum effort while watching the bike's speedometer dip below two and a half miles per hour — where it automatically zeroed out — I resigned myself to walking for a while. Pushing my bike was something I didn't practice nearly often enough, given the volatile weather and trail conditions I was likely to face in the Susitna 100. It goes without saying that once a bike can no longer be ridden, it becomes worse than useless. My feet, clad in floppy overboots, punched shin-deep holes in the snow as I dragged the anchor of a bike beside me. It was slower than wallowing without a bike, and definitely stupider than using a pair of skis. Still, the motion itself was meditative and strangely therapeutic — a Sisyphean grind whose rhythm echoed the impermanence of all efforts in life. The bike was a symbol of hope — of the pursuit of happiness amid an absurd and ultimately futile labor. Many people drag dead weight around for years in anticipation of a just few minutes of flight.

Here, beyond the End of the Road, I didn't need to wait so long. After forty-five minutes of wading through fluff, I reached a trail intersection where all of the neighborhood access trails converged on the main route to Caribou Lake. Crossing frozen swamps and forested hills, the higher-traffic trail was polished to a glistening sheen of ice. I mounted my bike again. With the breeze at my back, the sensation was like launching a kite. In a single breath I transitioned from wallowing in the snow to coasting effortlessly. Flying.

I accelerated to the precise speed of the wind, and its dull hum lapsed into silence. With gusts ushering the bike forward, I could no longer feel any wind or surface resistance. Moving at the speed of the wind had a similar effect to floating in space, in a vacuum devoid of sound or sensation. My body felt motionless as I continued to spin pedals and gaze at the landscape sweeping beside me — a blur of spruce, snow, and sky. Only the muffled crackle of tire studs and vibrating jolts on the front shock betrayed the illusion that I was no longer anchored to the Earth. In this virtual space warp, a seeming instant carried me seven miles from the ice road intersection to the shoreline of Caribou Lake.

Snowmobile tracks fanned in all directions across the frozen surface of the lake, accessing cabins and camp sites along the shore. Caribou Lake was Homer's backcountry getaway, and the vacation properties were the reason this ice road was so well-traveled. In summer, the land is mired in swamps and bumpy muskeg. The only way to access lakeside properties then is to fly in a float plane, or hike seven miles on a boardwalk trail. Like most of Alaska, winter conditions make Homer's backcountry more accessible. It seems counterintuitive that deep cold and long nights would create the best season for travel in this part of the world, but it's true. During the summer months, cross-country travel frequently involves mosquito-infested swamps, knee-deep sludge, turbulent rivers that can be crossed only by boat, raging creeks that can be crossed only at a hikers' peril, and alder-choked woods that could stymie an army with machetes. In the winter, when the land is blanketed by snow and waterways are frozen, travel can be as uncomplicated as drawing a line on a blank sheet of paper.

Well, perhaps not that simple. The ice road ended at Caribou Lake, and the public trail splintered in several directions. I wanted to head west, so I picked what appeared to be the smoothest individual snowmobile track. It was an illusion — a thin crust atop bottomless fluff. Although I could ride, the wheels dug in and I was once again churning through thick batter. My chosen trail veered at an acute angle from the ice road. A full half hour after I rode away from the lake, I could still see the occasional snowmobile zipping up the ice road across the swamp. I longed to just return to the easy seven miles of my route, ride laps out and back, regain that feeling of flying with every outbound trip, and then return home with a hundred miles on my odometer.

Those potentially quick and easy miles would bring a superficial buzz of accomplishment, but I knew they wouldn't provide meaningful training for the Susitna 100. The race course wouldn't offer effortless miles on a manicured road. Those trails were sure to be soft and unwieldy, veering away from the edge of civilization into true wilderness. This was the point of the race. It wasn't supposed to be fun — at least, not in the traditional sense of the word. It was supposed to be hard. It was supposed to invite pain and frustration. It was supposed to hinge on the likelihood of failure rather than success.

It was this promise of difficulty that kept me riding away from the ice road rather than rushing back toward the comforts of home. I craved this ache in my leg muscles, the tightness in my back, the burn of cold air in my lungs and frustration as I battled the wind and snow for forward progress. From a stranger's perspective, I must have looked ridiculous — cranking a mountain bike through deep snow, moving slower than a person walking. But if I could find a way to push through all of the obstructions, I was confident I'd discover something more enduring, and more meaningful than fun. Something like enlightenment.

Hours trickled away beneath the crush of heavy labor. My body began to break down in the way human bodies do — in that they're still physically intact, but the brain is besieged with signals of sharp pain, dull aches, and a distracting loop of negative forces that all echo the same protest: We're tired, we're tired, we're tired. Glycogen stores evaporated and my muscles turned to the slow-burning fuel source of body fat. I nibbled on peanut butter sandwiches in an effort to keep the inner furnace burning, but this was akin to throwing twigs of kindling on a nearly-extinguished log. The sandwiches were frozen, rendering the bread tasteless, the jam crystallized, and the all-natural peanut butter to a consistency of wet cement. Not exactly the most appetizing snack, and my stomach was churning from all the demands of my depleted body. This is the largest puzzle of endurance efforts — everything boils down to available energy, but when the body needs energy most is often when it's the most resistant to processing fuel. I had a handlebar bag full of sandwiches, but a diminished appetite and nausea prompted me to stop eating. Eventually my higher brain kicked in with a reminder: "Food is fuel. You need to eat!" After a few bites I'd start gagging, and the nausea would signal that I'd had enough. But it wasn't nearly enough.

My legs were wobbly by the time I reached the base of a large bluff. I would need to climb and then descend this steep ridge in order to complete my counter-clockwise loop and return to East End Road. I'd been traveling for six and a half hours, and although my odometer screen blacked out in the cold hours earlier, I guessed I'd ridden about forty miles. The effort lumped in my legs like hot lead. I could scarcely fathom the reality of surmounting this hill and pedaling ten miles back to the parking lot, let alone traveling the entirety of the Susitna 100. Sometimes it pays not to dwell on the big picture. Forward progress often depends on willful ignorance.

Climbing the bluff was more difficult than I feared. Powered by massive engines, snowmobiles laid a trail that cut directly up the steep face. There weren't even hints of switchbacks, and the grade was just a few degrees shy of a vertical wall. I had to kick steps into the packed snow for traction as I wrestled with my bike, pushing the wheels into the snow to leverage another step. My pace deteriorated from painfully slow to something otherworldly, like walking on a planet with fifty times the gravitational force of Earth. My legs felt like they weighed hundreds of pounds. Adding insult to insult, the frigid wind picked up strength as I gained elevation. Subzero wind chills sapped the remainder of my meager strength. I didn't have enough kindling left in the energy furnace to heat my core, and began to shiver.

Now I was not only tired, but increasingly cold and frightened. I wondered if I should flag down a snowmobile driver and ask for help. Of course, I hadn't seen anyone since the ice road, many hours earlier. I wasn't sure if any snowmobiles had ventured beyond the lake on this day. I was probably on my own, and my cell phone didn't work out here. Geoff likely wouldn't deduce something was wrong until a few hours after dark; in that amount of time, I'd freeze to death if I didn't keep moving. Panic gurgled in my gut, but I couldn't lose it now. I'd gotten myself into this spot, and I'd have to get myself out. There were no other choices.

After stopping to cram another sandwich half down my throat, I resolved to attack the remainder of the climb as though I wasn't running out of steam. I needed heat to stop shivering, and only hard-working muscles could make heat. Fear focused my efforts. I drove one foot into the trail as I picked up the other, fighting against gravity to move as quickly as possible. I gasped for air, and the cold fumes in my lungs were replaced with oxygen-starved flames. I didn't know what would kill me faster — hypothermia or hypoxia — but the hard marching did reignite my internal furnace. By the time I arrived at the crest of the bluff, feeling had returned to my fingers and trickles of sweat flowed down my face beneath my helmet.

I stopped briefly at the top to catch my breath, and crammed down another frozen sandwich. The calories helped stoke the furnace, causing the onslaught of shivery cold to retreat, for now. The wind continued to stir up swirls of snow, which swept across the plateau in a mesmerizing dance. This high plain was a nutrient-starved muskeg, and the few scattered spruce trees were no taller than me. The sun hovered low on the horizon, and long shadows cast the snow in dark blue hues. Twilight would arrive soon. I had a headlight but no desire to linger in this place after nightfall. Dark clouds and increasing winds signaled the approach of a storm, and the sun's retreat would strengthen the piercing cold. After several minutes on the plateau, snow flurries began to fall.

I mounted my bike and, still driven by fear, pedaled as hard as I could toward a white-capped Kachemak Bay. The water was still some distance away, but I was thrilled that it was in view again. At the edge of the bluff, the trail dropped just as steeply as it had climbed. I didn't stop to scout the descent. Duck into the handlebars and launch — that's the only way to do it.

As snow built up on the bike's wheels, the rims iced up and the brake pads became about as useful as a paper clip. I clenched the brake levers just the same, wincing at the brakes' ear-splitting squeals as the rear wheel shimmied back and forth like a salmon swimming away from a bear. Violent speed wobbles caused my legs to knock against the frame. All I could do was hang onto the handlebars and hope I met the bottom of the hill still attached to my bike, and not crumpled in a blood-stained snowball. My heart rate eclipsed the maximum effort of the climb.

As I relinquished all control, the landscape once again blurred in a black-and-white abstraction, and everything else — my heart, my fears, the wind — became quiet. For a few seconds I experienced a peace I had never before known, utterly paradoxical to the chaotic realities of the descent. Later, I wondered whether this tranquility engulfed me because my mind was convinced I was about to die. Or, perhaps involuntary serenity is the mind's greatest defense mechanism. When chaos can't be controlled — and it can never be controlled — the only choice is to flow through it, letting the current carry you to safety.

Just as suddenly as this quietness settled, the wind came roaring back and the bottom of the hill came into view. Momentum decreased and the bike shimmied to an ungraceful stop as I shoved my right heel into the snow and braced my legs. When I looked up, I saw three snowmobiles idling in a semi-circle on the trail. I hadn't noticed them at the top; clearly they were waiting for me to get out of the way so they could roar up the trail I'd just descended.

A man on the middle snowmobile lifted the visor on his helmet and smiled. "We've never seen a bicycle out here before," he said. "Where did you come from?"

"The trailhead off Basargin," I said, which I guessed at this point was fewer than five miles away. I didn't disclose the fifty-mile loop I'd embarked on eight hours earlier. "I'm just headed back now, before it gets dark."

A small helmeted figure poked her head from her perch behind the man and squealed, "See, Daddy, I told you! I knew it was a girl!"

A surge of pride filled my chest and I waved at her. Without trying, I had inadvertently pulled off a totally rad stunt, for an audience.

The sky had darkened from overcast gray to indigo by the time I returned to my car. Wind-driven snowflakes were accumulating rapidly. With numb fingers and stiff legs, I worked quickly to load my bike on the roof, knowing my window to escape this place on drivable pavement was closing quickly. Hunger gnawed at my stomach, and it was difficult to extract immediate satisfaction from my training ride. All I felt was soreness and fatigue.

And yet, as I rolled away from the parking lot with frigid air from the car's fans blasting in my face, I could already sense that something momentous had just taken place. I'd ventured across real Alaska wilderness, and not only did I survive, but I was strong. Even when I was most frightened, I didn't panic, or start crying, or lose hope. For a few glorious moments, I was a little girl's hero. Even if this hero status was short-lived and rather silly, the act of riding blindly down that hill had been daring, risky and completely beyond anything I would have dreamed of attempting as recently as five months earlier. I could hardly believe it had only been that long since I'd been so frightened of life that I purposefully avoided the outdoors, drowning my days in alcohol, shallow social interactions, and comfortable but mundane routine.

Here, in the Alaska wilderness, with no one to rely on but myself, I learned the value of embracing the whole of experience — the exhilaration, loneliness, fatigue, pain, terror, and triumph. The stakes were real, and the accomplishment was satisfying.

I came to Alaska when I finally accepted that the future would always be unknowable, and the only way to avoid being buried in the past was to keep moving. With Geoff and my newspaper job, it was still impossible to predict what the future held. But I had gained one hard-edged certainty: Alaska was not a dead end.

I Did, I Did, I Did ...

January 29, 2006

... The Iditarod Trail. Is. Slow.

Of course, everything about today was exactly what I would expect of such an excursion. Temperatures were cold, but not unreasonably so. The trail was soft, but better than I expected. Mount Augustine decided today was the fourth of July, but all the ash headed south. Yes, today was a good day. An encouraging day. And yet, I feel the cold grip of this daunting task tightening around me. It could be my neoprene gear. But, no. I think it's the Susitna 100. It's going to be hard.

Well, duh. But sometimes it's hard to grasp the reality of things until you're down in the trenches. Geoff and I went out for a half-day ride (Geoff, who's training to run the Little Su 50K, has no interest in ten-hour bike rides.) We drove up Point MacKenzie Road so we could start immediately on the Iditarod Trail. We planned to go as far as two and a half hours took us and head back. What we got was twenty miles. We made a lot of stops that were more indicative of the recreational nature of this particular ride. Still, twenty miles, five hours. One hundred miles ... well, the math isn't hard.

But I don't feel disheartened. My warm gear performed beautifully for temperatures that didn't even consider climbing above zero. The particular section we did was a roller coaster of short and steep hills, flat frozen bogs and snowmobile moguls. It was a lot of fun. The pace was laid back enough that the effort didn't even demand much energy (Though the one time I tried to gnaw down a deeply frozen Power Bar while pedaling was pretty funny. Well, funny ... not pretty. Without being too graphic, I'll just say that it involved a lot of saliva, a chocolate goatee and some blood.) Anyway, I have been planning this entire time for a race that would take about 24 hours. It's just, now, I'm starting to realize how long that actually is.

✳ ✳ ✳ ✳ ✳

"Hmm, minus twelve," I observed as we drove past a Palmer bank sign on our way to Craig's house.

"Perfect training weather," Geoff said with a smirk. I frowned, because he wasn't taking this venture seriously enough. Not only were we planning to scout part of the actual Susitna 100 race course the following day, but we would do so in the depths of a January cold snap. This was the coldest weather we'd seen yet. Temperatures were forecast to dip below minus twenty overnight. Cold air sinks, so in the low-lying swamps surrounding the Susitna River, we were warned it would likely be at least ten degrees colder.

We'd driven six hours for this training ride, so we couldn't back out at the prospect of minus thirty. Geoff didn't seem concerned. We'd both recently outfitted ourselves with all of the gear that we planned to use in our respective races. Hours of Internet research resulted in an ensemble that I looked forward to putting to the test: A pair of North Face winter hiking boots, one and a half sizes too

large; polyester liner socks; neoprene socks for warmth in wet and snowy conditions; large wool socks over that if it was really cold; neoprene kayaking gloves
for wet weather; zippered ski gloves for cold weather; inexpensive rain paints
(they were $8 on Sierra Trading Post, but those with more experience assured me
that cheap rain pants would block wind just as well as name brands); a polypro
base layer; fleece jackets to layer as needed (the most layers I had ever worn in
my cold office was three, so I figured three was a sufficient number); a Burton
shell; fleece hat; a thin polyester balaclava to protect my face from the wind; a
neoprene face mask; Burton goggles (also a remnant of my snowboarding days);
and what I viewed as my most important piece of gear — a knee-length pair of
waterproof overboots.

Several Alaska cyclists had warned me that the most immediate danger Geoff
and I would encounter on the trail was overflow. Overflow is a natural phenomenon in which water — either through groundwater seepage or weaknesses in
river and lake ice — rises to the surface and creates wet surface conditions even
when temperatures are below zero. After these pools form, they are often covered
with new snow, which insulates the liquid from freezing while hiding evidence
of open water. Step into a puddle at twenty below, and you're likely to freeze a
few toes. The best solution is waterproof footwear. Alaska's quintessential rubber
XtraTufs weren't insulated, and thus not warm enough for long ventures in subzero cold. Combining insulated hiking boots with overboots was the ideal armor
in the battle against hidden overflow.

Geoff, however, planned to wear only light trail-running shoes during the
Little Su 50K. He assured me his race was so "short," and he would be moving
so quickly, that he would need only minimal layers.

"It's like sled dogs," he said. "They run through the open water like it's no
big deal."

"That's because they're dogs," I replied. "We're not dogs."

"Yeah," Geoff said. "But we're not that different. People also generate a ton
of heat when they run. If I wear too much, even if it's twenty below, I'm going
to overheat and sweat, and then things will really suck."

I couldn't say I agreed. In my few morning runs with Geoff three years earlier,
temperatures around fifty above would leave me feeling chilled. I was drenched
in sweat after my Christmas Day run in Palmer, so I understood how running
generated more heat than my typical cycling efforts. Geoff insisted he would run
fast enough to go splashing through slush without freezing his feet, and I didn't
have the experience to argue otherwise.

Geoff also must have thought either his girlfriend or bicycling were too slow,
because he brought oversized Sorel winter boots for this outing. He also brought
his Trek 7500, a full-suspension mountain bike that was similar in style to my

Gary Fisher Sugar. Since he was still in training to run the Little Su 50K, this bike outing would do him little good in terms of training or gear testing. He was along solely to support me. This notion was endearing; while some women have to beg their boyfriends to see chick flicks with them, mine was willing to drive six hours and then spend the better part of a day dragging a bike through the snow in subzero temperatures.

Craig warned us about the cold snap as soon as we stepped in the house. "The high tomorrow is supposed to be negative eight. That's the high temperature, not low."

"Sweet, that's awesome," Geoff said.

"We know about the forecast," I interjected. "But that's good news for us. It's a good opportunity to test out gear for Susitna."

Geoff and Craig began talking gear and Craig showed off his newly acquired treasures: a pair of mountaineering boots from a secondhand store, and an insulated Carhartt jacket. While Geoff and I were still trying to make old winter clothing work for our current, more extreme purposes, Craig was sporting the latest in essential Alaska wear. This particular jacket was displayed in the window of every hunting and sporting goods store in Anchorage. Craig was unapologetically thrifty, but never held back on anything that might keep him from freezing. He was terrified of the cold.

"The only friend I have who's been hospitalized for hypothermia would be the one to move to Alaska," Geoff teased him.

Craig has had severe hypothermia, twice, both in the same slot canyon in the central Utah desert. The first was the incident he described to me when we met in 1998. He was hiking with friends in Lower Black Box, a narrow gorge of the San Rafael River, which — unbeknownst to them when they first set out — was at flood stage in the early spring. After several swims through icy cold pools, Craig lost consciousness and had to be evacuated by his friends. He went back the following year to lower water, but similar consequences. For this bout of hypothermia, however, Craig retained most of his mental faculties and was able to climb out without assistance.

The third time Craig returned to Lower Black Box, Geoff and I were with him, along with about a half dozen other friends. It was May — still early enough in the season that we needed wetsuits to swim through icy pools. Black Box became a toaster oven during the summer months, which is why we there in the spring, when nighttime temperatures still dipped below freezing. Our pre-dawn start promised a shivery hike until slivers of sunlight breached the canyon walls. Craig was certain to face his cold demons out there, but he was determined to hike the entire length of Lower Black Box, "without dying." He seemed optimistic.

Craig's expressive stories had incited anxieties about my own safety. The fretting continued as we arrived at our trailhead campsite after midnight. Starlight penetrated the desert air with an intensity I'd never before witnessed — stars upon stars upon stars. In front of these glittering depths was something else I'd never seen — streaks of green and white light, dancing through the indigo sky. We were setting up our tent when I first noticed the light, and I just let the stakes fall to the ground, mesmerized.

"What is that?"

Another friend of ours who arrived several hours earlier, Chris, emerged from his tent. "The Northern Lights," he said. "There's a major auroral event tonight, and they were supposed to be visible as far south as San Francisco."

"This is even farther south," I said, still gazing upward. "Wow. I've never seen the Northern Lights before. They're not quite like what I imagined."

What I imagined is something like animated films about the Far North, where colorful waves of light swirl around and morph into shapes of animals and ancestral spirits. These lights were more subdued — washed-out emerald greens and lavender hues that at times became so faint they were nearly indiscernible from the distant colors of the Milky Way. Then there was an unexpected element — white streaks, which were many times brighter than the green cloak, and moved rapidly through the sky like rising meteors. To see the aurora at all in southern Utah was rare indeed, and the white daggers of light sparked an eerie sensation. There were seven streaks of light. There were seven of us.

"It might be an omen," another friend joked. I didn't find this particularly funny. Glancing at the ashen look on Craig's face, it seemed he didn't think this was a time for superstitious jokes, either.

"Yeah, we're going to die," Geoff replied in a laconic but upbeat tone that made him sound both sarcastic and serious at the same time. He used this tone often, and until I got to know Geoff better, I found it difficult to extract his intended meaning from the things he said — was he serious, or joking? In this case, and in most cases, he was being facetious.

Craig laughed, but I sensed a shared dread. Logic reminded us that the rare presence of the aurora was just a beautiful coincidence. But the sweeping wilderness of the desert bolstered our vulnerability, making it difficult to brush off this "omen." For most of the night I lay curled on my side in the tent, gazing at the sky through the mesh door. The streaks of light faded and surged, stretched and retracted, until, one by one, they faded out entirely. When I could no longer see the last streak of white light, I crawled out of the tent and stood with my bare feet in the icy sand, shivering. Breath swirled around my face. I could still see the curtain of emerald light. But the streaks were gone.

"It's an omen," I thought, and this time fully believed it, even as my rational mind asserted the obvious — "You're in a beautiful place, witnessing a rare phenomenon, and all you can think about is the certainty of your death."

But death was all I could think about.

Of course, none of us died. We got up early buzzing with excitement and fear, shouldered big backpacks and descended into the canyon. We put on tight neoprene wetsuits as soon as we reached the first pool, and swam several hundred meters as our poorly-reinforced backpacks and all of the gear and food inside became soaked. We ate soggy crackers and swamped peanut butter in the afternoon, swam and waded some more, and then hiked out. Black Box was a stunning sandstone canyon, made more memorable and rewarding by the direct confrontation with fear.

Craig had conquered his cold demons, but he didn't seem as psyched about waging new battles in Alaska's wilderness. Geoff and I invited him to join us on skis as we pedaled toward Flathorn Lake on the Iditarod Trail, but he just shook his head and laughed. "My cutoff is minus ten, and that's only for short ski trips, no more than an hour. You guys are crazy."

"Come on, it's going to be awesome," Geoff reiterated, again with his signature vague sarcasm. Craig was unmoved.

Geoff and I set out not so early the next morning, at about 10 a.m. It was late January, and the sun rose a few minutes earlier every day, and climbed a few degrees higher on the southern horizon. Still, the winter sun was like a distant friend — someone whose warmth you remembered well, whose light still touched your life from a periphery, but who was too far away to feel any real connection. The January sun at least rose over the mountains, but it was a subdued sun, slumped against the peaks. Its muted yellow glow only made me miss it even more.

The thermometer at Craig's house read seven below zero when we set out — "Heat wave!" Geoff declared. But the temperature seemed to drop at an alarming rate as we traveled Point MacKenzie Road, where we parked at a spot that intersected with the Iditarod Trail. Geoff determined this was near mile eight of the Susitna 100 course. The air was deeply still, almost outer space-like, and clouds of icy breath stung the exposed skin above my neoprene face mask. Snow squeaked under our tires as we pedaled.

My toes began to tingle beneath my thick, knee-high wool socks, winter hiking boots, and overboots. My ski gloves did little to fend off numbness in my fingers, and I frequently shook one hand to reignite circulation while gripping the handlebars with the other. "Do you think it's minus twenty out here?" I asked Geoff.

"At least," he said.

It was fearsome, this cold, like a snake wrapping around my torso and slowly tightening its grip. There was an unsettling dynamic to temperatures this low — a wild swing from "So invigorating! I've never felt so alive," to "This is probably what death feels like, after I've already died." Once the initial surge of adrenaline wore off, there was only the sensation that warmth was leaking out of our bodies, never to return.

After a few hundred meters, Geoff hit a soft patch of snow and dismounted. I jumped off my bike and started jogging to catch up with him. It felt markedly better to run than it did to pedal; finally, some warm blood circulated away from my core and trickled into my legs and feet. I made a note of this — "When my feet are numb, I need to run."

When I caught up to Geoff, his face mask was coated in white tufts of frost. "How are you feeling?" I called out through my own rigid strip of neoprene.

"Fuck it's cold," Geoff growled. "Riding bikes in the winter sucks."

"I sort of agree; running feels warmer. In this sandy snow it's hard work just to keep the wheels turning. I'm sweating but my feet and hands are freezing."

Geoff brushed frost away from his eyelashes and turned to start pedaling again. The trail, which cut a straight opening through the forest, rippled across the snow like a wrinkled piece of fabric. These "whoop-de-dos" were a result of snowmobilers accelerating unevenly, which caused their machines to dig shallow trenches into the snow. Excess powder deposited behind the trench in a mound, and this ripple effect deepened every time another snowmobile followed. Whoop-de-dos were an obnoxious obstacle — worse than a road filled with potholes — but at a faster clip they were fun on a bike. Geoff and I swerved and giggled, cranking up speed on an undulating roller coaster until the trail flattened out again across an open swamp.

In swamps, the wind blew freely, and sandy snow obscured the trail. It was too deep to ride. Geoff was markedly faster while pushing his bike, and soon there was a large gap between us. As I rushed to keep up with him, I felt the dizziness of low blood sugar. I reached into my food bag and pulled out a chocolate Power Bar. It was the least appetizing food I could imagine, but Power Bars seemed like a good idea when packing for the trip. Geoff had acquired stacks of these energy bars at a discount store in Utah for five cents a piece. Even though the bars were already expired when he purchased them almost a year ago, they somehow found their way to Alaska and lingered in our cupboards like unwanted fruitcake. This Power Bar was probably not the softest piece of food material when it was warm, but at twenty below it was about as edible as a brick. Actually, even bricks have weak corners that a person could break with their teeth if they tried. This frozen Power Bar was harder than a brick.

Still, it was all I had, and my energy levels were plummeting. I decided to thaw the bar in my mouth, so I unwrapped the entire thing, shoved the block of food-like substance to the edge of my throat, and clamped down my teeth. I considered how I looked with an iced-over face mask pulled down around my neck and an unidentifiable brown rectangle sticking out of my mouth. Without the protection of the face mask, the tip of my nose began to sting. My whole face was numb, but I did notice a strange sensation of warmth oozing down my chin, onto my neck. When I brushed my glove over my face, it returned covered in brown slime — a mixture of drool and melted Power Bar.

"Ew," I said in a muffled voice, and took this as a sign that the bar was thawed and it was time to start chewing. My teeth clamped down, but they still didn't go all the way through the bar. I gnawed and gnashed and gnawed, finally wrestling a separated chunk away from my mouth. Warm liquid was dribbling down my chin again, but when I brushed my glove over it this time, it appeared bright crimson. Blood. My mouth was so numb that I hadn't realized I was also chewing on my own flesh.

Geoff was waiting for me at the end of the swamp. When I caught up with him, he gasped, "What happened?"

"Power Bar disaster," I said. "Is there still blood on my face?"

"It's all over your chin," he said. "Did you bite your tongue?"

"Maybe. I bit something, but can't feel anything. Doesn't matter. I'm okay but have nothing else to eat. Did you bring anything?"

Geoff shook his head. "Just Power Bars. It's probably time to turn around anyway."

I looked at my watch. "Two and a half hours. Yeah, we should turn around. How far do you think we've gone?

"I think about ten miles," he said. "Probably a little less. We're supposed to hit that Nome sign at mile eighteen of the Susitna, which should be coming up soon. But I haven't seen it."

I nodded and sighed. That was a grueling two and a half hours. How was it even possible that we'd ridden only ten miles? How would I find the energy for the return trip? And how would I ever find the energy to ride ten times that far on this trail? After just a few seconds of not moving the cold tightened its grip, reminding me that this was not the time to lapse into the inertia of despair.

Without bothering to wipe away the now-chilled layer of chocolate sludge and blood, I refastened my face mask and began pedaling furiously behind Geoff, who seemed unfazed by the paucity of edible food. Even though we left Craig's house with the first light of morning, pink evening light had already returned to the southern horizon. The heatless sun looked oblong, as though it was succumbing to the gravitational pull of darkness.

"Do you know what mountain that is?" I asked Geoff, gesturing toward a free-standing landmass beneath the sun. The Susitna River Valley was dominated by mudflats, swamps, and small glacial rises. It seemed strange for a mountain to rise alone above it all.

"That? That's Mount Susitna I think," Geoff said.

"Mount Susitna," I repeated, feeling a warm rush of affection. "Just like the race."

Of course, the mountain was named after the river that carved this valley as it flowed from a glacier in the Alaska Range to an ice-choked arm of the sea. The Little Susitna River was a tributary of the Susitna, and these swamps were known as the Sustina Flats. It made sense that the race would bear the same name as all of its major geographical landmarks.

"Susitna" was not a unique designation. The name was derived from a Dena'ina Indian word meaning "sandy river," and had no mystical implications. Still, ever since I embraced the Susitna 100 and everything it came to represent — taking risks, having faith, learning new skills, and making physical improvements in the name of personal growth — the word "Susitna" had taken on deeper meaning for me. In my mind "Susitna" was spoken in a drawn-out whisper, like a word one might recite at the beginning of a prayer.

Mount Susitna was a beautiful mountain — a rounded butte that cradled the oblong sun. Later I learned that locals referred to Mount Susitna as "The Sleeping Lady." I decided I'd look to her whenever I felt lost or afraid. The Sleeping Lady could guide me home.

Geoff and I retreated over the swamp and returned to the frosted forest. The undulating trail climbed interminably. As it turned out, a gradual downgrade was the reason for the effortless fun I enjoyed while riding this string of whoop-de-doos on the inbound trip. Outbound was a slog. A few small hills led to the top of a bluff over the Little Susitna River, where the trail plummeted steeply into a gorge. It appeared to disappear off a cliff, but I'd survived these steep descents before. Fearlessly, I launched into the canyon.

The rear wheel started fishtailing almost immediately, and the bike bucked me head-first into a snowbank. I landed only a few inches from the trunk of a birch tree. Happily, a pillow of snow broke my fall, but it also filled my face mask and coat with cold powder. I writhed as flakes of ice stung exposed skin and flopped out of the snow bank, breathing rapidly. Geoff had been waiting at the bank of the Little Susitna. As I hiked the rest of the way down the hill, he waved at me.

"You okay?" he asked.

"Just a little crash," I answered. "At least snow is a soft landing. Why do you think I like winter biking so much?"

"I crashed too," Geoff said. A little farther down than you." His coat also bore evidence of being recently packed with powder, but I could tell he was grinning beneath the ice on his face mask. "I guess biking isn't too bad."

"So do you want to sign up for the Susitna 100 instead?"

"Hell no. But now that I've seen the course I don't think the Little Su will be too hard. I expected more hills."

"More hills? There are a ton of hills," I protested. True, these hills were just geographical hiccups across a wide valley. But the combination of pedaling and high-friction cold snow had a way of making all grades feel like a steep hill.

"Have you looked at the course map for the Susitna 100?"

"I've looked at it a lot," I said. "But it's hard to conceptualize, when I know nothing about the landmarks on the ground. The topographical map makes it look completely flat through here. It's obviously not."

"From what I've seen, the hundred-mile course spends a lot of time right on top of frozen lakes and rivers. Should be easier once you get past these swamps.

"I'll keep telling myself that," I said.

At least the Susitna 100 was still weeks away and full of unknowns. I could still let false optimism conjure scenarios that made it possible for me to finish the race. But here, in the present, I knew exactly which obstacles I faced, since I'd ridden this same trail just hours earlier. I couldn't fathom why the trail felt so markedly different on the return trip — the hills were so much steeper, the snow so much sandier, and the distance so much farther. Hunger clawed at my stomach, and I was beginning to feel throbbing pain where I'd chewed a hole in my cheek. Still, I didn't dare try to eat again. The risk of further injury from frozen Power Bars was worse than biking with no energy. I was lucky I hadn't broken a tooth.

Twilight had taken over the sky by the time we returned to Geoff's Honda Civic. The purple hue was only a shade away from black, and yet streaks of crimson light from the lazy winter sun still clung to the horizon. My legs were exquisitely tired, but the rest of my extremities had finally achieved a pleasant equilibrium. My arms and neck were warm. My hands and feet were no longer numb, and hadn't been for hours. Somehow, without adding more clothing layers or consuming heat-producing calories, I'd managed to stay not only alive but comfortably warm, simply by staying on the move.

"Just keep moving," I thought as I looked toward the silhouette of Mount Susitna, now reclining beneath a blanket of stars. "That's the key. Just keep moving."

Gloom and Doom

February 14, 2006

With eagle feeding in full swing on the Spit, there's an eerily Hitchcockian feel out there — birds of prey peppered across the gray landscape, waiting out the silence with ominous glares. As for me, I've been feeling a little bit under the weather, in the more literal sense — as in oppressed by the weather. The local news is predicting lots of doom and gloom surrounding this week, which includes the Susitna 100. The Iron Dog snowmachine racers are tearing up the trails with as much force as they can muster in the soft snow. Several Yukon Quest dog mushers had to be airlifted off the trail after a storm (they're in a different part of the state, to be fair.). But still, weather reports call for the delightful-sounding "wintry mix/wind" for Wasilla on Saturday, complete with a 35-degree high. I feel sad. I blame global warming.

There are some encouraging reports at the MTBR

Alaska forum. Although one rider mentioned renaming the race "Ididaswim," another reported riding out to the Susitna River earlier today on hard-packed trails with a light dusting of snow. Mmmmm. If it could only stay cold enough to remain that way.

But with Saturday fast approaching, I'm going to have to decide beforehand how far I'm willing to "swim" without quitting. I've decided that as long as I feel healthy and am not suffering beyond reason, I should have no reason to quit the race before the official cut-off time (Forty-eight hours. That's right.) I have the option of sleeping along the way. I'll have enough food to stuff a luau pig. And if there's one athletic talent that I have, it's plugging along — even when the going is insufferably slow. How long will it take me to swim 100 miles? I don't know. But I'm fairly certain I could walk 100 miles given 48 hours to do so. Not that I'm about to enter this race in the foot division.

✳ ✳ ✳ ✳ ✳

January ended and took the cold snap with it, ushering in a sloppy thaw infused with aromas of rotten fish, dog feces, and wet soil. "This is what spring smells like," Sean told me.

On the first Saturday in February, I embarked on the last long ride of my training cycle, churning north toward an elbow of the road near Anchor Point. A sign announced this was "North America's Most Westerly Highway Point." With a designation like that, it wasn't too far a stretch to believe that I had pedaled to the edge of the world, which is how I liked to imagine the Cook Inlet shoreline. I dismounted the bike and waded through a cluster of spruce trees. Just beyond the thin strip of forest was the beach, coated in a paper-like film of ice. I took light steps atop the milky blue surface, giggling as it shattered and collapsed under my feet. The gray water of the Cook Inlet was calm, and a light breeze blew puffs of pink sea foam over frozen sand.

Across the water, the silhouettes of Mount Redoubt and Mount Augustine loomed above a hazy marine layer. Augustine was still spewing vapor one month after its initial eruption. Beneath the volcanoes, snow-covered peaks lined the distant shoreline. My thoughts drifted to the geographical expanse beyond this particular end of the road. In Homer, I could drink mocha lattes at the Starbucks stand inside the grocery store, and fire off blog comments to virtual friends in Norway. My Alaska life was as modern as it could be, and it was all too easy to forget about these primordial landscapes just beyond the edge of civilization.

These weekly long bike rides became a ritual of reconnecting with the wilderness beyond. They often fell on a Sunday, and the practice had become like church for me — acknowledging the spiritual elements that gave my day-to-day life a sense of meaning. Next to the ancient ash spewing from Mount Augustine, my own existence was inscrutably fleeting and small. It was gratifying to appreciate the trillions upon trillions of atomic collisions that had to take place for me to end up here, in this place, this moment, tiptoeing across paper ice that was surrounded by an primordial ring of fire.

In the pre-dawn hours a few days later, loud knocking startled Geoff and me enough to simultaneously jump out of bed. We braced ourselves on the hardwood floor as unseen forces rumbled underneath. "It's the bookshelf," Geoff said as the knocking persisted, followed by the sound of objects falling to the floor.

"It's an earthquake," I gasped, dropping to my knees to shield my head against the ceiling beams that would surely come raining down next. An eternity that was closer to thirty seconds finally brought an end to the tremor, and our cabin sustained no damage even though books and a few of Geoff's eBay supplies toppled to the floor. The U.S. Geographical Survey Web site reported a 5.3 magnitude earthquake centered just eighteen miles south of Homer. Several aftershocks prompted a tsunami warning, which in turn prompted my co-workers and me to drive out Homer Spit in the morning — the same spot everyone was supposed to be escaping to higher ground — and look through binoculars for errant walls of seawater.

It snowed heavily through the week, but by the following weekend — the last weekend before the Susitna 100 — snow turned to rain. I had become fixated on weather forecasts, scrolling through several different weather Web sites every day and weaving them together into a prediction I liked: one that was below freezing but not too cold — maybe twenty degrees — with only light winds and no precipitation. This optimistic compiling had become more difficult as the event neared and more forecasts called for a mix of snow and rain.

One week before the Susitna 100, the Tribune assigned me to shoot photographs at the Homer Winter Carnival. Hoping to squeeze in one final training ride, I strapped on my overboots, rain pants, and snowboarding coat, and rode the long way into town. This ride would be only forty miles on roads, so I didn't bother to pack extra layers into my backpack. Outside, the air was filled with snow bombs — snowflakes that were so wet they banded together into balls before they even hit the ground. I pedaled through the thick deluge, then descended in elevation until the snowballs turned to daggers of sleet, and then driving rain.

Despite terrible weather, the Winter Carnival went on as planned. Parade floats plied through several inches of standing water, and spectators lined sidewalks in their bright orange Helly Hansen rain suits, rubber gloves, and XtraTufs. A few people held umbrellas — fewer than I expected — and small children splashed through puddles that still held floating chunks of ice. It was one of those occasions where newcomers shake their heads and think, "Only in Alaska." Even with all the same modern conveniences as anywhere, Alaskans won't be mistaken for citified sissies.

The parade floats were similarly rugged and uniquely Alaskan. There was a small tractor with chains on its wheels, driven by a flannel-wearing homesteader and towing an unidentifiable wooden platform. There was a teenage boy dressed like a hockey puck and running in circles while another teen on stilts chased him with a hockey stick. There was an impressively massive taxidermy grizzly bear with leis draped around its neck. Alaska Native dancers swirled in traditional costume and the high school band marched in their drenched uniforms. No one seemed to mind the mud flowing through the streets. Alaskans don't let any weather rain on their parades.

I straddled my bike at a street corner, shielding my digital camera with one neoprene glove while taking snapshots with the other. Jane wouldn't permit use of the newspaper's camera in this weather, and I didn't expect any of my waterlogged images to turn out anyway. As I remounted my bike, I noticed water sloshing inside my overboots. My feet were so numb that I failed to notice rainwater leaking in from the top and flooding the interior. Waves of shivering soon followed. My core felt even colder on this rainy, thirty-five-degree afternoon than it did at twenty below.

"Wet cold is so much worse than deep cold," I thought. "No one ever warns you about that in the tropics."

Homer is sometimes jokingly referred to as "Alaska's Banana Belt," thanks to its location in a rain shadow formed by the Kenai Mountains (Homer's dryness is relative — on the other side of the mountains, hundreds of inches of precipitation fall over Prince William Sound every year.) The region also has relatively mild temperatures thanks to its proximity to the Pacific Ocean. This "Banana Belt" moniker has probably fooled more than a few Alaskans into believing the weather was always warm and dry in Homer. In reality, the weather was just a lighter shade of crappy.

Still, after only five months in Homer, I was already Alaskan enough to think nothing of returning from a five-hour bike ride, then dumping a half gallon of slush water out of my boots and wringing out my winter coat before walking in the door. My skin was chilled and my limbs were numb. The subsequent hot showers after these wet rides hurt so good, like a massaging mist of battery acid.

The following day brought another work assignment, the Nordic Ski Club's annual wine and cheese event. It sounded pleasant enough, but the caveat was that participants were skiing fifteen kilometers from a trailhead to the home where wine and cheese would be served. Saturday's rainstorm had fallen as more than a foot of dense snow in the hills, and my Geo Prism balked at the road conditions. I pumped the gas repeatedly as the car crawled through narrow tracks laid by stronger trucks and SUVs. Progress was glacial, even slower than biking. I felt like the car was barely moving, so it surprised me when I lost control and managed to skid all the way off Ohlson Mountain Road during an icy descent. The car plunged windshield-deep into a snow bank. I couldn't even see the hood.

It was laughable to believe I could dig my car out of several feet of chunky snow by hand, but I popped the trunk and pulled out the shovel I carried for this purpose. Just as I took my second stab at the cement-like snow, a man in a full-sized Ford pickup pulled up beside me. He was the first driver to pass, and I was surprised that he stopped.

"Need help?" he asked.

"I do, but it's going to take forever to dig out of here."

"No worries," he said, and got back into his vehicle. After maneuvering an impressive U-turn, he emerged again and pulled a wire cable out from beneath his truck, then attached the hook beneath the rear bumper of my car. I was confused for a few seconds before I realized that he planned to use his truck to pull Geo out by its ass.

As the wheels of his truck spun on the ice, locked in a vehicle tug-o-war, three other drivers stopped to help. I was flabbergasted. In Idaho I could potentially walk along I-15 with a gas can and my thumb out for an hour before anybody pulled over to offer a ride. In Homer, the default setting was to stop and help someone in need. Carey's explanation about weather extremes and inhabitants in Alaska rang true — the harsher the weather, the nicer the folks.

Also, by helping me, the Alaskan in the pickup truck had an opportunity to exhibit the power of his vehicle, of which he was clearly proud. The snowbank put up strong resistance, and the truck emitted a chorus of guttural roars and squeals. Even though I told others who stopped that we had it all covered, they got out of their vehicles anyway and retrieved their own shovels. Now there were four different people shoveling snow away from my car's front end as the truck bucked and growled. Finally, in a burst of powder, Geo broke free. Everyone cheered.

It took only nine minutes for my situation to change from seemingly hopeless to solved. The pickup driver unhooked his tow cable and tipped the brim of his hunter's hat like a real cowboy. The turnover was impressively fast, but combined with my late start and slow driving, I arrived at the trailhead thirty-seven minutes after all the scheduled start of the ski outing. Homer's skiers, always a punctual bunch, had long since departed. Since I didn't know exactly where they planned to meet for wine and cheese, I had no choice but to race after them. Anyway, people skiing would make for more interesting photographs than people standing around and drinking wine. The fact that they'd be doing so in their ski clothing was the only uniquely Alaskan thing about it.

The skiers' course was marked with pink ribbons tied to trees, and started at the base of a tiny, tow-rope supported ski hill on Ohlson Mountain. I strapped on my secondhand skis, warped with age, and scooted along the groomed trail. Although I had continued to join Geoff for ski outings at least once a week, I seemed to only get worse at it with every attempt. I'd shuffle along slowly like a prisoner with chains strapped to my feet, only to start careening out of control on any remotely downward-angled slope. If I were to rate my skill level in winter activities, hopping uphill on a snowboard and shoveling my car out of a snowbank would rank above my skiing abilities.

To top it all off, the morning's snow flurries had transitioned to a full blizzard. Gusts of wind swirled from all directions, disrupting my already precarious sense of balance. I scooted down a small hill into the disorienting whiteout. Since I couldn't discern the trail from the hills from the sky, I continued to search for pink ribbons that were now tied to lathe stabbed into the snow along an open meadow. Often I'd have to stand in place for several seconds before I could locate the next one. At this rate, I would never catch the other skiers before the wine drinking began. It seemed a lot of trouble to go to for a photo that Carey was probably going to bury on page fifteen next to the classified ads for Toyo stoves and outboard motors.

At the end of the meadow, I crossed into a stand of spruce trees. My relief about shelter from the blizzard was short-lived. A hundred meters into the forest was a paper plate stapled to a trunk, scrawled with the words "Caution" and an arrow pointing straight down a long, steep hill. Peering over the edge, I couldn't see the landing zone beneath a swirl of blowing snow. It could have been fifty feet down, or it could have been five hundred. There was no way of knowing.

"They have to be kidding me," I said out loud. Even if I took off my skis and walked down, it was steep enough that I was likely to slip and careen down the slope on my back. Injury appeared inevitable. Even a small thing like a twisted ankle would sabotage my participation in the Susitna 100 one week later. The thought of dropping out of the race with a work-related injury made me feel queasy.

Where self-doubt was the wiser inner voice, ego spoke louder. I was trying to be an extreme winter athlete, damn it, so surely I should be able to handle a fifteen-kilometer ski. I pointed my skis in the classic "A" formation and scooted toward the ledge until gravity took hold. Unsurprisingly, my skis crossed about twenty feet into the descent, pushing my right knee in one direction and my left foot in another until my body toppled in a swirl of powder and limbs and skis. During the rumble, I managed to stab myself in the back with one of my poles and wrench my left knee before I finally skidded to a stop halfway down the hill. By that point I could see the meadow below. It was still a long way down. I didn't bother to fasten the death planks to my feet again. As it was, those skis were lucky that I bothered to collect them on my way up the hill rather than toss them into the woods.

"Carey should know better than to send a non-skier to the ski n'cheese," I grumbled to myself as I started my car. I rolled away from the trailhead without taking a single photo. My boss would likely be annoyed if I used the excuse of my car going off the road for not attending the event — as it was, she continued to remind me that I needed to upgrade to something with four-wheel drive. But I wasn't sure I wanted to admit the truth — that my ski skills were simply too poor to manage a casual Sunday outing involving wine and cheese. Some extreme winter athlete I was.

Of course, beneath these layers of ego I had so carefully bolstered with training rides and praise from the Internet, a deeper part of me feared my less desirable, hidden identity — I was not an extreme winter athlete. I was not even an athlete. I was Just Jill, scared little Mormon girl from Utah, who once had an anxiety attack while sitting on a couch indoors, and who followed a boy all the way to Alaska not because she was fearlessly adventurous, but because she was afraid of being alone.

The events leading up to that anxiety attack also revolved around Geoff to some degree. For much of my youth, I pursued adventure travel. In high school, I joined friends for trips into the desert of western Utah to trip out on LSD (but never partook, largely because I was afraid). I dated boys who were into backpacking and invited me on overnight trips in the Wasatch Mountains. Then, shortly after I met Geoff, I became convinced that quitting my career job as a graphic designer and following this man I barely knew on a three-month road trip across the United States was a fantastic idea. It was. The life experiences I amassed traveling through the Deep South and into the boreal wildernesses of northern Ontario eclipsed three years of college education.

Still, there was always a lingering suspicion that Adventure Jill was a fraud. After our road trip in 2001, I landed my second career job as an editor at a bi-weekly newspaper in Tooele, a bedroom community west of Salt Lake City.

Five days a week I commuted seventy miles round-trip from our crowded house in the city to this town at the edge of the West Desert. I interviewed conspiracy-theory-believing commanders at Deseret Chemical Depot and routinely fielded phone calls from readers screaming because a name had been spelled wrong in a wedding announcement. This proved to be a stressful position for a twenty-two-year-old. Meanwhile, Geoff worked part-time as a server at a bistro near the University of Utah, earning just enough to scrape by in our already inexpensive living situation, and continued to embark on adventures.

I'd join him for weekend excursions, but often he'd leave for weeks at a time. Early in the summer of 2002, Geoff left for a two-month rafting trip down the Green and Colorado Rivers. Also during this time period, I developed a mysterious but pervasive fear. It was subtle at first — a gray curtain of dread that followed me through my day-to-day activities. Then, just like subzero cold, fear started to seep into every aspect of my life. I'd drive to work and fret about car accidents. I'd watch television with my roommates and imagine devastating earthquakes.

In June, a teenage girl named Elizabeth Smart was kidnapped from her home just a few blocks from my house, and I started obsessing about danger lurking outside my bedroom window. This anxiety wasn't completely unprecedented. I'd exhibited hints of a potential anxiety disorder when I was a child, but thought I'd shaken it off as I developed into a rational, objective adult. Now, I was sinking back into a disturbing pattern. It did seem crazy for a twenty-two-year-old to fret about being kidnapped from her bed by a stranger, and yet there I was, shivering next to an open window that the rational side of my brain told me needed to stay open because it was too hot inside the room to sleep.

In July 2002, something snapped. I drove home from work with a throbbing headache, then slumped down on the couch in the front room. An afternoon thunderstorm moved in as I tried and failed to read a newspaper, and instead stared out the window at the darkening sky. Thunder rumbled, and without much warning the storm seemed to explode over the slightly run-down houses of our neighborhood. Gale-force winds whipped the branches of the gnarled willow tree in the front yard, and garbage can lids bounced down the street.

"Tornado!" my imagination screamed, and my body became paralyzed with anxiety. I felt helpless and disoriented, clinging to the arm of the couch as the room appeared to gyrate around me. Long seconds passed as I neglected to breathe. When I started again, my breaths were short and panicked, hyperventilating, gripped with terror. My vision went dark and my body went from rigid to limp in a strange sort of melting sensation, and I slumped to the floor. Nausea swept in, followed by chills and shivering. Did the tornado kill me? Was I dying of a disease? My body just laid in a useless heap as my mind raced in impotent hysteria.

The thunderstorm moved on, and the wind calmed. There was never a tornado, and I knew that. Still, several more minutes passed before I found the courage to rise. When I looked out the window again, daggers of sunlight were slicing through the clouds.

"What is wrong with me?" I questioned, aloud, to no one. I didn't have the answer. But the storm panic did set off an alarm. After several months of shrugging off my unstructured fear, I could finally understand that something was very wrong. I remembered other bouts of heart-racing anxiety I had experienced — while hiking in Moab, while dancing at clubs with my roommates, while stewing about Geoff's safety on some far-away trip, while attending Memorial Day breakfast with my extended family at a cabin in the mountains. Finally I could connect the dots. These were not isolated incidents. I wasn't just afraid of scary things. I was afraid of everything.

The second big wake-up call of adult life would happen three years later after a drunken blackout in Idaho Falls, but this was the first. I was not even twenty-three years old and already becoming a stress-riddled, anxiety-driven, otherwise boring adult who couldn't even handle a thunderstorm without a having a meltdown. Something clearly needed to change. I wasn't quite ready to quit my job and join Geoff on eight-week-long river trips, but I needed to meet Adventure Jill halfway. The following week after returning from work, instead of plopping down on the couch, I pumped up the tires on Geoff's mountain bike and took it out for a ride.

Although I'd embarked on big adventures in the past, there was something unique about those first bike rides through Salt Lake City's avenues. The evening sun would cast the valley in glittering gold as I made my way up a maze of suburban streets toward the forested corridor of City Creek Canyon. Most of my self-powered adventures up to that point had been backpacking trips, hoisting forty or fifty pounds of gear and trudging through most of a day to hike ten miles. I was amazed at the ground I could cover on a bicycle, seemingly without effort. The sensation can only be described as flying. It was their ordinariness that made these rides so incredible — the world continued to hum along as it always had, but I was floating above it, free from my perceived anchors.

Avid cycling didn't eradicate all of the symptoms of my anxiety, but the effect was profound. Initially cycling was a calming distraction, and then it became an empowering motivator. Pedaling drained away stress while generating strength, well-being, and self-sufficiency. Once I discovered I could travel between two points while relying entirely on my own body and wits, I started testing the limits of this independence. Twenty miles became an achievable distance, and then fifty. Geoff and I formulated a plan for a six-hundred-mile bicycle tour across the remote reaches of Utah's deserts. The trip necessitated carrying two days worth of water and food at a time, camping on open mesas where coyotes howled through the night, and climbing an icy 11,000-foot pass in Colorado after a September snowstorm. We would embark on this tour less than two months after my anxiety breakdown. Somehow, my bicycle made me immune to abstract fears. I wasn't even concerned with more rational fears when I was riding my bike — the sheer effort of turning pedals required all of the energy I would have used to fret about traffic collisions, wild animals, and dehydration.

My anxieties weren't so much a fear of the unknown as a fear of powerlessness in the face of the unknown. With hands on handlebars and feet on pedals, I was in control of my situation — come what may.

✳ ✳ ✳ ✳ ✳

My emotional state in the days leading up to the Susitna 100 was the most pronounced anxiety I'd felt in years. It was markedly worse than the unease I managed to overcome when I abandoned my job, routine, and most of my possessions to follow Geoff to Alaska. In that case, there was a sense that a chapter of my life had rightfully closed. Accepting the inevitability of change subdued my fear of the unknown. But the Susitna 100 was something I had chosen —something unnecessary, irrational and maybe even certifiably crazy. Adventures were my way of battling existential turmoil. New familiarities necessitated upping the ante at regular intervals. But surely this was taking it too far?

Geoff and I drove up to Anchorage two days before the race to attend a pre-race briefing and purchase last-minute supplies. At the meeting, the race directors warned us that warm weather had caused overflow to flood parts of the trail, and that thawing temperatures and even rain were a possibility. Volunteers parsed out and weighed our gear to make sure it met the requirements — one sleeping bag rated to twenty below zero, one sleeping pad, bivy sack, a stove, fuel and pot for melting snow as drinking water, one headlamp, two-liter insulated water container, a rear flashing light, and 3,000 calories of emergency food that we were instructed to not eat under any circumstances, unless we were dying — and either way we'd be disqualified from the race. Since no one has ever died because they went without food for a few hours, I considered this rule particularly condescending. But every other requirement was welcome. I would need to protect myself from elements I didn't fully understand, and I appreciated the direction.

The day before the race was particularly gloomy. Streams of gray slush flooded Anchorage streets, and the sky was similarly murky. Sleet pelted our faces as we waded through puddles to buy waterproof matches and ingredients for peanut butter sandwiches at Fred Meyer. I felt hollow, as though anxiety had corroded through my emotions until only the mechanics of my body remained.

Throughout the day I moved in robotic motions — eating energy-storing meals without joy, pacing the hall at Craig's house, and packing and repacking my supplies, which included obligatory gear as well as spare clothing, water containers, and food. The gear was bundled inside of a dry bag that I strapped to a seat-post rack on the back of my mountain bike, or stuffed into an empty sleeping bag sack and strapped to my handlebars. A small square bag attached to the frame held most of my "fuel" — sandwiches, chocolate, and Power Bars. Inside this bag, I opened several hand-warmers to "heat" my snacks and prevent them from freezing to inedible bricks. In hindsight, my conviction that this would work was amusingly naive.

Geoff planned to only carry a small hydration pack with water and some Power Bars. His preparations for the Little Su 50K were less involved, but he was visibly nervous as well. He stared quietly at Craig's television — Geoff never watched TV — as I made fumbling efforts to glue the bead of my studded tires to the rim. A few blog readers recommended this technique for low tire pressures, which snow bikers often run to increase the surface area of the tire and improve flotation. With the tube mostly deflated, tires had a tendency to slip along the rim, often tearing the tube's valve stem in the process. Glue would prevent this slippage. Still, the gooey adhesive didn't immediately stick, requiring long minutes of wrestling with the tire as layers of glue flaked onto the carpet. My fingers were cemented together by the time I completed the job.

"Do you need any help?" Geoff asked ninety-five minutes after I'd started the tire-gluing project, when I was clearly almost done.

"No," I grumbled, wishing that he had just offered in the first place, as he was so much more skilled — or at least more willing — in mechanical work. I wanted to just get on my bike and start riding it somewhere … anywhere. Waiting for the race had to be tougher than racing itself. It just had to be.

Susitna Sustained

February 20, 2006

Did I finish the Susitna 100 with a smile on my face? Well, based on this photo Geoff took (that I don't remember him taking) — not quite. Actually, I look like a drunk zombie. But I gave that smile my best shot. Just like the race.

Also, I forgot to mention in yesterday's post that Geoff won the foot division of the Little Su 50K. He came in first with a time of 3:54, just ahead of elite ultra-marathoner Julie Udchachon. I biked the first 25 miles of my race in about that time. He ran 31. Geoff's the champion. I'm not even a contender. But I do feel good about what I did. Really. I did something that as recently as six months ago I would have never imagined myself doing, and I had an incredible journey.

Yesterday, when I was mulling over some of the decisions I made on the trail — and the times I posted — Geoff told me, "Only you know what you did out there." He's right. The ideology behind the Susitna 100 is not necessarily to be the fastest runner or best rider. It's about pushing into the Alaska wilderness and making some tracks in the snow, whether they're tire tracks, footprints, or a swerving combination of both.

There are some ways I could have been better prepared. I knew it when I lined up next to my fellow racers, most equipped with specially-built snow bikes, wide rims, four-inch tires and rigid forks. And there I was, straddling my rock hopper. I felt like I was standing at the startling line of the Tour de France with a beach cruiser. In conditions where flotation was everything, that analogy isn't that far off. But I did the best I could with what I had. And, for its highs and lows, its loneliness, pain, joy, beauty and desolation, the experience was amazing.

❋ ❋ ❋ ❋ ❋

By 8:47 a.m., sunrise had nudged hints of morning light over the Chugach Mountains, but it was difficult to discern the transition from pre-dawn to day. The sky was a dark pall, choked with storm clouds. After days of sleet and rain, snow on the ground was dull and saturated. Silhouetted spruce trees lined the horizon, drawing the only distinction between competing shades of gray. The race itself was the only splash of color. Clad in brightly hued gear, dozens of skiers, cyclists, and runners funneled toward the official start of the Susitna 100 — the referee box of the Aurora Dog Mushers racing track. Someone had spray-painted a yellow line across the snow, and about sixty people gathered behind it, perched at the edge of a monotone infinity.

True to character, Geoff and I got a late start in the morning, and Geoff nearly rolled Craig's truck off Big Lake Road as we raced toward the start. By the time I pulled my bike from the truck and strapped on my hydration pack, it was 8:52 a.m., and the race director was already calling out instructions from a megaphone. I sprinted toward the crowd, dragging my gear-laden mountain bike alongside, and nudged my way into position behind most of the cyclists, next to skiers and runners strapped to sleds. Geoff's race didn't start until 11 a.m., so he buzzed around shooting photographs. I was so nervous that I couldn't bear to smile at him or make eye contact with any of my fellow racers. Instead I stared at my legs. Covered in rain pants and overboots, it looked like I was wearing an astronaut suit. I tried not to think about the alien landscape beyond.

I blacked out for a second, or lost my focus, or there was a crack in the space-time continuum, but when I looked up again, I saw skiers and runners streaming around me. Loud cheers and the sound of skis scraping over icy snow erupted out of silence. I felt like a competitive diver, rising from the depths of a swimming pool to a roaring auditorium. I shook off my daze and joined the surge.

The dog mushing park was a maze. Yellow-striped laths marked the Susitna 100 course, but I was still distracted by trails jutting off in every direction. Adrenaline surged through my blood and I spun my heavy legs as fast as I could muster, skirting around several skiers while scanning ahead for course markers. Ten miles passed quickly, in less than an hour, and I reached the edge of the mushing park. From there, groomed trails ended, and real Alaska began. What had been a light breeze in the trees became a stiff wind as I crossed an open swamp. Drifted grains of sugar snow covered the trail, and my wheels spun out on the soft surface. I got off the bike and walked, rolling my ankles repeatedly as I punched through a fragile crust. High humidity gave the wind a sharp bite. Even though the temperature was just below freezing, the air felt alarmingly cold.

As I walked, all of the skiers I'd overtaken on the groomed trail glided past me with ease. Most of the other cyclists in the race were riding Surly Pugsleys or the similarly designed Wildfire fat bikes, and their tracks indicated they were able to ride atop this breakable crust. When I returned to the woods, I found better surface conditions, and was able to crank my way up the short, steep climbs that Geoff and I had scouted three weeks earlier. Descents were jerky and fast, and compression in the shock caused the rear wheel to slam into my seat post rack. I stopped to readjust the rack, but positioning it higher on the seat post pushed the gear bag uncomfortably into my lower back. There was no way I was going to endure back pain for ninety miles, so I was just going to have to gamble on repeated collisions with the tire, and hope the rack didn't blow apart before I was done.

Sunlight was beginning to filter through the clouds when I pulled into the first checkpoint on the shoreline of Flathorn Lake. My pace so far — three hours and forty-five minutes for twenty-five miles — was respectable enough. My legs still felt peppy, although fatigue was creeping around the edges. The checkpoint was an idyllic lakeside cabin with smoke pouring out of a chimney. Even though it wasn't particularly cold outside, the interior felt like a sauna in comparison. Sliced oranges and homemade brownies were piled on plates at the table. While filling up my water bladder, I shoved several orange slices into my mouth. I was astonished at how rich and flavorful they were. It was as though the proprietor had taken regular oranges and injected them with some kind of mood-enhancing drug. It just wasn't possible for food to taste this good. I closed up the water bladder and attacked the brownies, stifling little moans as the warm morsels slid down my throat. I wondered if I'd ever again experience such a taste sensation. I doubted it. After all, there's only one first time for everything; never again would I be surprised by the bliss of food consumed during a race.

After spending a little too much time indulging in the exquisite satisfaction of sitting in a chair, I was one of the last cyclists to leave the checkpoint. I pedaled away from Flathorn Lake feeling guilty. Still, I was on pace for an eighteen-hour race — my best-case scenario. The trail hugged the shoreline of the lake for two more miles before cutting back into the forest. Before making this transition, I stopped to look back across the lake I had just crossed — a white expanse illuminated by the soft, filtered light of the overcast sky.

My heart fluttered, at once terrified and exhilarated. Only the gusting wind broke a primordial silence. Spruce tress lined the far shoreline, again drawing a harsh black line between the muted grays of land and sky. Mount Susitna, the Sleeping Lady, loomed in regal repose. I looked toward her with a grateful smile, knowing she was watching over me. It was amazing that such a place existed, so distant from the din of modern life, so frozen in time. And I had pedaled my bike to this place, by myself, under my own impetus, so I didn't have to be afraid. Sugar and endorphins surged through my blood, and I didn't know whether to cry or sing. Then I remembered that I was racing, so I turned away and continued pedaling into the woods.

At mile thirty-three, I crossed the Susitna River, the corridor that cut through the heart of this overwhelming landscape. The surface of the river was flat and white like Flathorn Lake, and similarly frozen in time. The wind had quieted, and the world was so still that I wondered whether I really had entered a hiccup in the space-time continuum.

Suddenly, a gray figure darted through the trees across the river. A wolf? A lynx? What else could it be? My heart raced faster. This was not a place for humans. It was a place for predators, for wind-ravaged trees and scavenging birds, for hulking moose and snow-cave-dwelling rodents, all eking out their survival from an ice-encased land. My presence here had no relevance. I moved through the landscape like a ghost. The wind-driven snow would sweep away my tracks, and nothing else would change. In the human world I was insignificant, but out here I was less than that — just a shadow, bearing every part of myself to a wilderness that had the power to take my life in a whisper. I was at once humbled and amazed, and felt as though my fingertips were grasping something truly beyond the physical world — something sublime.

I crossed the river and again returned to the woods, where I reconnected with the human world in the form of two snowmobiles. They buzzed past, churning up the snow to mashed-potato consistency. The softened trail reduced me to pushing my bike again, and I made slow progress to the second checkpoint at Eaglesong Lodge. Despite fond memories of the magical food at Flathorn Lake, I felt edgy about my slower progress and wanted to keep moving. A race volunteer was waiting outside, so I gave him my name and continued without venturing inside the building.

As I approached checkpoint three — a cluster of cabins on the Yentna River called Luce's Lodge — soft snow atop the lightly used trail forced me to walk for most of the next ten miles. Daylight slipped away almost imperceptibly behind a ceiling of clouds that had progressively thickened throughout the afternoon. Physical discomfort was beginning to consume most of my thoughts, and my brain rebelled by withdrawing useful functions, such as appetite. My stomach churned, so I opted to skip the spaghetti dinner offered at the lodge. In the span of less than six hours, the sensation of eating had switched from euphoric to repulsive. I wanted nothing more of food and the nausea it induced.

The sauna-like heat inside the building added to my wooziness, so I made a quick exit from Luce's as well. A skier on the porch was removing his hat as I stepped outside. His face and hair bore an uncanny resemblance to a friend of mine back in Utah named Curt. "Hi Curt," I blurted out before I caught myself. The skier looked up but didn't acknowledge my inaccurate greeting. Without another word, I rushed away.

"Huh, I must really be out of it," I thought as I hurried down the hill to the frozen Yentna River. It was unsettling to realize that my mind, which I needed to be sharp in order to make the best decisions, was incapable of making rational assessments about other people on the course.

The sky was black without a hint of moon or stars. The once-expansive landscape narrowed to the flickering beam of my headlamp. Snowmobile tracks veered in many directions along the wide corridor of the river, and I strained to pick out yellow-striped Su100 stakes. I was terrified of losing them, as though these wooden lath were the only thing tethering me to Earth. The river was too wide and the night too dark to see anything beyond the tiny island of yellow light. I might as well have been pedaling across the Bering Sea.

My breath was becoming increasingly labored, and my lungs and throat were raw. I'd never felt more small. This place was outer space, and I was a molecule, floating through the void. All-too-familiar anxiety started to creep around the periphery, so I focused on my hands. I stared at them for long minutes, wrapped in gray neoprene gloves and gripped around the handlebars, occasionally making slight movements to guide the bicycle's front wheel. These were hands capable of piloting a bicycle across frozen swamps and over snow-covered hills, I thought. I looked at my legs and feet, hidden beneath rain pants and overboots, and saw limbs that could propel my body no matter how tired I became. As clouds of breath swirled in front of my face, I saw shadows of myself — shadows of fear and doubt and insecurity — dissolving into the hard air. And when I glanced behind me, I could see a sweepingly empty expanse that I had somehow managed to cross, under my own power, under my own impetus, by myself. With every passing mile I was transforming — from "Just Jill" to "Adventure Jill," and then to something else entirely. A racer, perhaps.

Ahead, a bright circle of light broke the darkness. Another point of civilization! I grinned and increased my cadence. Soft snow kept my speed to a minimum — the odometer often dipped below four miles per hour — but at least I was pedaling. I was pedaling hard. The distant light flickered. Minutes passed, and then miles. An hour passed. Through sharp breaths, a lump began to gather in my throat. Why wasn't the light getting any closer? Was I moving at all? Was time passing, or had I entered another hiccup of space-time? My odometer still registered a slow progression of miles. I breathed out a sigh. The only power I possessed was to keep pedaling.

Two hours passed between the moment I first noticed the light, and the moment I finally arrived at a small canvas tent pitched on the ice at the confluence of the Yentna and Susitna rivers. A humming generator powered the floodlight, which garishly illuminated a campfire crackling on the ice. A man in a thick black coat stepped out of the tent and waved both arms toward me. I was still fifty feet away and apparently on the wrong tangent in a multitude of snowmobile tracks. The man continued to gesture wildly, so I stepped off my bike and pushed it directly toward him. Off trail, the snow was hip-deep, forcing awkward lunges. I was annoyed that the otherwise purposeless electric light had been taunting me for eight miles, but at the same time grateful that this encampment prevented me and others from turning the wrong way up the Susitna River.

The man introduced himself as Rich Crain and welcomed me to his "five-star tent camp." He dished up a cup of lukewarm noodle soup. I downed it in two gulps and asked him about the trail ahead.

"It's all stuff you've done before now," he said. "You're almost done with the lollipop" — referring to the forty-mile loop the course took after it crossed the Susitna River. "Might snow tonight. Shouldn't be too bad. You have about thirty-five miles left."

I pumped my fist, my first non-zombie-like gesture in many hours, and thanked Rich. Sixty-five miles done! And it hadn't been all that hard — at least, not as hard as I expected. The Susitna River ice stretched out in front of me, wide and flat. Everything else was terrain I had already ridden, and knew to be mostly good trail. My energy-deprived brain indulged in smug, but premature, satisfaction.

About a half mile from the five-star tent camp, I rounded a sheer bluff towering several hundred feet over the river. My shadow, which had been sharply defined by Rich Crain's floodlight, slipped into the darkness. I was alone again. The small serving of soup provided just enough energy to re-engage my brain, which only served to shine a spotlight on my physical discomforts. My hands and feet were tingling — whether from cold or pressure, I didn't know — and my back was sore from weight pressing against it, again. I stopped to tighten the straps of my gear sack and contemplated adding another layer and changing my gloves from neoprene to the thicker ski gloves. There was an odd chill to the air. I couldn't quite place it. It didn't feel like bitter cold. It wasn't frosty or sharp. It was more of a dull, saturating chill. I looked up at the starless sky and felt tiny needles of moisture bounding off my nose and cheeks. Until that moment, I hadn't realized it was raining.

Rain? Rain wasn't good. How often does it rain in Southcentral Alaska in February? I had planned for blizzards. I had planned for Arctic blasts of cold. I had planned for snow, ice, sleet, open water, and even the unlikely ideal of twenty-degree temperatures and clear skies. I hadn't planned for rain. Just as soon as I noticed it, the light drizzle began to pick up volume until large droplets were bouncing off my breathable — and therefore minimally water-resistant — Burton snowboarding jacket. Beneath rain pants my tights were also damp, and I could feel cold streams of water trickling down my neck, which meant my hat and balaclava were saturated. There was no warding this off; I was already wet. It was thirty-five degrees outside. The situation was not optimal.

Anxiety about the weather prompted me to pedal harder. Rain penetrated the snow, and the trail was already beginning to break apart. The bike's tires spun through deteriorating crust, digging into the snow as they inched forward. Eventually the wheels stalled altogether. There were several instances where I nearly tipped over while furiously spinning the pedals, so reluctant was I to admit to myself that the trail was no longer solid enough to ride. Rain continued to pelt the snow like acid. Conditions were not going to improve, but my brain, still numbed by fatigue, let me cling to futile hope. Then I descended into not-frozen-over Hell — churning up slush until the wheels seized, stopping to push my bike for a few yards, trying to pedal again, stopping again, and again and again.

Yellow race stakes made a sharp turn toward the riverbank, where a trail climbed into the woods. I was back on the inbound trail, but it no longer bore any resemblance to the smooth path I had ridden earlier in the day. Rain had transformed it into a quagmire, choked with gray slush and occasional puddles of standing water. Snowmobile tracks had carved irregular ruts into the surface. Optimism had ceased and riding had become impossible. There was only pushing now. Even then I wallowed, frequently punching shin-deep holes into the soft snow. The insides of my overboots were utterly soaked. I could hear water sloshing around but couldn't feel it, so numb were my toes. My fingers felt like slabs of half-frozen salami. The rain kept coming down, cold and endless.

After a seeming eternity of wallowing in purgatory, the churned remnants of trail emerged from the woods and faded into an open expanse. A paper plate stapled to a stake indicated this was "Dismal Swamp." The sign might as well have read, "Abandon all hope, ye who enter here." The low-lying clouds dully illuminated the white plain, enough to pick out sporadic spruce trees from an otherwise bleak moonscape. I could see a long way across the swamp, but I couldn't discern the end of this dismal place. I wavered for long minutes at the paper plate sign, utterly terrified.

The sound of my feet plunging into slush had becoming maddening. When I stopped to collect my bearings, these sounds were replaced with screams from inside my head — the hot and cold throbbing of blisters and waterlogged skin, the dull ache in my legs, the sharp pains in my knees. My throat was raw and prickly; I hadn't eaten anything since Rich Crain's five-star soup, which was now about three hours back. The oranges and brownies at Flathorn Lake were a lifetime removed. I felt ill, not hungry, and I couldn't bear the prospect of cramming a Power Bar into my roiling stomach. Although the rain had tapered off, cold water continued to trickle down my spine. My gloves were dripping as well. When I gripped the corners of my coat, I could easily wring out a large volume of water. There was no more plausible deniability — I was officially soaked.

Even though I was saturated on the outside, I felt as though the last drops of vitality had drained from my body. I looked in the direction of Mount Susitna, which darkness and clouds hid entirely from view. My bike was so deeply embedded in the slush that it didn't even fall over when I let go. I knelt down to rest my shoulders, and ended up crumpled in a heap. With great effort, I rolled onto my back and stared at the starless sky. Its charcoal emptiness was so serene, so restful.

"Maybe it would be better to be dead and nothing, than to spend an eternity in Hell." A whisper of wind whisked over the swamp. The chill was sharp, like needles in my skin. I turned back onto my side and buried my face in my wet gloves. I wanted someone to come rescue me, to take me away from this hopelessness. But I hadn't seen a single person besides Rich Crain since I left Luce's Lodge many hours ago. No snowmobilers would be out at 2 a.m. No one was coming.

The chill found its way to my core, and I began to shiver. The numbness of my extremities had become absolute. The nihilist in my head — the voice who was musing about the nothingness of death — whispered how wonderful it would feel to let this numbness settle over every part of my aching body. Of course I didn't want this. I wanted the pain to end, but I didn't want to die. Logic waved urgently behind a hazy veil of indifference brought on by fatigue. It was thirty-five degrees outside, and my wet clothing no longer provided any barrier from the heat-sapping air. I could abandon all hope, but the consequences of failing to extract myself from this snowbank were clear. If I didn't keep moving, I would die.

I stood up. Once again, my cold salami fingers found a hold around the handlebars, and my exhausted shoulder muscles nudged the bike forward. After a few more steps, primordial instincts took over. My legs moved as necessary. The voices of pain and fatigue no longer screamed. The nihilist's whispers quieted. My mind was as blank as the charcoal sky, as open as the featureless swamp. Only a single voice remained. It told me to march, so I did.

There were brief moments of clarity. Occasionally I'd stare up at the sky, scanning for stars that I never found. The clouds lifted enough to reveal distant light pollution from Anchorage, which cast an eerie orange glow over the horizon. Amid the daze, I found my way across Flathorn Lake and into the wood-heated cabin high on the bluff. The lights were still on at 3 a.m. A volunteer with sleepy eyes fed me a warm bowl of paella and brownies, and helped me refill my Camelback bladder when it became clear I was still too dazed to figure out the complicated function of a zipper.

As the food settled into my stomach, more clarity returned to my brain. I learned the volunteer was named Peggy, and she was irrationally cheerful for being awake as long as I had, if not longer. The cabin was one of several buildings on a property she owned with her husband. They owned a small plane that they could land right on the lake, in winter or summer. Peggy had offered her home, fresh food, and warm hospitality for racers ever since this event was known as Iditasport, back in the nineties.

"Does anyone else look as bad as me?" I asked.

"You don't look bad at all," she exclaimed. "Most people look far worse. You should see some of the runners. Some people won't even get here until tomorrow night."

"Tomorrow?" I shook my head. That span of time was unfathomable. Of course, even on my schedule, it was already tomorrow.

Peggy gave me two brownies in a plastic sandwich bag and made me promise that I'd eat them. "You have to eat," she said. "It's a lot harder when you don't."

I crammed my hands back into wet neoprene gloves — like wedging a squirming child into a wet suit — and returned to the dull night. But in my calorie-assisted, newfound clarity, I noticed several things had changed. Large, chunky snowflakes replaced the drizzling rain. The slurping sound made by my footsteps had transitioned into an icy crunch.

"It dropped below thirty-two," I thought. Perhaps the slush on the trail would freeze, and I'd be able to ride my bike again. Despite the falling snow, the sky was beginning to clear. Hazy moonlight filtered through scattered clouds, and shadows of spruce trees plodded beside me. I didn't want to listen to my footsteps anymore, so I removed my backpack, dusted away a fresh layer of snow, and fished out a little AM/FM radio.

I turned the dial to the weather band. I often listened to this frequency when cycling, and as always hoped the soothing drone of a computer-generated voice would deliver good news — that the storm was over, temperatures would continue to drop, and the trail would be hard again. The channel was filled with loud static, but I was able to catch a garbled report. The temperature in Wasilla was 37 degrees, with scattered showers and light winds. The signal cut out before the monotone voice recited the forecast.

"Ugh," I growled. I switched the radio to FM, and found only one clear signal — a top-forty channel out of Anchorage. Pop music wasn't my favorite, but any noise was more soothing than silence, so I listened as I walked. The station played songs I remembered from high school, one-hit-wonders and formulaic ballads that opened a floodgate of memories. There was dance music that injected some more pep into my legs and prompted me to try to ride my bike again. When these attempts ended in swerving failures, I marched in anger to Britney Spears. The early morning broadcast was pre-taped. There was no DJ, but every commercial break brought the same jingle — a gratingly upbeat tourism advertisement for the very place I was slogging through, the Mat-Su Valley. Even though every repetition made me want to rip the ice-encrusted hair from my scalp, I couldn't help but sing along, out loud: "Yahoo, Mat-Su! Fun is at its peak in the val-leee."

For a while, the music faded into the background. I forgot I was even listening still, when a haunting melody filtered into my disconnected thoughts.

"It's coming up ... it's coming up ... it's coming up ..." I stopped walking, held

my breath, and listened. The music caught my attention in the way certain songs just do sometimes — a mesmerizing blend of surreal melody, movement-matching rhythm, and lyrics that speak to a certain mood.

"You've got to press it on you … you just think it, that's what you do, baby … hold it down, DARE."

"DARE" by the Gorillaz. It was just another pop song, but it injected my slow march with a sense of meaning. The distant orange glow of Anchorage still lit the horizon. I licked my lips, cracked and crusty, and felt a surge of comfort, as though this remote connection through FM radio bridged the bewildering gap between me and the familiarities of the city.

The chorus cracked like a whip, slinging my mood from fathomless depths to a new height of elation I had never before experienced. Having given up all hope hours ago, I again attempted to mount my bike. The bike churned and swerved, and I was laughing even though these jerky movements were futile. I had no options but to mash pedals to the threshold of my physical strength. It was either that, or dance, or sprint to chase the joyful surge that was bursting out of my body. This was my first true encounter with the miracle of endurance euphoria — the phenomenon of having been so miserable for so long that even the tiniest hints of positive emotion resemble ecstasy.

Many write off these emotional surges as nothing more than a natural high produced by hormones and neurotransmitters. Those who seek out these moments of ecstasy know they go considerably deeper than that. After all, getting high is easy. Synthetic drugs are undoubtedly simpler and arguably safer than riding a bicycle a hundred miles across frozen Alaska wilderness. Endurance euphoria requires an astronomical investment — hundreds of hours of training, hundreds of dollars in gear, more in race entry fees, vacation days, travel costs, and a healthy dose of suffering that usually exceeds even the worst hangovers.

And yet, once athletes get a taste of this — this feeling — they never want to go back. Endurance athletes are the worst kind of junkie, scheming new ways to get back out there, to recapture the magic, to increase the speed or distance, or both. When I read about such endeavors in magazines, as much as they captured my imagination, I never really understood. Not until that moment. And it was more incredible than I could have ever imagined. With legs weighed down by fatigue and waterlogged overboots, I engaged in an awkward, beautiful dance, moving in synchronicity with the whole of the universe. All of the energy that had ever been created flowed directly through me, and I knew, with certainty, that I would never be "Just Jill" again.

Still, because endurance euphoria only emerges in the midst of prolonged misery, and because it's accompanied by muscle fatigue and poor nutrition and, in this case, the dangerous edge of hypothermia, it never lasts. Soon enough, I was back to being just miserable again, pushing my bike through the still-mushy snow, and screaming at the "Yahoo Mat-Su" commercial but too lonely to risk turning off the radio.

Another hiccup in time happened, and then the sun began to rise over the Chugach Mountains. I blinked into the ochre light, reflected under a thin cloud cover. This meant I had been out there grinding away at the Susitna 100 for nearly twenty-four hours. An entire day. Not only did that more than double any amount of time I had ever spent engaged in a non-stop activity, but it exponentially surpassed the stress, fatigue, strain, and soul-crushing tedium of any other experience in my life. It was, by large degrees, the hardest thing I had ever done.

And yet, it wasn't necessarily becoming harder. Dull pain simmered in my legs, and a chill continued to encapsulate my core. And yet legs kept walking, arms kept pushing, and my body temperature continued to keep me alive. Even as flickers of lucid thought begged me to find a way to stop already, I wondered how far these newfound abilities could take me.

For now, they returned me to the far edge of the dog mushing park, the final ten miles of the race. The trail was still well-groomed; rain hadn't damaged it too badly. For the first time in twenty-five miles, I was able to pedal more than a few yards at a time. Endurance euphoria ignited again, and my excitement sent me into a renewed sprint. Through this, I failed to pay attention to the yellow stakes that had guided me for ninety miles. After forty-five minutes, it occurred to me that I hadn't seen a yellow stake in a while.

I rode forward another half mile before deciding that I was, in fact, on the wrong track. Wrong turns are common in an endurance race, but this was my first unintentional detour, and I took it badly. I spun around and pedaled as hard as could muster back the way I came, fuming with frustration. Still-fresh happy tears were doused by angry tears, which dissolved into fatigue more crushing than any I'd felt yet. By the time I backtracked nearly three miles to a trail intersection with no stakes in sight, everything was spent. I was still lost and there was nothing left. I slumped off my bike and let it fall to the ground as I knelt into the snow and screamed. I was ready to surrender. My odometer had surpassed a hundred miles, and I didn't care anymore about finishing the race. I already proved I could do it, hadn't I?

Just as I laid down to indulge in "quitting" — in the center of a swamp with no extraction opportunities in sight — I saw a skier skating along the far side of the swamp. I jumped up before he disappeared into the trees, and tracked his direction until I found a yellow stake. Even though my mind had just convinced my body there was no energy left to burn, my legs had no issues spinning pedals once I was back on track. Happy tears drowned the angry tears. Two and a half miles later, the snow-caked front wheel of my mountain bike rolled across the finish line. It was just after 10 a.m.

I pulled up next to the sleep-deprived and sallow-faced race director, who made a note in his clipboard but didn't so much as mutter "congratulations." I stared in disbelief at my surroundings — a tiny warming hut with smoke billowing from the chimney, a mostly empty parking lot, and a yellow line drawn in the snow next to the dog mushing referee tower. It was the same scene I had left twenty-five hours earlier, but there was something odd about it now. Everything had shifted, as though I'd made my way through space-time and emerged in a parallel universe. The differences were so subtle that they were undetectable to my senses, but they nagged at my subconscious all the same.

As I made my way toward the building, Geoff emerged and wrapped his arms around me. He had tears in his eyes and a grin stretched across his face.

"You did it!" he exclaimed, and raised his camera to take a photo. I tried to smile but my face felt frozen. The emotions in his eyes mirrored the joy in my heart, but my body was too drained to emit expression. I stood there like a shell, unable to think of any reply except, "I finished."

The words sounded raspy and foreign, echoing from the hollow chamber of my throat. Any fumes of remaining energy drifted away like smoke. I looked blankly at Geoff, who hugged me again. He was talking quickly, and some distant part of me realized that I needed to find out about his race, and what he'd been doing for the remainder of the past day, and what we were going to eat for dinner. But for now, it was all the energy I could muster to hand him my bike follow him to Craig's truck. Somehow, someway, I was eventually going to have to accept that I had finished the Susitna 100, and things could never be the same.

Tough to Quit

February 25, 2006

Today Geoff and I went to lunch at our favorite organic greasy spoon, Cosmic Kitchen. (There are two types of restaurants in this town: the swank places that welcome XtraTuf-wearing locals with open arms, and the carrot-juice-brewing hippie places that also serve beef and cheese burritos the size of your head.) After months of hugging the horizon, the noontime sun ventured toward mid-sky, bathing the whole restaurant in white light. We took our plates into the glare of a south-facing window just as a family settled in next to us — only on the other side of the window, where snow-covered picnic tables lined the balcony. There they sat for nearly an hour — sipping coffee, munching on corn chips, soaking in sunlight, with steam pouring from their burgers and breath in the subfreezing air.

That's when I decided it would be a great day for a bike ride. I left work a little later than I'd hoped, but I still thought it would be good to go out for an hour, absorb some vitamin D through that narrow slit in my balaclava, and come back with time to spare before Foreign Film night.

One aspect of the Susitna 100 that I didn't anticipate was letting go of this whole training thing. Giving up the multihour, four-times-a-week bicycle rides I've become so accustomed to almost feels like losing a job. I fear that suddenly I'll find myself sprawled on my coach, pouring through classifieds for used bicycle parts and struck with that hollow feeling that my life is slowly sinking into uselessness ... meaningless ... joblessness. Sure, I could get some other hobby. Find a new passion. Maybe even get a life. And while I'm at it, I could apply for new jobs. It's not as easy as it sounds.

✳ ✳ ✳ ✳ ✳

When the Susitna 100 was over, I just expected that spring would follow us to Homer. It was jarring to roll into a town still coated in ice, with snow clinging to bare branches, and realize it was late February in Alaska and winter was far from over. My body was in a state of shock. After Geoff drove me back to Craig's house after the race finish, it was early afternoon on a Sunday, but felt like the middle of a summer night sometime decades later. The air inside the house was hot and musty, and I felt like an 90-year-old creaking my way along prickly carpet, grasping at walls for support. The skin on my feet tingled, and was so sensitive that it hurt to wear socks. I attempted to take a nap, only to be rattled awake numerous times as various muscles seized with painful cramping. My limbs seemed locked in rigor mortis. Even reclined on the couch, I'd spend long minutes battling a desire to roll my body over to a more comfortable position, knowing how much it hurt to move. Usually I'd give up and just lay frozen in the same twisted posture, staring at the gray gloom out the window. Geoff purchased a pizza for dinner. I thought I was hungry, but could only manage a few bites before wincing from its strangely salty and metallic flavor. In fact, everything I tried to consume tasted salty, even candy. My stomach churned so violently that even eating was a battle.

"Probably an electrolyte imbalance," Geoff speculated. "Everything tastes too salty because your body actually needs more salt. If you ate some more sodium, that might help with the cramping."

I nibbled on a potato chip but only made it through one. There was no flavor behind the unappetizing saltiness. It seemed as though my body had shut off some of its unessential functions, like taste, in order to reset the whole system.

"How are you feeling?" I asked Geoff.

He shrugged. "Pretty much fine," he admitted. "My legs are sore, but it's not really worse than after any of the other long runs I did."

Geoff finished first in the Little Su 50K with a time of three hours and fifty-three minutes. He started racing at 11 a.m., and he was done before 3 — about the span of time I spent riding less distance between Flathorn Lake and Eaglesong Lodge, when trail conditions were still good. He won the race handily. There was one other runner, a well-known female ultra-runner, who nearly caught him around mile fifteen. After he crossed an open swamp, he looked over his shoulder and saw her emerge from the trees on the other side, so he picked up what until then had been a relaxed pace. But he never pushed his limit. He didn't just complete his first ultramarathon, first winter race, and first serious race in a decade. He dominated it.

I wasn't entirely surprised — Geoff had always been a natural athlete. On the other hand, in the five years I'd known him, I had never seen this competitive side. I'd hiked with him, backpacked with him, ridden across the country on loaded touring bikes with him, and embarked on plenty of shorter mountain bike rides with him. All of these opportunities to compare our abilities allowed me to cling to the impression that Geoff and I were closely matched in strength and endurance. His Little Su 50K performance proved we were nowhere near the same league. He had a penchant for long-distance speed that I couldn't even fathom. My race pace had wrung every ounce of my strength, and it still only produced a comparatively mediocre performance. I was thrilled for his win and proud of what I'd accomplished on my own, but it was difficult not to feel inadequate.

We drove home later that evening— Geoff graciously did all of the driving — and I slumped back into work on Monday morning. Carey offered a exuberant congratulations when I walked in the door, and told me to go look in the refrigerator. Inside, beneath the unidentifiable Tupperware containers and age-old remnants of birthday cakes, was a six-pack of Pepsi. On my desk was a package of Goldfish crackers — two of my favorite things, according to my blog, where the intro at the top of the page flippantly declared that I was a "small-town journalist who likes to ride my bicycle in horrendous conditions and eat Pepsi and Goldfish for breakfast."

"Aw, thanks," I said with a lopsided grin; my face still felt numb. "I'm just starting to get my appetite back, so this will taste awesome for lunch."

"How are you feeling?" Carey asked.

"Oh, you know, like I got run over by a truck," I replied. "I am glad I finished, but I'm even happier that it's over."

Carey just shook her head. "It's crazy, but congratulations. What now?"

I shrugged. "That's a really good question. I guess for now we put out this week's paper. And maybe later this week I'll think about riding my bike again."

"If I were you, I'd take at least a week off," Carey said. "Lay on the couch or something. Once you have kids, you'll be wishing you could do stuff like that."

"I suppose," I said, letting my voice trail off. There was work to do, but more than resting my body, I wanted an opportunity to turn off my brain and zone out for the rest of the day. I still needed to process a large amount of fear, anticipation, elation, and anxiety that consumed me during the past week. My emotional center, more than my legs or my heart, was ready to flatline for a while.

Newspaper work, of course, never makes that easy. That same afternoon, Jane pulled me into her office to point out several nitpicking customer complaints about two ads I had designed for the previous week's edition. The advertising intern, Emily, quit in December. Rather than hire a new intern, Jane delegated the job to me. Designing ads was a time-consuming job that I juggled along with my editorial assignments — reporting on arts events, editing sports and news stories, compiling community news items, and designing pages. After Jane started dropping advertising assignments in my inbox, I was incensed. But I knew the "too much work" argument would get me nowhere, so instead I protested the ethics of having someone from the newsroom cross over to ad work.

"How can I be objective about news items from local businesses if I'm also designing their ads?" I protested.

Jane didn't have an answer for that, because she didn't believe it to be a valid question. "Julie is still going to deal with the customers," she told me. "I just need you to put together the ads."

But that wasn't true. I still had to deal with the customers, only through the convoluted channel of fielding their complaints through our ad representative, Julie, who then complained to the publisher, Jane, who often complained to the employee who was technically my boss, Carey. ("Why is she telling me this?" Carey would wonder aloud.) Eventually this time-consuming game reached its intended source, and by then any issue had been blown out of proportion and twisted beyond recognition. I wondered if most people who worked office jobs had to endure similar moments of impotent rage — standing in a cold, cement-walled room and staring ashen-faced at the floor while their boss berates them for getting a numeral in a phone number wrong, because the instructions were scrawled in bad handwriting.

"Now I have to give them a free ad," she barked. "You're lucky they didn't pull their contract altogether. Julie is livid. It cuts into her commission, too, you know."

Of course it was all my fault. I was just the person at the end of the chain, the low woman on the totem pole who was slowly being crushed. It didn't matter that Julie was supposed to review every ad and send proofs to the customer to have them approved before printing. I doubted any of this actually happened. It was easier to blame me in the aftermath.

"I'm sorry," I stuttered. "It's been a really busy week." I looked up. Jane knew, at least on the periphery, about my bicycle race. She never mentioned it but sometimes made quips about my mountain bike chained outside, or my wet bike clothes drying near my desk. Of course I couldn't use my hobby as an excuse for mistakes in my work. Still, I was becoming more convinced that my hobby was the only thing keeping me anchored in my work. Having bike rides to look forward to most days of the week helped me tolerate an endless stream of deadlines and demands that I viewed as unfair. Hard efforts helped me burn off frustration. I did what was asked of me, mostly without complaint. Couldn't she tell I was limping around the office right now, and maybe infer it was because of this extremely difficult race I'd just completed? Couldn't she cut me some slack, just for today?

"Don't let it happen again."

I hobbled back to my desk, fuming.

"Everything all right?" Carey asked.

"Just ads," I said, my voice shaking slightly. "When is she going to rehire Emily's position already?"

Carey shook her head. "She's not."

✳ ✳ ✳ ✳ ✳

The following afternoon, the throbbing soreness in my legs had dissipated enough that it seemed possible to lace up my New Balance shoes and hit the street for a recovery run. The road was slicked in a layer of hard ice, which was subsequently coated in just enough frost to give the ice sand-like traction. It was an ideal running surface, actually. Overcast skies and light wind made for an ideal day for a run, but there was a sharp bite to the air and daylight was fading at 4 p.m.

"How is it not spring yet?" I wondered as I plodded along the neck-high snow drifts lining the driveway. A rush of hot blood flooded my sore muscles. My feet throbbed with sharp pains from still-open blisters. Logically I understood the slow progression of the season, but a deeper part of me just expected that the Susitna 100 would mark a grand, ceremonious end to my first winter in Alaska. After more than three months of pedaling through slush, pickling my skin in a marinade of grit and cold rain, braving long outings in below-zero air, and blinking against blizzards, I succeeded in overcoming the hardships of winter training. I vanquished fear and emerged victorious in an intensely difficult endurance feat. I had done this impossible thing. I had finished the Susitna 100. Yet I was still a lackey at my work, and it was still winter.

I supposed I couldn't expect everything to become different. And yet, everything was different. I hadn't yet managed to pinpoint any tangible reason why.

I widened my stride as I crossed Diamond Ridge. It felt like prying open a rusty hinge. Forced into movement, muscle tightness began to break apart, until all hints of soreness subsided. The sun slipped into a narrow opening between the cloud ceiling and the sea, and the ice road reflected a dazzling shade of tangerine. I had to squint against light that was suddenly everywhere; there was no turning away from it. Even the snow was on fire, glittering like a disco ball as light shifted from orange to coral to ruby. If I had any unknown superpowers residing in my body, then beauty was their elixir. I picked up my feet and started sprinting, breathing the searingly cold air and running as though the hundred-mile slog never happened, and my legs were healthy and strong, and the energy of the universe was all mine to absorb and release.

Two miles earlier, I wasn't even sure that I'd make it to the end of my driveway. I'd convinced myself that the nutrition deficiencies and muscle breakdowns I'd sustained were debilitating, and that I'd be broken for weeks. But it my mind — where it mattered — the fast and free runner still resided. She was always there, even at my lowest moments of the Susitna 100. She never left.

Perhaps that's what shifted during the Susitna 100. The inner runner, or Adventure Jill, whatever I wanted to call her — that free-spirited side of myself that I all too often buried beneath anxiety and obligation — had finally broken free. In many ways, my past adventures had been well-calculated to minimize risks. I leaned on others to make decisions and put safety nets in place. I kept close to my comfort zones so I could avoid discomfort. I thought experience expanded my comfort zones, but in reality they narrowed as anxiety and fear gained leverage. All those years, I kept Adventure Jill on a leash to prevent her from dragging me into terrifying and dangerous situations. That had been the mistake. Backing away from unknowns only trapped me in a suffocating corner surrounded by my own misperceptions. It took long enough, but I finally realized it was worse to be trapped than it was to be afraid.

✳ ✳ ✳ ✳ ✳

For the weekend following the Susitna 100, Geoff and I indulged in our first lazy morning in a while. Our local paper boy, who was actually a middle-aged man in a Ford pickup, plowed through four new inches of snow covering our driveway and delivered the Anchorage Daily News. "Hey, now I can probably actually get my car out of the driveway tomorrow," I announced to Geoff as I cracked the front door just enough to pull the thick Sunday edition inside and wave at the driver as he backed away.

"The plow guy is coming later today," Geoff called back from the loft, where he was answering e-mails on the desktop computer.

"Even for only four inches?"

"He's been good about that. Charges us twenty bucks every time, but at least he's consistent."

It was true. Our snow plowing bill averaged a hundred and twenty dollars per month, which was more than we paid for heating fuel. I wondered if Geoff ever pondered the irony that we invested more money in leaving our home comfortably than we did in living there, but I didn't say that out loud. Our driveway was more than a hundred feet long, and I didn't want to shovel it, either.

"So what do you feel like doing today?" I called back toward the loft as I threw the newspaper on the table and filled up my espresso maker with whole milk and chocolate syrup. It may have been a week, but as long as I could feel Susinta aches in my legs, I was going to indulge in hot milkshakes for breakfast.

"You want to go for a ride?" Geoff asked.

"You want to ride? A bike?" I replied, surprised. Geoff's interest in two-wheeled activity seemed to wane with each training run. His studded-tire mountain bike, which at least saw some commuting action early in the winter, had gathered a layer of dust nearly as thick as the one on my road bike trainer. His Honda Civic worked better for post office trips, and he didn't want to waste energy that was better conserved for running, skiing, and construction work. After his Little Su win, there was no doubt that running was going to continue to be a major part of Geoff's life. He was already talking about summer races, and had even registered for a couple of spring events in the Alaska Mountain Running series. In the meantime, I was becoming more entrenched in endurance cycling, researching twenty-four-hour mountain bike races and four-hundred-mile road rides under the midnight sun. I wondered if our outdoor interests would ever realign.

"Sure, why not?" Geoff said. "We could just do something mellow."

"Crossman Ridge would be fun. Usually it gets enough local snowmobile traffic to always have a decent trail even when there's new snow."

Crossman Ridge was a strange neighborhood, even for Homer. A strip of cabins and other rustic structures lined the crest of the hill above Bridge Creek Reservoir, about a mile beyond the end of the town's winter road maintenance. These homes were snowed in for six months out of the year, requiring residents to commute by snowmobile and shuttle all of their supplies — heating fuel, food, and water — on cargo sleds. Despite this inconvenience, about a dozen residents lived there year-round. It was arguably an ideal living situation — wild Alaska living just a few miles from all the conveniences of a city. Building codes didn't seem to apply to the Kenai Peninsula in general, and Crossman Ridge residents especially seemed to not adhere to standard protocol. There were all manner of structures up there — plywood and Tyvek shacks, yurts, and even an old blue school bus that had been partially converted to a dwelling. It was abandoned for the winter, but a peek into one of the broken windows revealed a clean living space and newer cans of food as evidence that someone had resided there recently.

I enjoyed riding my bike on the snowmobile path beside these mysterious residences. It had the mischievous excitement of trespassing through backwoods properties where reclusive residents would shoot first and ask questions later (I reminded myself the trail was legally a public road, although this was only marginally reassuring.) Even as a trespasser, I felt a connection to the place — the promise of Alaska, the appeal of self-sufficiency, romance of escaping societal constraints, and gumption to carve out a life from the land.

"When do you think we'll move to a cabin out in the woods? Like, really out in the woods, where we have to chop wood and mush dogs into the nearest village?" I mused to Geoff as we pedaled away from our driveway, just a few minutes after it had been freshly plowed by a contractor with a large truck and twenty more of our dollars.

Geoff laughed. "What do you mean, when we move? It's perfect here. Anyway, where would you ride your bike?"

"We'd live on a hundred acres and I'd slash and set my own trails with a chainsaw, then groom them with my snowmachine. I saw one for sale when I was putting together the classifieds this week — an Arctic Cat. Only seventeen hundred dollars. I could probably sell my Geo for that much, or make a trade. We'd be set."

Geoff shook his head and pedaled ahead of me on the muddy gravel of Diamond Ridge. "So now you want to move to the Bush? You're always saying that you'd get cabin fever and probably die."

I pulled up beside him. "Probably. I mean, a world with no bike trails, maybe that I could live with. A world with no Internet? Yikes."

"Yeah. If it wasn't for your blog, I would never know what you're thinking about."

The words hit like ice water and came out just as we launched down the steepest section of Diamond Ridge. The roar of wind drowned out the conversation, and we refocused on the bumpy descent. Verbal communication had never been one of my strong traits, and e-mail and text messaging was more than a convenience for me. Written communication bypassed the part of my brain that always became bogged down in speech, and I relied on it heavily. I went to great lengths to avoid confrontations, even benign ones. There was a reason I found my way into the editing side of newspaper work — reporting caused far too much anxiety. Every time I needed to call a source for an interview, it often took three or four tries to build the courage I needed to dial all seven numbers on a phone and let it ring through.

As difficult as it was for me to talk to strangers, it was exponentially more difficult to address uncomfortable subjects with people I knew well and loved. I was willing to lie through my teeth, even though I was a terrible liar, just to avoid expressing difficult truths. I spent the entire previous summer telling Geoff I was "still working on it" when he broached the subject of moving to Alaska, even though at the time I had no intent of doing so. Pretending I was going to move to Alaska was easier than admitting to him or myself that I suspected our relationship had run its course. The idea broke my heart too deeply to ever say it out loud. It was more comforting to lie, until the lie became truth. I was grateful on so many levels that it had. But I couldn't deny that the roots of this lie were still firmly in place. Even though our life in Alaska had evolved into a beautiful truth, it didn't fix our communication problems.

We rode in silence for several miles. I didn't bring it up again, but continued to stew in the upsetting realization that Geoff thought he needed to read my public blog to understand my heart. My blog didn't really say much of anything. I wrote about biking almost exclusively, mentioned weather frequently, mused about quirky Alaska culture occasionally, and only a few times hinted at frustrations with my work. I almost never wrote anything about Geoff, unless it was a report on some outdoor activity we shared, such as this ride. Is this all I revealed to him — the same parts of me I revealed to everybody else? I had let myself believe we'd never been closer, and in many aspects this was true — we were living together, and mutually working toward our individually determined ideal lives. But I continued to clasp onto the fear that self-actualization would eventually drive us apart. It seemed our passions were already diverging, and our partnership might not survive this bridge we built hastily, then reinforced with shaky connections. This was the same issue I worried about when I was still resolved to stay in Idaho. It was only a matter of time. One day I'd prove too domestic for

Geoff, he'd be too flighty for me, and that would be the end.

I reminded myself that it was useless to fret about the future, and vowed to try to be more open with Geoff about my thoughts. Usually I felt the most willing to expose myself during an outdoor adventure. Fresh air and endorphins pumping through my system opened up a floodgate of emotions that I was bursting to share. Paradoxically, this was always when my communication skills were at their worst. Happy chemicals would inundate my brain, rendering me incapable of forming sentences more complex than "this is awesome, isn't it?" I'd say these words and Geoff would agree enthusiastically. Amid this swirl of emotion, I believed we had shared something intensely meaningful. But outside the limitations of my own perspective, I could never be sure. Maybe Geoff's frontal lobe was similarly inundated, and we were simply two animals getting high on our own pleasure sensors. But our humanity prompted us to reach through the deluge embrace one another, forging a connection that would sustain us during the dry spells of our lives.

We rode Skyline Ridge Road to the far end of the snowmobile trail that would take us up and over Crossman Ridge, where it would then loop back to the main road past the reservoir. We opted to ride the known conditions of the plowed road first, and saved the surprises for later, past a point where returning the way we came would be more inconvenient than just enduring whatever lay ahead. This was by design, because I expected the trail to be soft and hoped Geoff would stick it out anyway. I was right about the trail. If fact, no one had traveled over the ridge since four inches of heavy powder fell overnight. Both of our bikes knifed through the new snow to the platform of the trail base below. We were able to ride, but only barely. New snow created a wall of resistance that reduced our speed to something just above a trudge. I ended up being the first to suggest just turning around, but Geoff wanted to ride it out, reasoning that perhaps one of the Crossman Ridge residents drove out the other end of the trail.

He was wrong about that, and we struggled together for the better part of four miles. I mashed pedals until my quad muscles felt like they were about to burst through my skin. My bike swerved wildly on rolling descents. A couple of times the front wheel disappeared into deeper drifts, causing the bike to stop cold as my body hurtled forward, which resulted in slamming my crotch into the bike's stem. (Happily for Geoff I was the only one to make stem contact. He tended to crash at higher speeds and launched Superman-style over the handlebars.) It was exhausting work, and those four miles consumed ninety minutes of our purportedly "lazy" Sunday afternoon. All the while, smoke streamed out of the occasional cabin stove pipe, the sun drifted low on the horizon, and nothing else in the quiet neighborhood moved.

"So much for a mellow ride," I said to Geoff as he crawled out of another snow drift, where he had landed several feet from his overturned bike. "I sus-pected the trail might be soft, but you never know how bad it's really going to be."

"You know, I have a lot more appreciation for what you did last weekend," he replied. "This is way harder than running, and you did this for a hundred miles."

"The Susitna 100 wasn't all like this. Some of it was, though." Quietly, I brimmed with pride. Geoff was clearly the better athlete in this relationship, but he respected my ability to tough something out. Maybe we could reconcile our passions as well. Because while Alaska had set my adventurous side free in many ways, it also sharpened an understanding of the points where Geoff and I might always diverge. I cherished outdoor experiences, but also required the balance of civilization and routine. And I craved opportunities to confront my fears, but I couldn't throw all caution to the wind, either.

Geoff remounted his bicycle and I followed his serpentine track up a hill, trying to hold his line through the trench left by his tires. A stiff breeze blew, whisking puffs of snow that resembled silver ghosts in the afternoon light. As ground blizzards swirled around Geoff, he wrestled with his bike in a comical kind of dance, rocking side to side as the white landscape pulled all around him. I felt a surge of love that I could scarcely describe, and would never try. Our connection always felt strongest in these quiet moments, with all of the unsaid, unnecessary words scattered in the wind.

Work Too Hard

March 30, 2006

Squinting against radial gusts of wind, I waver at the intersection. Which way to go — left or right? One way is West Hill, the short way, the traffic-clogged highway spewing mud and melted snow. The other is East Hill, the long hill, the beast, the lung-searing climb that chews up my studs. The wind goes both directions. I go east.

The hill sets in fast, pulling hard at legs that sat unmoving, atrophied, dead weights for nearly eight hours prior. Wind grit builds up on my teeth and I clamp my mouth shut, squint downward, watch the odometer. 5.8 mph ... 5.9 ... I'm already sick of being out here. It's gray with little flecks of snow blowing around. And around and around. Wind hits from new directions. I tilt again. Studs grind into the pavement. I stand. 6.4 mph .... 6.7.

How high does your heart rate have to go to find that

place where frustrating thoughts dissipate? I ask myself this question but don't really think about the alternative. 6.8 mph ... 7.0. I round another switchback. More wind. More snow. I think about April in the desert. I think about winter in Alaska. 7.2 mph ... 7.4.

Mouth wide open, I swallow bits of musty grit and road goo. I no longer have a choice. The tunnel closes in. First pavement. Then tires, patches of rubber tread, handlebars. Then only the odometer, encircled in blackness. 7.6 mph. 7.7 ... The iPod speaks to me in gasps and whimpers ... 7.8 mph ... 7.9. Involuntary thoughts tear through. Thoughts that long for anything but the present, long for old times, the days of after-school jobs and riding the banana seat Huffy to work, greeting the dead morning hours with the time-worn smells of flour and bleach, of baking bagels at Einstein's with Sam.

Sam and I were equals in our dead-end job. We worked the 4 a.m. shift on Saturday mornings, baking bagels for the blurry-eyed people who no longer cared. We were brothers in arms, hiding in the walk-in refrigerator, eating frozen cookie dough, recounting our adventures in snowboarding and caving and skipping out of classes. We both went on to become cyclists. He became a racing roadie. I became a cycle tourist. I quit the bagel shop and went to college. He stayed and worked his way up to general manager. He made many thousands in savings. I made many camping trips to southern Utah. Now he manages a large hotel in Argentina. I pull in migrant worker wages at a small-town rag in rural Alaska.

The world seems black and white at 8 mph.

Tinted by choices.

❋ ❋ ❋ ❋ ❋

Aquietness would wash over me at unexpected moments — during a pause at a traffic light, or while shoving a shopping cart across the gravel-strewn ice of the Safeway parking lot. A cold breeze would sting my face, I'd gaze upward at the yellow light of a street lamp, and I'd remember the moon, and the bronze glow of a distant city, and a place that was far away from any I had known. A place far away from the world most people knew.

Amid this quietness, I would wonder whether I'd ever entirely return to the known world. The Susitna 100 was a new galaxy, and my explorations there prompted a paradigm shift that I couldn't quite reconcile upon touchdown in my regular life. A sense of separation had occurred. The other shoppers wrestling their carts across the parking lot, my co-workers, even Geoff — no one else seemed to have ventured to the same outer edge. No one else acknowledged the maelstrom that raged just beyond our veneer of convention, the infinite chaos and encompassing void. We were just going about nanoscale routines, purchasing milk and eggs, eyes glazed over with boredom, when all around us, the whole universe was on fire. How could people not see this? How could they not even notice the sprawling darkness beyond the street lights?

The things I thought I knew were drifting away into an ever-expanding big picture. There was no going back. I frequently caught myself in daydreams, fixated on stars or the distant mountain skylines, lost in wonder at what it must be like out there. I immersed myself in imaginary adventures — scenarios involving my tiny figure atop an expansive ice field, or pedaling along an ice-coated beach as waves crashed on rocks. These daydreams had expanded beyond the realm of wishful thinking to something more encompassing. I'd jolt "awake" to my computer desk with some half-finished ad displayed on the screen, and smile sadly. Not because my fantasies weren't real, but because they had become so vivid and dominant that they were taking over my ability to live in the moment. How would I ever reconcile the desires that made me feel alive, with the tasks that helped me stay alive?

I couldn't deny that the requirements of income, bills, and day-to-day chores were increasingly a source of frustration rather than satisfaction. Even pedaling to and from work — a chore I enjoyed — couldn't compete with the adventures in my imagination. When I was finally outside, breathing cold air and feeling warm blood surging through my veins, my routine commute never failed to be invigorating. I reminded myself of this. But unless I could find the time for new explorations, or longer distances, everyday cycling no longer held as strong of a grip on my interest as it had just a few months earlier.

Entrenched routine allowed me to go on autopilot in the morning. I hardly had to think to ride my bike to work. I simply grabbed fleece layers and rain pants to throw on over my khaki pants, cotton T-shirts, and sweaters. The arrival of March brought enough direct sunlight to warm the office, but outside temperatures still hovered well below freezing. Still, spring was undoubtedly on its way. The sun now stayed up past seven in the evening, offering plenty of time to take the long way home with a comfortable buffer of twilight.

One Thursday evening, I left downtown Homer pedaling in the wrong direction so I could climb East End Road and ride Crossman Ridge trails home. I wore the same number of layers I'd descended into town with during the frigid morning, and within a mile I was overheated and drenched in sweat. Although I stopped midway up the hill to strip outer layers, the damage had been done. My cotton pants and T-shirt were soaked, and even the brief pause to stuff the shell and fleece jackets in my backpack resulted in a shivering chill.

"No matter. I just need to ride harder," I thought.

It seemed a good day to go hard, with the afternoon sunlight glittering on Kachemak Bay, and a cold breeze wafting at my back. My head ached from a tedious day of database entry in the Tribune's classified ads files, and cortisol levels were high. I might not have huge mountains or new galaxies to explore every day, but I certainly had adventure within reach. This was still Alaska, and it was still winter. I ratcheted into a high gear and leaned into the handlebars, inhaling ice and exhaling fire.

March brought warm days yielding to freezing nights, which had the effect of solidifying the snowpack. The Crossman Ridge trail was packed with a slick layer of ice, as solid as pavement. I sprinted up and down the rolling crest of the ridge as the wind cooled the sweat on my skin. My hands tingled, and the needling sensation spread to my arms. Soon I felt the familiar numbness of cold salami fingers, but I didn't want to break my momentum just to put on mittens. I could do that at the bottom of the ridge.

The sun slipped below the horizon, and the woods fell into shadow. Wet khaki pants clung to my skin, and the single fleece jacket I pulled on at the base of Crossman Ridge felt like an ice wrap. The final descent brought a tear-inducing blast of cold. By the time I finally reached the reservoir, my whole body was rigid. After I peeled my dead fingers away from the handlebars, my arms continued to hang limply at my side. Even as I tried to lift them, the muscles seemed unresponsive to the imperatives of my brain. As I turned to remove my backpack, my shoulders stiffened and my whole body moved as though I were deep under water. Meanwhile, thoughts raced. "I am not just cold, I am really cold. I am in trouble."

Just as I finally worked the backpack to the ground and began to maneuver my seemingly disconnected hands toward the zipper, my body erupted in shivering. The initial onset was so violent that I lost motor control and had to sit down in the snow to avoid toppling over. Trying to open my backpack seemed futile in this state. Instead, I stood back up, lifted the backpack onto a shoulder between convulsions, pushed my palms against the bike's handlebars, and started running.

Initially, I loped on wooden legs. Eventually my core released some heat into my leg muscles, loosening the joints and sparing some warmth for my arms. With shivering somewhat abated, I stopped again, and pried open the backpack zipper with my teeth. With a jilted, slow-motion kind of frenzy, I pulled on all of my fleece jackets, shells, and mittens. I was three miles from home, engaged in a race for survival that felt more real and more urgent that anything I had experienced on the Iditarod Trail.

With layers applied, I mounted my bike and began the infuriatingly slow process of working heat back into my sluggish muscles. All of my extremities felt like frozen meat, and the painful tingling had extended to my torso and butt. My mind, which was convinced it was freezing to death, screamed to ride harder, but my body was slow to respond. My veins seemed to be filled with icy sludge. I continued to shiver and convulse. My teeth chattered so wildly that I accidentally bit my tongue, and yet in cruel irony my legs would barely move.

After a half-mile of "warm-up," I finally achieved enough motor function to add some power to the laughably slow spinning. With increased power came the relief of increase heat. My hands and feet were still numb, and the rest of my body was far from comfortable, but at least I achieved the necessary momentum to propel myself home. Once inside the cabin, I peeled off wet layers of clothing and stumbled stiff and naked into the shower. The plumbing tapped into a private well, then pumped it into our house at such low pressure that it was often difficult to coax more than a trickle through our single shower upstairs. The well water was steeped in sulfur that left an unpleasant smell, and other minerals clogged up the fixtures. Our diesel-powered water heater was also a relic and would often only provide five to ten minutes of near-boiling water before running completely cold.

Still, I cherished these showers. They were often my favorite part of the day. Given my brush with hypothermia, I expected my most sublime hot shower yet. Perhaps I should have known better. I expected similar ecstasy from my post-race shower after the Susitna 100, which I took at Craig's house. That shower provided real water pressure and a modern heater that didn't scald and then chill. Yet the experience proved to be the opposite of heaven — burning raw and chafed skin, beating tender muscles that throbbed with pain at the slightest pressure, and pulling my tangled hair out in clumps.

This post-hypothermia shower was even more insidious. My fingers and toes felt as though I was dousing them in water that was actually boiling. The sudden temperature swing opened up all of my nerve endings in tingling so intense that I became nauseated. I slumped against the side of the shower stall and slid onto my butt when I could no longer endure the agony of standing. The shower continued to douse my body with fire water until it was beaten into submission. Electric shocks subsided, and I was left feeling thoroughly numb.

Even a hundred miles of Iditarod Trail hadn't quite prepared me for this brush with danger. It was an important lesson. Hypothermia lurks where you least expect it. It would be another two days before the numbness in my fingers and toes subsided, and I felt recovered enough to ride my bike to work again.

❋ ❋ ❋ ❋ ❋

On the first of April, Geoff and I finally got around to trying real winter camping — the tent and fire pit variety. Daylight now extended past 9 p.m., so after I returned from work, we drove out to the Caribou Lake Trailhead with all of our gear — his in a sled and mine in a pack. Geoff cut a trail with his skis and I slogged behind in snowshoes. Because we were using this "backcountry" mode of transportation, he wanted to avoid snowmobile trails. Instead, we paralleled the main route to the lake, with the easier path just beyond sight. Wind-driven snow pelted our faces and I had to squint to see his silhouetted figure a hundred feet ahead.

We wallowed for four miles in the blizzard and then set up our tent in a thin stand of spruce trees. Geoff had recently purchased a used mountaineering tent from a friend. Desire to use this tent at least once before spring thaw was the main catalyst for this weekend's trip. I had mostly reached acceptance that it wasn't spring yet, but resented being coerced into another survival trip when flowers were already blooming in other places I had recently lived.

"I can't believe tomorrow is April Fool's Day," I whined as Geoff and I trudged through thigh-deep snow to gather twigs for a fire.

"April Fools," Geoff laughed as he broke branches from a downed tree and piled them in my outstretched arms. With the ground still buried in several feet of snow, I didn't think we'd find any wood for a fire, but eventually we had enough ruler-sized twigs to stoke a few hours of small flames. Geoff fished the camp stove from his sled and we made dinner out of soupy rehydrated vegetables spooned up with tortillas, because both of us had neglected to bring bowls or silverware. We devoured our sloppy meal over the campfire, dripping vegetable mash everywhere.

"The bears are still asleep, right?" I joked.

"Hope so," Geoff said with a shrug.

We hovered over our tiny campfire for the next two hours. It kept us warm, but only because we had to repeatedly get up, trudge through the snow, and hack away at a dead tree until we collected another armload of wet spruce branches to feed the tiny flames. Finally it was dark enough to feign sleep, so we crawled into our tent only to discover that moisture from the wet snow had already soaked through the floor. My base layers were drenched in sweat from walking and wood-hauling, and my outer layers were soaked from wallowing in waist-deep drifts in search of wood. My sleeping bag was now damp as well, from condensation dripping overhead. This mountaineering tent — built for the extreme climates of high altitudes — apparently wasn't waterproof. An overnight camping trip on a date that technically qualified as spring suddenly didn't seem so benign.

"What do you think about hiking out tonight?" I asked Geoff as we slithered into wet sleeping bags.

"We'll be fine," Geoff said. "If we get cold we can always build another fire."

"Great," I mumbled. Heavy flakes of snow continued to pummel the tent as I shivered and tossed in my bag. I wasn't hypothermic, but I certainly wasn't comfortable, and no amount of meditative counting could take my mind off the fact that my skin felt like it was wrapped in a cold pack.

Somehow I fell asleep, and woke to gray morning light and six inches of dense snow. Geoff heated up similarly thick oatmeal. We shoveled it into our mouths with spruce twigs, only able to sit still for only a few seconds before we started shivering.

We left our packs and most of our remaining food behind, and set out for a six-mile walk to the shoreline of Caribou Lake and back — the day hike we'd planned before we trekked out later that afternoon. A dark, low-lying cloud ceiling washed out the spring daylight, giving the landscape the appearance of a pencil sketch that had been doused in dishwater. Temperatures hovered just below freezing. The new layer of snow was soft to the touch, but it would freeze to a concrete-like crust around my shins after my snowshoes punched through the surface —a veritable trap. Geoff fared better on skis, but our strained progress ensured this stroll was going to consume more than four monotonous hours.

By the time we returned to our campsite to pack up, heavy snow was falling again, and my body was weary. I'd lapsed into shivering, and yet I felt too weak to generate my own heat. Since there were only three miles left in the journey, I felt incredulous about my fatigue, rather than concerned for my own safety. We'd slept outside in moderate cold and then hiked six miles. How could this be so difficult?

"Turns out camping is tougher than racing," I said to Geoff as we followed the faint remnants of our own tracks toward the car. The wind drove snow daggers directly into our face. We had to scream over the machine-gun-like clamor, and discussed potential plans for the upcoming summer as a weak distraction. Geoff wanted to complete the Alaska Mountain Running series and canoe the Yukon River. I wanted to enter a twenty-four-hour mountain bike race at Kincaid Park in Anchorage. Without a regular job commitment, I just figured Geoff would spend the entire summer linking ambitious adventures that didn't include me. At least this would be a good opportunity for time-intensive endurance training.

"I'm feeling much better now than I was this morning," I observed. "It is actually easier to just keep moving."

"We should do this more often," Geoff said without sarcasm. "I miss camping. It's more work here than it is in the desert, but it's still fun."

"I suppose," I said. My thoughts drifted to all of the luxuries I was going to enjoy when we returned to our cabin. Eating Fruit Loops out of the box. Curling up in a blanket on the couch and watching DVDs. More blankets. All of the blankets.

The reprieve didn't last long, because the following morning brought the Homer Sea to Ski, an annual triathlon that involved a five-kilometer run along the Sterling Highway, a seven-kilometer mountain bike ride up West End Road, and then a five-kilometer ski on groomed trails. This would be my first triathlon, and second race ever.

The weather made a dramatic turn toward spring since the blizzard just sixteen hours earlier. Clear skies and temperatures above forty degrees made it almost feel like it really was April 2. I wasn't a skier, but I was arguably even less of a runner, so I felt disproportionately nervous as I joined sixty other participants in a gravel parking lot at Mariner Park, at the base of the Homer Spit.

After an unseen race volunteer called out "go," I slithered toward the back of the pack with the middle-school-aged girls and even younger boys. My heart rate shot skyward and I was breathing fire, but only managing about a ten-minute-mile pace. The rest of my energy was consumed by nerves and adrenaline. Soon I fell behind the children and joined a few stragglers at the very back of the pack — other non-runners and hobby joggers coerced into taking the undesirable running leg for their relay teams.

Mine was one of six or seven bikes remaining at the school parking lot where we picked up the cycling leg, and I dashed to vindicate my poor performance with a show of cycling prowess. West End Road was my usual commuter route, and I had memorized every point where the grade steepened and where it eased, and every section where I could ride hard and then recover. I sprinted toward the other back-of-packers and was soon passing the little boys, the teenage girls, and even other racers who I'd been nowhere near during the run. I felt a surge of power in passing people with such ease, and I could understand why people like triathlons — after all, most people have only one sport they're actually good at, and it's gratifying to show up others struggling through a sport that for them is a weakness. If all of us stuck with only our good sport, our competition would be more directly matched, and the mediocre would never have an opportunity to shine.

I surged up the hill, passing one cyclist after the next, and basking in the illusion that I was the strongest cyclist on the road. The route turned onto a slush-coated gravel road. Here I also excelled, thanks to efficient handling skills learned from a season of riding through marginal trail conditions. I elevated my position to something legitimately mid-pack when the mountain bike leg ended all too quickly, and it was time to strap on my secondhand skis.

A handful of ski outings since the Susitna 100 still hadn't transformed me into a skier. If anything, I was getting worse at the sport. When it came to simply propelling myself forward in the snow, attaching planks to my feet made about as much sense as strapping on a lead-weighted vest or hopping in a potato sack. On this groomed trail, I'd be much faster using either my running shoes or my bike. Instead, I had to drag the sticks for five kilometers. This was the point of a triathlon — to build us up as athletes before tearing down our poorly-constructed delusions.

The trail cut into the woods, remaining mercifully flat for all of two hundred meters. My inefficient scooting technique at least allowed me to move at walking speeds on flat terrain, but the course rolled through the drainages just below the crest of Diamond Ridge. Beyond the initial run-out, the entire trail either climbed or descended steeply. The course trended downhill, which was not an advantage.

The first upward pitch prompted frantic chopping. When the skis began to slide backward, I resorted to squatting down and hopping, like a frog, using the plastic-edged skis to dig a shallow anchor into the icy snow. As the trail plunged into the next drainage, I flailed halfway down the hill, lost my balance altogether, and rolled shoulder over shoulder until finally slowing to a stop near the bottom. After I rose, I had to climb in the wrong direction to retrieve both skis and poles. I considered just chucking them into the woods and leaving them there, but I didn't want to forfeit the race on account of finishing the ski leg with no skis.

In the meantime, the cyclists I'd passed on the mountain bike leg passed me once again. A few asked if I was okay. "Yeah, not much of a skier," I'd reply with a weak laugh. By then they had already glided out of sight. I continued to strap the skis back on my feet and make choppy, frog-hopping attempts at every climb, but started taking them off at the top of hills because I was afraid of breaking a bone. I'd step off the trail to avoid collisions with skiers as they zipped past me. Soon I just stayed off the trail. I wasn't just walking downhill; I was wallowing in thigh-deep powder.

I finally scooted into the finish, wearing my skis for show, with a final time of one hour and forty-three minutes. Geoff had finished more than thirty minutes earlier, and was already shivering from waiting for me in his sweaty clothing. He came in eighth, having dominated the race until the ski leg, where he employed classic cross-country technique while all the other top competitors skated. I was fifth from last among thirty-five solo competitors. I needed forty-one minutes to finish the five-kilometer ski, which obliterated the next slowest time of thirty-two. The thirty-one-minute run was also pretty dismal, but not quite to the level of total embarrassment. However, I pointed out to Geoff later, my bike time rivaled the fastest women.

"Maybe you should just stick to racing bikes," he said playfully.

"Hey, triathlon is hard," I retorted. "Everything here is hard. Commuting. Camping. I can't even do a fun sprint-distance race without risking death by impaling myself with a ski."

Geoff shrugged as we loaded my disappointingly not-broken skis into his car.

"Next winter, I'll spend more time practicing skiing," I resolved. "And running."

"Doesn't matter to me," he said. "Racing is fun; it's not important."

"I'm excited for summer," I said. "I have some ideas."

"Crazy long bike rides?"

"Of course. And all the other Alaska summer adventures I can squeeze in."

"Well, yeah."

Just for the Halibut

April 20, 2006

Today I was finally indoctrinated into the tourism side of Homer, which is known far and wide as the "Halibut Fishing Capitol of the World." (Note the addition of the word "Fishing" to that motto. If you just want to eat halibut around here, you still have to dish out $12 a pound.) I hooked up with the Chamber of Commerce crew to tag some "little guys" for the annual halibut derby. After we tagged the requisite number of fish, they let us catch a couple of our own.

Compared to the rest of the boat, I had an awful morning. I caught three cod, had four incidents of snagging other peoples' lines, and then nothing — for hours. I just stood out there in the wind and blowing snow, wielding a fishing pole that weighs as much as my road bike, and practically tap dancing to maintain an on-board (as opposed to overboard) position in the rising swells. I had taken two Dramamines to ward of seasickness but wound up feeling pitched and drugged instead. After a while it was hard not to ask myself, "and this is fun, why?"

At about noon, I was reeling up what I was certain was another cod, thinking about the Popeye forearm muscles I could build if I did this kind of fishing every-day, when my first flatfish finally surfaced. No sooner had I reeled him in the boat and dropped my line back down when I felt another familiar tap-tap-tap. Second halibut, within seconds. And just like that, I was done. Four hours of nothing. Eight minutes of fishing. Done.

But there is a certain satisfaction, a feeling of warmth and independence, in pulling up your very own "little guy" — one that will net you a cool 10 pounds of moist, melt-in-your-mouth fillets. It makes the whole morning of mindlessly bouncing a four-pound sinker with frozen fingers seem entertaining, even exhilarating. In this way, fishing can be a lot like bicycling. Or mountaineering. Or hitting yourself repeatedly with a hammer. It doesn't feel good until you stop.

✳ ✳ ✳ ✳ ✳

By mid-April, daylight lingered until ten in the evening. Diamond Ridge, however, remained stubbornly defiant of spring. The snow in town had mostly melted, exposing a winter's worth of trash and amid ankle-deep mud and the occasional sheet of ice. At our cabin a thousand feet above town, the land was still gray and white. There wasn't a streak of mud to be seen.

Because the roads in town were nearly clear, Geoff and I discussed the possibility of switching our costly studded car tires with summer tires. But the tires remained where he left them when he switched them over in October — stacked outside the shed and buried under six feet of snow. "It will take at least an hour to dig them out," Geoff said. "And it might snow again."

Precipitation that fell as rain in town still came down as sleet and ice pellets on the ridge, and I still had to bundle up to ride my bike to work. I was no longer training for anything specific, although I had nearly committed to a twenty-four-hour mountain bike race in Anchorage on the summer solstice. That race covered multiple loops of an eleven-mile course with mud, roots and rocks — technical features I had not seen since October and might not see before the June race.

Even as days warmed, nighttime temperatures continued to fall below thirty-two degrees. Sunlight thawed the surface crust, saturating and condensing the snowpack into a viscous slush. The crust would freeze again overnight, becoming increasingly more dense and solid. I found the freeze-thaw cycle frustrating, because it was beginning to seem like summer would never be warm enough to melt the glaciers forming on the ground. Still, the hard layer of textured ice had its own intriguing quality. I could walk across it, jump on it, roll wheels across it, probably even drive my car on it without sinking in (I did not try this.) Petrified wind-drifts became ramps; stream beds became half pipes. The surface crust was a ready-made mountain bike pump track.

Duties at work continued to pile up, and I found myself sitting at my desk later each day. Even with more hours of daylight to work with, I still returned home with only an hour, perhaps two, before the sun sank below the horizon. Often I used the time to ride faint remnants of Geoff's backyard snowshoe trails, leaning into the corners and pretending I was sprinting for the win at the 24 Hours of Kincaid.

On Easter Sunday, a particularly low overnight freeze left the snow as hard as concrete. Geoff woke up early to embark on a long run. He'd set a rigid training schedule to prepare for the Alaska Mountain Running series, and for the time being we didn't have any weekend adventures planned. I wanted to take my road bike down to the Homer Spit and ride sprint intervals along the bike path — my own weak nod to structured training. But after removing both wheels and stuffing the bicycle into the back seat of my Geo, the car refused to budge. It started up just fine, and the engine revved when I pressed the gas, but the car was stationary amid loud squealing and clanking noises.

I turned off the engine and popped the hood to assess the situation. Everything looked okay. There was no smoke. All the fluids were full. I bent down to examine the undercarriage, and noticed ice built up around all four tires. There had been heavy snowfall a few days earlier, and I hadn't driven since. Subsequent thaws piled up wet snow around the tires, and now the wheels were frozen in clumped ice. Chipping at them with my hands did nothing, and I didn't have a pickaxe or better tool that wouldn't damage my car. I speculated that in order to free the car, I'd have to boil a large amount of water to melt the ice. It seemed like more work than it was worth.

"Well, guess I'm mountain biking around here today."

The outside temperature was twenty-seven degrees as I suited up in my usual winter uniform of a fleece pullover, Burton shell, and rain pants. When I pulled my mountain bike onto the ice-slicked driveway, I noticed the air had a kind of earthy sweetness to it, almost springlike in quality. In town, spring mostly smelled like wet newspapers and dog feces, so this was a welcome aroma. I veered onto Geoff's snowshoe trail. It had been hard-packed during previous evenings, but today it was like pavement. The bike swooped down the flowing path, flawlessly gripping the hard turns cut by Geoff's running strides. I giggled out loud. How could I have even considered riding in the muddy part of town? This was going to be the best day for crust riding yet!

When the snowshoe trail ended, I pulled a small wheelie over the berm and rolled onto the snow crust. I felt a rush of freedom as I cut across the pristine surface, and began weaving erratically through the trees. I imagined myself as a snow rabbit evading a wolf, darting into gullies and sprinting up knolls. My leg muscles throbbed with the urgency of escape, and my throat burned in the cold air. Every breath was an audible marvel at how easy it was to transition from computer-screen drudgery and boxed breakfasts to this thrillingly primordial state of being.

Stamina faded as the forest corridor continued snaking upward, and logic reminded me that I wasn't actually being chased by a wolf. I continued climbing toward the crest of a ridge that I thought paralleled the reservoir. When I arrived at a small clearing, however, I didn't spot the frozen reservoir. I saw only forested hills, in all directions.

It occurred to me that I hadn't necessarily ridden in a straight line. I could have turned any number of directions while weaving through trees, and I had no idea which direction I was facing. The sky was a gray pall that hid the position of the sun, and I couldn't locate any of the taller mountains that might give an idea of which direction pointed east, south, or north. The snow I'd been riding atop was so hard that even my footprints didn't make an indentation. Bike tracks were nonexistent. I was, unintentionally, quite lost.

A small whimper escaped my throat. I chased it with a long, collecting sigh. "It's all right, it's okay," I whispered. I grasped for rational justifications to quell a surge of panic. "There are hours until dark, and it's pretty warm. I've been riding for only forty-five minutes. I just need to head down this hill and I'll find Geoff's trail in no time."

I reached for the water bottle on my frame. Only a few ounces of water remained. There was little in the way of food in my pack, but I had some extra clothing layers. I knelt down to collect snow to put in my bottle, but the bullet-proof crust would not break. Even after pounding at the snow with my fists and a tire lever, I only managed to free a few small chunks. The ground was a veritable road made of water, and had neither a real road to follow nor water to drink.

"Well, this is pretty stupid," I grumbled to myself. As I turned around, every corner of the forest looked the same. The clearing made a semi-circle, and I couldn't even say with certainty which line I'd ridden only moments earlier. Every tree I passed was another decision to make: do I turn left here, or right? Or straight? Backtracking forty-five minutes worth of erratic decisions started to look like an impossibly long distance.

"People die in the woods in Alaska, just like this, all the time," the little voice of panic whispered despite my best efforts to shut it out. I was only a few miles from my house, but that bastion of civilization was surrounded by thousands of acres of wilderness. It felt big even when I clung to the thread of trails that, no matter how faint or primitive, always promised to reel me back to safety and comfort. Without thinking I'd ventured off trail without a compass, maps or any extended sense of the region, and had to accept that I was hopelessly lost in my own back yard.

I jumped off my bike and walked slowly along the crust, scanning for any indication of my own bike tracks. After making several criss-crosses with no luck and fearing I'd lose my tentative bearing once again, I came up with the idea to mount the bike and flow like water down the hill, toward its inevitable arrival at the narrow gully I'd ridden when I first left Geoff's trail.

The hill that had seemed almost too steep to climb barely slumped downhill. I resisted the urge to pedal, having convinced myself that coasting with gravity would put me back on track, but the wheels stalled frequently enough that I had no choice. I sipped my meager water supply laced with dirty ice chunks and watched the overcast sky for hints of the sun. The temperature climbed with early afternoon, and droplets of water began to rain down from ice-crusted tree branches. It wasn't enough water to collect, but the continuous pitter-patter on the snow was maddening. I was very thirsty. But that felt less urgent than finding my way.

"People die in the woods in Alaska, just like this, all the time," an unhelpful mantra continued to loop through my head. As journalists often do when they find themselves in a tough spot, I imagined the headlines. "Homer Tribune arts reporter found dead near Bridge Creek." And the content of the article: "Homer's partner, construction worker and up-and-coming endurance runner Geoff Roes, was mystified by her disappearance. 'She trained all winter on these trails back here,' Roes said of the criss-crossing network of ski and snowmobile trails near their home on Diamond Ridge. 'After getting through something like the Susitna 100, I thought she at least knew how to use a compass. Plus, she told me she was going biking in town, so I just figured she'd been abducted or something. I didn't imagine she was lost in our back yard.' A neighbor who was out on his snowmachine collecting firewood discovered Homer's body less than a mile from the cabin she shared with Roes. A K-9 unit investigated the site and determined she had been circling a small area without stopping for three days before she succumbed to dehydration. No foul play is suspected in her death."

The heat of the day beat down, and each gulp I took to push back anxiety only further parched my dry throat. Clouds continued to hide the position of the sun, but the glare was so bright that the sky turned a withered shade of white. Snow began to collapse beneath my wheels, where weaker layers were melting beneath the icy crust. I reached my hand into the holes and scooped out handfuls of sugar snow to eat, but this did little to quell the thirst. Steeper slopes rose to the left, and I was hopeful that this was the Bridge Creek drainage, where I could climb directly uphill to reach Diamond Ridge. But in this barren maze of stick birch and spruce, I was fooling myself if I believed I could read the contours of the land against a vague memory of maps I hadn't looked at in months. How could I even be certain I was following a drainage? Maybe I was wandering in circles in a wide basin, or cutting due north toward the vast unpopulated interior of the Kenai Peninsula. Or, maybe, I'd entered a ripple in space-time and was stranded on Mars. How could I know?

The crust no longer held my weight. I could not ride my bike, and each step punched through icy snow up to my knees. Forward progress had been reduced to a trudge, but I took heart in the idea that I was at least making tracks now. At least I'd leave something behind, some indication I was here. And if I stumbled across these tracks again, I'd know it was time to panic.

With every wallowing step, my situation seemed more hopeless. And yet, my anxiety continued to diminish. It felt as though I'd gone through the initial realization and reaction. Once I had that adrenaline-driven episode out of my system, instinct took over the motions of doing what I needed to do to survive, which is stay calm and collected. I suckled the last droplets of water from my bottle and squinted through trees at the upper slopes for any sign of a cabin, or road, or anything. I'd become so uncertain of my direction that I started looking to the right as well, in case Diamond Ridge was in the opposite direction I expected it to be. I couldn't just pick a bearing and stick with it, because any wrong choice in direction would have me wandering long enough to die of dehydration. No, I needed to go west, then south. Boy, it was dumb not to carry a compass.

My mind entered a dull space as I trudged across the collapsing snow, scanning for any sign of civilization. Looking for random clues was the only idea I had at this point, but the odds of finding anything in this expanse of taiga were low enough that I couldn't let myself think too hard about it. Thinking about arriving safely at home only upset the delicate grip I held on my emotions.

Instead, I focused on Geoff, out for his Sunday run, and how surely he was somewhere nearby and would somehow find me out here, wandering through the woods. Illogically, I stopped every few minutes to hold my breath and listen for Geoff's footsteps. Droplets of melting ice continued to hit the snow with a rhythm and cadence that fooled me every time. Was that him? Was he here?

Only the melting snow answered, and the countless quiet "whomps" that preceded each collapse of the now-delicate crust under my feet. Underneath the shattering layers of snow were trickles of meltwater and larger streams that were waking up for the season. Moss growing around the trunks of the spruce trees glistened with an almost iridescent shade of green that I hadn't noticed before. Squirrels leapt between branches with a drunken awkwardness, as though they had only just awoken from hibernation. A spring that had taken months to emerge from winter was now accelerating toward summer at an astonishing rate.

The timing was not ideal. My legs crashed through the crust with every other step at this point, and I'd given up all hope of riding my bike — although going nowhere more quickly wasn't exactly going to end my predicament on its own. Still, instinctual urges kept inching toward the panic button, and my ability to sprint had been reduced to a glacial trudge. Even if I knew where I was going, I was not going to arrive there soon, but at least the slow pace gave me ample opportunities to continue my Easter-egg hunt for remnants of civilization. I found rusted tin panels and twisted metal beams only half exposed after a winter under the snow, but nothing promising for more recent human presence. Moose tracks were everywhere, and I glanced around nervously for unwanted glimpses of this territorial animal.

All the while, I strained to listen for sounds from Geoff. Not just another human, but Geoff specifically. I had no logical reason to believe he was anywhere near this spot, at the bottom of a canyon without established roads or trails, but the conviction that he must be nearby wouldn't let go. I hoped this was a glimmer of intuition, but suspected this was just another emotional coping mechanism — I couldn't let myself believe I was utterly alone. The truth was too dispiriting, so I created an impossible hope and clung to it in the face of all evidence to the contrary. "Geoff?" I called out as loud as I could muster. "Can you hear me?"

An afternoon wind was starting to pick up, and it answered me with un-settling eeriness —no. No one could hear me. Even though temperatures had climbed enough to melt snow, they were still well below comfortably warm. The breeze cut through my damp clothing and chilled my skin, reminding me of that edge on which I still teetered. There were still many hours before dark, but if night came before I found my way, I'd have no choice but to hunker down. I wondered whether I should start building a snow cave sooner, while the snow was still softened, rather than later, when I'd no doubt be desperate and clawing at ice. But even in a cave I'd struggle to make heat in my damp clothing with no fire. I had no fire starters and no headlight. I had no water or food. I had nothing I needed.

"People die in the woods in Alaska, just like this, all the time," the low, ominous warning cycled through my thoughts. "Geoff?" I called out loud, again, in response. "Anyone? I'm lost. Can you help me?"

The overcast sky lightened to a degree where I could see the obscured orb of the sun, almost directly overhead. Just as I pondered its position, I stumbled across a snowmobile track, faint and clearly old, but it continued to press a path into the crust along a frozen stream bed. This discovery didn't spark the joyous reaction I would have expected. It was something, but apparently not enough to quiet the jitters still vibrating just below the surface. I followed the track to where it intersected with other tracks. It was just a maze within a maze, drawn by hunters looking for game most likely, and any track I picked was just as likely to lead nowhere as somewhere.

But, it was something. The snow beneath the tracks remained compacted enough that I could ride my bike again, and I figured I'd just ride until I either found my way out or came across my own tracks, after which I'd at least know which trail not to take. The idea that I was doing something tangible toward my escape brought a new sense of purpose, and my anxiety relaxed enough that I became more acutely aware of my thirst and hunger.

Even as it quieted the panic, the snowmobile maze had an effect of causing me to feel even more unmoored than I was before. I'd managed to convince myself I was following Bridge Creek, and if I continued to move with my back to the sun, which was generally east, I'd find the dam. But now I wasn't so sure, and the tracks only took me deeper into the forest, possibly following different drainages. Still, it was something. Thoughts drifted back to Geoff. Now that I could no longer convince myself he was out there, I speculated where he might be. Probably back at home after his long run, showered, and tinkering with one of his eBay projects, or maybe he drove to town to browse the latest shipment of tools and materials at Ulmers, Homer's quintessential "everything" hardware store. Although our landlord refused to let us put a wood stove in the cabin, Geoff was determined to make our heating more energy and cost efficient, and had been researching options, putting up weather stripping, and coating the windows in plastic. This project was leading to more home improvement ambition, and our outdoor shed was slowly filling up with scrap wood, extra nails, and other dumpster finds in anticipation of future usefulness.

After six months in Alaska, Geoff had become more enamored with self-sufficiency and subsistence. The previous evening, we'd had a long conversation about stockpiling local foods over the summer for the following winter. He planned to start a garden and pick berries where he could, and wanted to find a local charter fisherman who'd be willing to let us clean boats or do other odd jobs in exchange for halibut and salmon. I'd managed to land a spot on a charter later that week as part of a tagging crew for the Chamber of Commerce halibut derby. Geoff was especially excited about the prospect of me catching two of my own fish. Our bedtime conversation revolved around making sure to keep the halibut cheeks and why twenty-five-pounders are tastier than hundred-pounders.

As lost as I was in the woods, I couldn't help but shake my head at the pretenses of home life. I loved these acts of nesting because it meant Geoff and I were building something together. But where it mattered, did it matter? By many standards we were barely scraping by. Did swabbing decks in exchange for a few pounds of fish really make a difference over longer hours at work? Geoff seemed to take the stance that food gathering was a virtue while slaving away in an office was a waste of life. Trading time for goods, or money, or personal gratification — each is infused with subjective standards by which deem our lives worthwhile. I craved interludes to the outdoors, which felt almost stolen from "real life." Because of this, I wanted them on my terms. I wanted to wander and observe; I didn't want to fixate only on what the land could give back to me.

These meandering and disconnected thoughts continued, as though I was subconsciously trying to distract myself from the bleak knowledge that while the land can provide bits and pieces of life over time, it can take away everything in an instant.

Lost, I imagined, was a strange state of limbo not unlike what one might experience in the final moments of life. It feels as though an anchor has been wrenched away, and there are moments of desperate grasping as we're set adrift. Unlike death, of course, lost is a conscious state. After the initial dismay comes acceptance, then rationalization, then a sort of curiosity. "Why have I never come down here before?" I wondered. "I live here. I should know this place."

Snowmobile tracks flowed through the forest, and I clung to the conviction that this was the right way, definitely the right way. I came across a faint mark over the trail that could have been my own tire tread, but I chose to interpret it as something else. As I followed what appeared to be the main track, the trail indeed became more defined from side tracks until it spilled out onto a corridor of what was almost certainly a road, at least in the summer. It climbed through the forest until I reached a bluff above a frozen body of water that was almost certainly Bridge Creek Reservoir, with a plowed road leading toward Skyline Ridge. Relief washed over me, but I was so emotionally drained that the joy I expected to feel was subdued. That came later, as I pedaled up Diamond Ridge

Road, processing the experience. I remained unsure of where I'd been or how I ended up above the reservoir. I was astonished with how lucky I'd been to stumble my way out.

"What am I going to tell Geoff about this ride?"

I didn't want to admit to getting myself lost in the woods, especially since it turned out to be a relatively short period of time. And yet, now that it was over, I felt only the thrill of adventure, of having survived another day, another wandering through the wild. As much as I was loathe to demean my own intelligence by admitting to being a thrill-seeker, it was impossible to connect with this invigorating sensation without the presence of risk. Whether the risk involved exposure to cold, or the fatigue of great distances, or the uncertainty of losing my way, the experiences reverberated with an intensity that I never experienced in my day-to-day life.

I found Geoff at home, on the couch reading a paperback novel. He said he was worn out from his run.

"I had an exciting ride," I told him. "I followed your trails into Bridge Creek and climbed up to the ridge above the reservoir. I rode on the crust and got a little bit lost."

Geoff asked me a few more questions about my route, and I admitted I couldn't piece it together entirely, other than weaving through the woods to was likely the western edge of Crossman Ridge, descending back into Bridge Creek, and feeling way more hopeless and lost than I actually was.

Geoff laughed. "Sounds awesome."

"I was scared," I admitted. "But important lessons were learned. I kept hoping I'd run into you out there. It was all in my head, but I had this strong sense that you were right there, really close by. Where did you go running?"

"Just around here. Homestead Trails. I came back just when things were starting to get sloppy. I followed the ski trails down that way, so who knows? Maybe we were close together."

"Huh. Well, I sure could have used your help. My sense of direction is awful."

Geoff laughed again. "I'm not touching that one."

I tended to lean on Geoff as a compass, both in adventures and in life. Maybe we did nearly cross paths in those meandering woods, or maybe I was just discovering what it felt like to navigate on my own, without anyone else showing me the way.

Indecision

June 4, 2006

Sorry for my absence. I spent a few days wallowing in indecision, like an uncomfortable dreamer locked in a losing fight for consciousness.

It's a strange state of discomfort — never quite in the moment, yet never able to completely let my mind wander. I'd stare vacantly at the back of the cereal box or watch my cat cross the yard and wonder where my mind had been. Did I draw any conclusions? What would I eat for dinner tonight? Would it really be all that unhealthy to eat cold cereal again? Finally, I'd give up and go for a bike ride.

That's how I did all of my riding this week – setting out without really deciding to do so. That's the conse-quence of having a big decision to make. It erodes your ability to make even the smallest decisions — decisions that are usually unconscious pieces of an everyday routine. One minute, I'd agonize over whether to take out the trash or wait until tomorrow. The next, I'd be spinning my mountain bike down Diamond Ridge and wondering how exactly I got there.

As a result, I generally had no idea where I was going. So I've been frequenting some old winter haunts — places I hadn't even thought to ride since breakup gave way to summer because, well, it just isn't that appealing to ride a full-suspension mountain bike on a smooth gravel road when so many clear trails and good pavement have opened up. But when autopilot kicked in, I'd find myself coasting down roads I'd ridden dozens of times, when they were cold, barren and covered in ice.

On Friday evening — before a long night of rockabilly at Kharacters and dancing with spit rats who chided me for my "affluence" (because I have a washer and dryer) — I had a rare moment of clarity at the top of Ohlson mountain. I had been really lost in thought for the better part of an hour. I remember little of the 13 miles that took me there and only vaguely recall the switchbacking climb to the top, mostly in short gasps. But I do remember standing beside a grove of lupine at the summit, emerging from my stupor just long enough to realize how lush and blindingly green everything was — as though I had expected the snow and silence and gray.

It really surprised me, not because the view was beautiful (although it was), but because my expectations of it deviated so drastically from the obvious. It's summer, I thought, and I'm in Alaska, and I've been here ten months, and I've never taken the time to really look at a devil's club blossom, and it's already summer. Suddenly, everything around me had a thrilling sort of novelty.

Sometimes I become so mired in the miles and routine that I fail to notice my world changing all around me. Such is the root of all indecision.

❋ ❋ ❋ ❋ ❋

Despite the seemingly sudden arrival of spring on Easter Sunday, it still took five more weeks for the snow around our house to disappear. By late May there was enough exposed grass in the backyard for Geoff to build an outdoor fire pit. Using a small chainsaw, he felled several dead trees around the perimeter of the cabin and cut them into logs. Outdoor lounging took over our evening routines — sitting next to the fire, reading New Yorker magazines and watching lazy sunsets paint the sky at eleven at night.

Our five-dollar thrift store television still broadcast only two static-filled networks, but outside our cats were a reliable source of entertainment. Midnight, the stoic black cat, kept her vigil on the porch as Cady, the hapless Siamese/tortoiseshell, went on laughably futile hunting excursions. A chorus of songbirds had arrived with the dandelions. Dozens of birds were pecking at the grass where Cady assumed a crouched position. Her stalking technique was so obvious that every single bird gave her the avian equivalent of the side-eye. Finally, an awkward pounce forced them into the air. Every time, Cady looked to the sky with a mournful gaze, as though this bird had been the ultimate prize — the one that got away.

Early in June, I spotted another young grizzly bear in our yard. She prowled through the carpet of dandelions and munched on grass for several minutes before sauntering back into the woods. While this didn't dampen my enthusiasm for our backyard campfires (bears are afraid of fire, aren't they?), it did give me pause about letting our cats roam free.

"I don't think it's safe for them," I told Geoff one evening.

"Do you really think they're going to be eaten by a bear?" he asked.

"I'm not sure," I said. "My co-worker Sean told me the story about a dog he used to have, one of those little dogs. He let it outside so it could run around the yard in the snow. One day, it just didn't come back. Sean went out and followed the dog's tracks in the snow until they just abruptly ended. There was a splatter of blood, and the dog was gone. Sean thinks it was carried away by an bald eagle."

"So eagles are going to eat the cats?"

I shrugged. "I don't know. But that grizzly bear is back. She looked hungry."

"Look at it this way," Geoff said. "The cats were miserable when they had to stay inside all winter. Midnight is so much happier now."

"And Cady's nemesis is making me crazy," I said. Cady was regularly engaging in cat fights with one of Carey's cats, a long-haired female named Tasha. Their yowling brawls woke us up nearly every night. Recently Cady had limped home with one of her ears pierced and bleeding.

"Do you really think we should confine them inside because there are wild animals in Alaska? What kind of life is that?"

"For a cat, a pretty normal one," I retorted.

"Yeah," Geoff replied. "That's the problem."

As our cats enjoyed a more feral lifestyle, Geoff and I adapted to the relative ease of summer. He landed fewer construction jobs as temperatures rose and more qualified workers stepped back into the employee pool, but his eBay business was thriving. Now that roads were no longer slicked in ice and snow, he used his car every day to transfer packages to and from the post office. He still trolled the city dump for treasures, but more often went to the hardware store to purchase supplies for his home improvement projects. He constructed fire pit benches from new two-by-fours, and re-enforced the shed with more shelves for his eBay inventory. On the other side of the yard, Geoff cleared a small patch for a garden and planted seeds.

"Carey says moose are going to eat everything in that garden unless we buy an electric fence," I said.

He shrugged. "I just want to see what I can get to grow up here."

The rest of the yard was bursting with manic growth. Besides the golden carpet of dandelions, thick stalks of cow parsnip opened their white, umbrella-like blooms. Purple lupine lined the road, and magenta fireweed blossoms opened all at once. Most of my nine months of Alaska residency had been shrouded in white and gray, and this sudden burst of color was startling. The neighborhood moose, which had retreated elsewhere during the depths of winter, were back and more active than ever. Several cows had tiny calves that tottered alongside them on the road.

June meant leaving work when the sun was still bright and hot, and riding home without any of the urgency to which I'd grown accustomed. Often I'd stay in my bike shorts and jersey while Geoff and I ate dinner, and head back out for a few more miles of cycling in the evening. As the sun made its wide arc over the horizon, I pedaled the perimeter of Diamond Ridge neighborhoods, sniffing out new trails. The ski trails had flooded with snow melt and were too boggy to ride, but several ATV trails revealed themselves after the snow melted. The discovery of a new spur was always cause for exploration, even if it meant pedaling through thick mud for half a mile before reaching yet another dead end.

There were other nights when I coasted back into town to watch sunset over Kachemak Bay, photographing bald eagles as they circled a background of sky and water that exploded with crimson light. Riding home from these late-evening excursions, I'd marvel at the utterly empty streets. Where was everybody? Time seemed to stand still as dusk lingered in the midnight sky.

Both Geoff and I kept the fitness routine alive with our summer goals in mind. While I trained for the twenty-four-hour race, Geoff registered for the Alaska Mountain Runners Grand Prix. The first event of the season was an up-hill-only race just south of Anchorage, ascending Powerline Pass from a roadside rest stop on the Turnagain Arm. The course followed a popular hiking trail that gained 3,500 feet of elevation in about four miles. I opted to miss the start of the race in order to catch the finish, setting out an hour before the runners.

It was the first truly hot weekend of the year, with ambient temperatures in the high seventies. Despite the warmth, the seasons regressed as I ascended the mountain, from the green plumage of summer, to the closed buds of spring, to rocky tundra still covered in snow. A narrow strip of dirt trail along a sheer cornice allowed hikers to skirt around the snow fields, but the trail still frequently disappeared beneath slushy drifts. The steepness of the grade was unrelenting — a muddy staircase without the benefit of stairs.

"Damn, this is going to be a tough race," I thought, and just as soon as I thought it, I heard a shuffle of footsteps from behind. I turned to see the beet-red face of a runner who momentarily looked up from his hunched position. Even though the steepness of the trail nearly forced me on all fours, he was moving at a solid running pace.

"Crap, they're here already," I thought.

After another man passed I raced behind him, but failed to hold his pace. My lungs burned and I could feel my own face twisting into an agonized grimace. Disappointment injected itself into gasps as I realized that either Geoff wasn't going to finish well in this race, or I wasn't going to see him finish. I checked over my shoulders as I continued to run — well, trudge forcefully — beside the neck-high cornice.

Geoff caught up to me about a hundred meters from the finish, in fifth position. Just ahead were crowds of spectators gathered along a saddle and four runners in various states of collapse next to the trail. I pulled over just before the finish line, drawn with flour in the dirt, and took his photo as he passed. He was hunched over almost in an L-shape, pressing his hands into his knees.

"You're doing awesome. Almost there!" I yelled.

Geoff just exhaled. "Hmmmph."

I didn't want to steal his thunder, so I hung back and waited until he crossed the finish line before I hiked the rest of the way to the top. He gave me a hug and then went to shake the podium finishers' hands. Geoff looked winded but not as shattered as the other guys, one of whom was sprawled face down on the dirt.

"How was it?" I asked.

"Shit," he said, still panting. "Fuck, that was hard." As he uttered a few more expletives, a grin peeled across his face.

"You got fifth place, that's so awesome," I said.

"Those guys are strong," he said. "It would take a lot to win." I could see by the expression on his face that by the end of the season, he intended to rise to the top of Alaska Mountain Running. After forty-five minutes of running, he was ninety seconds back from first place.

We lounged at the pass for another fifteen minutes, greeting a steady stream of finishers. Despite the warm morning, there was a cold wind at the ridge. Geoff was shivering, so we started back down the mountain. All of his muscles had stiffened up, and he limped rigidly along the edge of the cornice.

"I can't believe it only took you forty-five minutes to climb this," I said. "It was really hard in an hour and forty-five."

"I bet you'd like these mountain races," Geoff said. "They favor hiking and you're a strong hiker. I'm probably better at running flat and fast stuff, but this is more fun."

I regarded the faces of runners still ascending the mountain, some almost twisted in agony. I'd had some tough moments in the Susitna 100, but all of these people appeared to be in real pain.

"I don't know," I replied. "I think I'll stick to hiking for fun."

✳ ✳ ✳ ✳ ✳

The 24 Hours of Kincaid took place on the weekend of the summer solstice, when the sun made its widest arc through the northern sky. Geoff and I arrived at the staging area late in the evening, just as sunset took a brief intermission behind the Alaska Range. We set up my "pit" and crawled into the tent to rest before the start. Geoff would serve as my race crew, lubing squeaky bike parts and making sandwiches. I would race to discover just how far I could ride a bicycle in one day.

Hour zero arrived at high noon. The first lap launched in a flurry of confusion as racers dashed across a soccer field toward mountain bikes lined up in a mismatched row. I was one of the last to find my bike, and rushed to catch up with the field. At the edge of the park, the trail funneled into a narrow corridor beneath a canopy of birch trees, often no wider than my handlebars. The serpentine trail had many spurs. Despite straining to pay attention to the neon ribbons that marked the course, I veered off route early and had to backtrack in the first half mile. Cleanly in the back of the pack, I mashed the pedals over roots and around tight corners, desperate to catch the others. I'd never be able to sustain this pace, not even for one lap, but the urgency of competition sent me into a panic.

Despite the intense effort, tenths of miles clicked by too slowly as the surface of the trail continued to deteriorate. Thick roots braided through a patchwork quilt of mud, wet leaves, and devil's club vines. I plummeted off rocky drops and dabbed my feet against trees. At mile three, the bike bucked me off the saddle into a thorny patch of Devil's Club. I stood up with mud smeared across my face and blood trickling down my arm.

"Damn it!" I called out, to no one, because I was still in last place. Amid my recent transition to hardcore endurance athlete, I'd neglected to acknowledge that my past experience included almost no technical mountain biking. I went straight from road touring to snow biking, and neither of these disciplines developed the skills necessary to pilot a bike efficiently over roots, rocks, and mud. The unsettling realization that I actually had no idea how to ride technical singletrack overshadowed my physical distress. I walked my bike down the next steep descent, and pedaled lightly through the forest maze as tree branches grabbed at my shoulders.

"I'm going to have to quit after just one lap," I lamented. "I suck."

"No!" Adventure Jill shouted back. "What has endurance racing taught you?" It didn't matter how slowly I moved, as long as I kept moving forward. I had twenty-four hours, after all, and I didn't have anywhere else to be. If I could just finish one lap, I had no reason to believe I couldn't do it again and again.

The course crossed a road onto smoother double track, and I threw my new resolve into powering up a steep climb. I even managed to pass a few people to relinquish last place, and finished up the eleven-mile lap on a squeal-inducing roller coaster of a descent. One hour and sixteen minutes had passed since the start, and I'd already forgotten how upset I'd been.

"That was awesome," I exclaimed to Geoff as he approached me with a peanut butter and strawberry jam sandwich that he had lovingly cut into quarters. "Oh man, the first half is hard, really technical. But the second half has one amazing descent. It's really fun."

After three more laps, the effort ground into my back and legs. My stomach lurched at the sight of Geoff's peanut butter sandwiches, and I doubled over as I stepped off the bike, gulping from an urge to vomit.

"Maybe you should lie down," Geoff suggested. I sprawled out on the grass and drew in quick, shallow breaths. A soccer scoreboard, broadcasting the race clock, spun in my peripheral vision.

"I don't feel good at all," I whined. "I'm not sure I can go out again."

"Take as long as you need," he said. As I took exaggerated deep breaths, Geoff filled me in on the action in the staging area. "Pete comes in every hour, grabs a bottle out of his cooler, throws the empty bottle on the ground, and then just leaves," he said, describing the rider currently leading the solo race. "That's all he has. That one cooler."

Geoff had been noting my lap times on a piece of paper, and regularly checked my position on the board. He was kind enough not to divulge exactly where I fell in the standings, only telling me, "You're doing so well."

Geoff had a large capacity for compassion; this was something I appreciated most about him. He distributed this compassion evenly to everyone he met, which is why as his girlfriend I sometimes felt left behind. But when all of his empathy was focused solely on me, I felt a surge of love that had the power to pull me out of dark and hopeless places.

"I was going to go for a run," he said. "Maybe we could go out for this next lap together."

"You want to run while I ride?" I asked, skeptical.

"Yeah," he said. "It will be fun."

It seemed an unfair but potentially motivating competition — although in Geoff's defense, he never used the word "race." We took off together, and hopscotched positions frequently on the technical trail — mostly because he stopped to wait for me and take photos. After the downhill hike-a-bike, he took off and I never saw him again. The laps were now taking me more than an hour and a half to finish, and Geoff ran the eleven-mile course faster than that.

I felt demoralized. Sure, I still appreciated the loving support Geoff had shown me, and "racing" was probably the farthest thing from his mind. But this was a race — I was racing other bikers, and I was racing myself. In this regard, I had failed. A runner shouldn't be able to beat a biker. It seemed like another example of all the ways Geoff excelled at life while I floundered.

"Hey how did it go?" he asked when I returned to the pit. He'd made another sandwich for me. "Are you feeling better?"

"I suppose so," I replied. Racing Geoff around lap five had taken my mind off my sour stomach. I choked down the sandwich and realized some of my energy had returned. Maybe I needed a little hurt and anger to shake up my complacency. That's what it took to move to Alaska, and that's what it was going to take to stick out Kincaid.

Twenty-four-hour racing has elements that mimic years of a life. We circle an endless loop as a clock keeps ticking, striving toward a destination that is not a place, but simply a finish. Hearts flutter and legs flounder. People orbit in and out of our periphery, in a place where anguish and compassion can be shared amid a midnight conversation about television cartoons. Through these brief connections, we feel an intensity of empathy and understanding that binds us together as a community. Each circumnavigation leaves us wiser, more familiar with the obstacles ahead, and also more skilled. As miles add up, they also leave us more broken, leaning on aged muscles and overstretched tendons, nursing scraped skin and bruises — the scars of experience. Eventually the clock simply runs out and we limp into the finish, stooped over handlebars, bodies utterly spent, with a depth of satisfaction that can only echo from a race well lived.

Sometime around two in the morning, sunlight finally faded below the horizon. I was in the prime of my race life, with a comfortable routine to each mile and a technique for even the most difficult obstacles. Nine laps were behind me and I was nearing expert status for this single strip of trail. I threaded the wheels through root mazes and deftly navigated rock gardens. Smooth doubletrack was a place for contemplation, to marvel at the salmon-hued sky and the fact that I had ridden my bike nearly one hundred miles — and there was so much life left in me.

During the darkest minutes between dusk and dawn, I switched on a tiny headlamp and cast flickering shadows on the tree maze. Birch trees twisted into menacing silhouettes. My mind was foggy, flickering imperceptibly between the past and the present. Along the roller coaster descent, I rounded a corner and nearly collided with the backside of a bull moose as he reclined in the grass. Brown haunches materialized from a shadowy blob, and I had slammed on my brakes and squealed to a stop before I even realized what I was about to hit. As my vision focused, the moose looked up with infinitely black eyes and antlers as wide as my whole bicycle. I exhaled a timid squeak; the moose just blinked and regarded me with indifference. As he lowered his head and went back to ignoring me and the other cyclists who continued to pass without stopping, I stood for several more minutes, paralyzed with primordial instinct. Clearly the moose didn't care about a mountain bike race; he was king of the forest and he would nap wherever he liked. I mustered courage and tiptoed around him, shaking with adrenaline. By the following lap, when the moose was still there, I was fully desensitized and roared past like everyone else.

The hours began to blur together. The sun was bright and hot again, but the race clock was still many hours away from twenty-four. Geoff went to sleep for two laps, leaving me sandwiches, still lovingly cut into quarters, in the cooler. The staging area was almost completely still, with the beer-drinking team racers in their tents, and the solo racers scattered along the course. I arrived at my pit at the same time as Pete, whose shade tent and cooler were positioned next to our site. Pete's legs were crusted with mud, and he stooped painfully to open his cooler. He regarded me with a smile and I grinned back, feeling as though we were sharing a wonderful secret. "Good luck," I said shyly as he surged away, a ghost in the sunlit night.

I lost track of my emotions — fear, angst, fatigue, and excitement all boiled together into a beige contentedness. I was a machine built to ride bikes. Technical descents no longer slowed me at all. I may or may not have been riding well, but I was too tired to care about the consequences. I released the brakes and barreled down minefields of roots, tossed from side to side. I gripped the handlebars and tucked my butt behind my saddle, instinctively holding onto the only thing that mattered to me at this point — momentum.

My forearms felt like they were being pierced with needles. My hands were so rigid that I could barely peel them away from the grips, and my shoulders burned as though the bones had been replaced by fire irons. I didn't want to visualize the horrors that were happening under my bike shorts, but stinging pains gave me an idea. Still, I was thrilled with how forceful my momentum had become. Geoff told me there were no solo women left in the race, and I was now behind only a handful of men.

"If you can wrap up this lap in time to go out for another, you might end up in third overall," he said.

Energized by this news, I pedaled into lap sixteen about fifteen minutes before 11 a.m. I would need to put in my best effort to finish the lap before noon, wherein race rules would let me embark on another. But if I arrived after noon, my race would be over. My aches and pains had amplified to the point that I could no longer ignore them. I did not want to do any more laps, but the little voice of Adventure Jill still resonated.

"Just imagine, third place. Geoff will be so proud."

I gathered the beige mass of emotions to muffle the excess noise in my head. Hunched in, I let the trail come to me. Now that my race life was nearly over, I had nothing left to lose. My body would be needed for only a few more miles, and then rest would come either way. I intended to go out with a bang.

Legs aching, heart pumping, every muscle in my upper body searing in pain, I rolled to the staging area having given lap sixteen everything I had. It wasn't good enough. The race clock read 12:04. The race official made a single check on her clipboard, and that was it. I was done. My lips curled into a numb half-smile. A warm satisfaction surged in my chest, and that was all that seemed to matter. Geoff jogged up from our pit and wrapped his arms around me while I continued to straddle my bike.

"Awesome job," he said. My effort was still good enough for fifth place. I had beaten a couple dozen men, as well as the three other solo women in the race. Just by moving forward.

Moving on Up (er, Down)

July 18, 2006

Well, I'm moving to Juneau. It sounds a bit rash, I know, but it's actually the culmination of several weeks of events that started the day they handed me number 111 at the 24 Hours of Kincaid (Elevens, my friend Ryan always told me, signify shifts in universal or personal patterns.) Anyway, the next day I received a cold call from the Juneau Empire. Next month, I'm going to be working there. Crazy how quickly life can shift gears.

While Juneau is technically in the same state I live in now (and who am I kidding ... it's the capitol), moving there is no small matter. It's about the distance equivalent of moving from Denver to San Francisco, if the only way to get to San Francisco was to drive to a tiny up-state town like Arcata and then hop a slow-moving ferry down the coast. Oh ... and throw in an international border crossing as well. I might as well move to Seattle. At least it stops raining there once in a while.

But that's precisely the reason I'm excited. Juneau is this mysterious community isolated by a wall of steep, vast mountains and hundreds of miles of remote coastline. With 30,000 people, it's the second largest city in Alaska and the center of its government — all squashed into this unlikely place teeming with bears and avalanche danger. As a former denizen of the wide-open Mountain West, who grew up with Interstate dependence flowing through her veins, I find this kind of lifestyle very intriguing. So I'm going to give it a try.

Also, I'm completely in love with Alaska, and I realize that I've scratched only a small surface of this bewildering state. Moving to Juneau, I know, isn't exactly going to open up opportunities to move freely through the Arctic. And yet — it's another piece of a vast puzzle. For that reason, I couldn't resist.

When I think about leaving Homer, I feel sad. I feel anxious. I feel anticipation. I feel angry at myself. I feel excited. I feel terrified. I feel like I need to stop thinking about it even if it does make the hill intervals go faster. Change is so hard, and unfortunately I'm one of those people who thrives on it, craves it, consumes it with reckless abandon. I like the fact that there's something new around the corner. It gives the present so much more meaning.

✳ ✳ ✳ ✳ ✳

The call came just a few days after Kincaid. A tattered number plate was still pinned to the handlebars of my bike. I huddled next to it in our shed, unintentionally brushing clumps of mud from the frame onto my jeans. I swatted at them vigorously, removing evidence of the fact I was hiding in the shed. As soon as the caller had identified herself as "the managing editor of the Juneau Empire," I knew that I needed to find a private place to continue the conversation. She told me the Juneau Empire was in need of a weekend editor. The job entailed working nights and weekends on the copy desk, editing wire stories and designing news pages. She noticed I'd won an award from the Alaska Press Club, and based on that alone, offered me the position up front.

"Are you interested in working for a daily newspaper in Southeast Alaska?" she asked.

Was I interested? I had been unsatisfied with my current job for quite some time. At the Homer Tribune I made twelve dollars an hour, had no health insurance, and felt no particular sense of loyalty to an employer who shuffled me into advertising work without my consent. But how could I move away from Homer? Just the thought of losing the beauty of this region was enough to break my heart.

And speaking of broken hearts, would Geoff be willing to start over with me again? I couldn't be sure he'd choose our relationship over the life we'd established in Homer. It didn't seem likely that he'd be excited about Juneau. Geoff and I had visited Juneau once before as well — three years earlier — arriving by the state ferry during our big Alaska road trip. We huddled in tents at a "campground" that was actually a city-sanctioned homeless camp. Most of the other tenants lived in tarp shanties, and the designated kitchen shelter was a dilapidated haven for mice and rats. Our only hope for (cost-free) respite from constant sogginess was the local library. Days were gray and melancholy, nights were damp and cold, and my sleeping bag was growing mold by day three. The weather forecast promised at least another week of the same, and locals told us that nonstop rain was not unusual. Juneau makes Seattle look like a sunny paradise. It was enough to convince us both that Juneau was the worst place in all of Alaska. Still, we'd also bestowed that designation on Homer, and look how Homer turned out for us. Even Geoff agreed that ignoring first impressions and moving to Homer anyway was one of the best decisions he ever made. Maybe he'd be equally interested in expanding our Alaska adventure to the soggy Southeast.

The editor offered six weeks to make the transition, a salary that was nearly double what I was earning, moving expenses, and benefits. No interview was required — the job was as good as mine. I all but said yes over the phone, but still waited several more days before I broke the prospect to Geoff. His reaction was both understandably skeptical ("Juneau, really?") and surprisingly indifferent, ("Sure, why not?")

"Aren't you going to miss Homer?" I asked.

Geoff shrugged. "Yeah, definitely. But there's so much I haven't seen in Juneau. There are big mountains right outside town there. And yeah, the weather sucks, but it's not great here, either. I don't mind running in the rain." In Geoff's view, newness and exploration was always preferable to comfort and familiarity.

A few days later — before I'd yet broken the news to my boss — my co-workers gathered for a bonfire on the Homer Spit beach. It was nearly the Fourth of July, the third anniversary of our initial escape from Homer. Sand-blasting gusts of wind kept the crowds away, and we huddled next to burning driftwood as cold air pummeled our backs and salty moisture clung to our skin. At midnight, an electric sunset faded into the bay, and Sean broke out a bottle of Jagermeister. I'd been saying no to beer all night, but relented to a few shots of liquor to "warm the core." Layton showed up with the Kilcher cousins, and my heart fluttered as I shared a long, tipsy gaze with Eivan.

Geoff didn't seem to notice as he knocked back more Jagermeister with Sean, and I wondered how much he'd care if he did notice. Geoff and I had a wonderfully symbiotic relationship, and I felt love for him in the only way I ever understood love. Still, Geoff was the first to remind me that life is impermanent, and it was futile to expect that nothing would change when, in fact, everything changes, always. The prospect of something new and exciting tugged at both of our hearts. Eivan and Layton danced along the shoreline, almost too drunk to stand. Geoff and Sean cackled wildly at nothing, and I felt a surge of affection for the people I was going to leave behind. I understood in that moment that nothing could ever be the same, and that was okay.

I staggered back to my car in the violet dawn of 2 a.m., realizing that I was too drunk to drive. It was the first time I'd been drunk since my blackout the previous summer, and I was angry at myself for returning to this state — inebriation and the amplification of shallow emotions. Excitement and acceptance of change swung back to disgust and fear. Was I really different than I was a year ago? Had Alaska changed anything, or had I just drifted from one escapist mechanism to another, pretending that change was my only choice because the other option — inertia — was so terrifying?

✸ ✸ ✸ ✸ ✸

The Soggy Bottom 100 was another mountain bike race I'd signed up for in my post-Susitna 100 frenzy. The hundred-mile race over Resurrection Pass was two weeks before my first day of work at the Juneau Empire. Stress had gotten the better of me, and I was mired in the logistics of moving to a new city that was seven hundred miles away. I felt underprepared and undertrained. Geoff had signed up for a trail-running race in the same region that weekend — Crow Pass Crossing — so we agreed to keep this trip on the schedule. On my blog I feigned excitement for another endurance challenge, but quietly I felt like the Soggy Bottom was just another hurdle I had to clear.

Geoff and I drove north to Girdwood, where his race was set to start. We kissed each other for good luck, and then I drove his Honda Civic back to the coastal community of Hope, alone. I set up my tent on the grass next to the Seaview Cafe and Bar — a rustic building with white paint peeling off the wood, and loud bluegrass music vibrating through the walls. Riotous laughter rang out through the night, and deepening twilight reminded me how much sleep I was missing. Around 3 a.m., I crawled out of my tent and ate dry cereal several hundred yards from my campsite, just in case there were bears nearby. I missed Geoff, and wished I'd accompanied him to cheer for his race. Riding my mountain bike a hundred miles over muddy mountain trails was not something I wanted to do at this point in time. What did I have left to prove?

An hour before the 9 a.m. start time, the race director, Carlos, rousted the group by walking among the tents and calling out, "Time to ride!" About two dozen bleary-eyed bikers eventually funneled toward a starting line, which Carlos had drawn with chalk on the street in front of the Seaview Cafe. As far as I could tell, I was the only woman in the crowd. Carlos yelled "go," and we took off in a pace line that quickly fractured in two — fast, aggressive racers at the front, and not-as-fast-but-still-aggressive chasers in the back. Even the not-as-fast group held a pace that was near the limits of my abilities. My vision blurred and legs burned, and I had to sprint to keep up with them. I felt dangerously close to burning out in the first five miles, but I couldn't afford to fall off the back of the race yet. The course wasn't marked, and I didn't know the way to the Resurrection Pass trailhead — a 38-mile long strip of singletrack that connected Hope to Cooper Landing. If I lost my way at this point, it would be the end of my race. A forceful inner voice asked whether that mattered, and I shoved the thoughts away.

Sheer desperation let me hang onto the pack long enough to reach the trail, which cut away from the smooth gravel road onto an unpleasantly rocky and jarring path through the forest. I continued to chase after boys, convinced that this is what racers did. The pace remained fierce, and by the time I climbed above tree line — about twenty-five miles into the race — I'd entirely unraveled. Besides burning all of my energy on the climb, I'd been thrown from the bike several times when I slammed the front wheel into a rock or overshot a hairpin turn. Knees bloodied and face smeared in mud, I knew that slowing down was my only hope for survival. Maybe I'd come in last, and maybe that was okay. Not finishing at all was a concept that filled my heart with dread. Even though I wavered on starting the race, I hadn't given much thought to the prospect of dropping out. I went into the Susitna 100 with such fierce dedication that I just assumed I'd either finish the race or die trying. The 24 Hours of Kincaid was an automatic finish — even one lap counted. The Soggy Bottom 100 traveled over the Resurrection Pass trail and back with a spur out the Devil's Pass trail, offering multiple chances to leave the course. I could drop out at the next trailhead and no longer have to push through the pain in my knees, or endure the crushing fatigue. It would be easy, and I'd be the only one who cared. Why was I so afraid to quit?

I let these thoughts fester as I descended through the glacier valley beside several lakes and a raging stream. It was a beautiful course, and I had to admit that nothing was inherently wrong with me. I reached the far end of the trail, Cooper Landing, with forty-five miles on the odometer. Carlos stood next to his vintage camper in the parking lot, doling out Vanilla Wafers and Gatorade.

"Isn't the Devil's Pass spur twenty miles out and back?" I asked him.

"That's about right," he said.

"So that would make this race more like a hundred and ten miles," I croaked. Cookie crumbs were lodged in the back of my throat.

Carlos shrugged. "That's about right."

Mud-splattered cyclists were still descending toward the trailhead as I climbed out; this surprised me, as I'd just assumed I was at the back of the race. As I pedaled, masticated Vanilla Wafers tumbled around in my stomach like wads of paper in a washing machine.

"Those were a mistake," I thought. I felt desperately thirsty, and had two liters of water in my backpack, but felt too nauseated to ingest anything else.

Wispy clouds descended into the canyon, hanging like silk drapes over the mountains. The lower canyon was choked with overgrown shrubs, which whipped me in the face in slow motion. The trail was a thin ribbon of mud sliced with deep bike ruts, many of which had already been trammeled by fresh bear prints. My race-required bear bell hung from the saddle, cheerfully jingling in a way that was beginning to rattle my sanity. "Hey bear!" I called out to nothing. "Hey bear!"

Hemlock forests became groves of spindly shrubs, and then rocky tundra as I gained Resurrection Pass for a second time. Purple lupine lined the trail, and yellow blooms emerged from a patchwork of matted grass — summer erupting from a landscape that had been covered in snow very recently. Clouds were beginning to lift; I could see patches of blue in the sky. Despite all this vibrant beauty, my mind was still foggy, and my gut was raw. The Soggy Bottom was my third endurance race, and I understood well the consequences of bonking. I knew calories were the only solution for my woes, but even thoughts of eating upset my stomach. I could still taste Vanilla Wafers — a flavor that had become extremely unpleasant — and battled an urge to vomit. Peanut butter sandwiches would never work. My snack stash also included a single packet of Gu, which was a remnant of my swag bag from the 24 Hours of Kincaid. The Gu was vanilla flavored. I pushed the packet of sludge to the back of my mouth, squeezed it into my throat, then gagged immediately. Choking forced me onto my knees, hands pressed into the mud as I spit up most of the snot-like substance. Finally I caught my breath, and promised myself that Gu would never pass through my lips again. But what to do about the bonking? I'd think about that later.

My odometer told me I'd traveled seventy-eight miles when I descended to the Devil's Pass trailhead, where Carlos was waiting. He'd run out of Vanilla Wafers and Gatorade, so the roving aid station had no aid. This didn't matter to me. "Bout thirty-five more miles," he said, and I nodded. The concept had become too abstract for me to visualize. What was thirty-five miles? Or a hundred? Or a thousand? Several riders were sprawled on the pavement. Some were rifling through packs, and others were lying on their backs and staring vacantly at the sky. I understood that their races were likely ending here. Their defeated postures looked so appealing. Did I have a good reason to quit? This concept also was too abstract to quantify.

As I climbed toward Devil's Pass, I didn't see anybody else. In all likelihood, I was at the back of the race now. Bear tracks were everywhere, all but erasing evidence of other cyclists. "Hey bear?" I called out weakly. I imagined families of black bears prowling for racers they could scare away from their backpacks. "You can have my gross peanut butter sandwiches if you want," I shouted. "Just don't eat me."

The trail again rose out of the forest, where fog-shrouded mountainsides curled into the tundra. Sunlight flickered through rolling clouds, and I felt as though I was looking at the surface of a clear lake that had just been broken by waves. I blinked rapidly to shake away a sudden dizziness, but it was too late. My front wheel veered off the rocky slope and plunged into a steep embankment. My shoulder hit the rocks as a loud crack reverberated through my helmet, and then I tumbled for several seconds before an alder thicket broke my fall. I'd tumbled more than twenty feet from the trail, into a dry creek bed. Alder branches were tangled around every limb. It would take a few minutes of thrashing to free myself, and in the immediate aftermath of the fall, I felt too weak to fight this battle. For an indeterminate amount of time that might have been a second or hours, I lay very still, draped like a rag doll over the alder bush with my chin angled to the sky. My heart beat in synchrony with the streaming clouds, and my breathing slowed to a tranquil rhythm. It was nice to stop moving.

Eventually common sense knocked from behind the stupor and demanded to find out whether I was broken or bleeding. Alder branches clung to my jersey and tights as I writhed, finally rolling onto the steep embankment next to my overturned bike. The motions necessary to free myself assured me that I wasn't badly hurt. I wondered what might have happened if I had broken a bone; there was a chance no riders were approaching from behind, and Carlos was not the type of race director to fret about long absences. I might have been stranded here for a long time.

"Be more careful," I breathed as I wrestled the bike up the steep embankment. Endurance mountain biking was such a ridiculous endeavor. If the constant physical strain wasn't enough, we were taking our efforts to the wilderness where bears and moose lurked in shadows, rugged terrain demanded constant vigilance, the consequences of mistakes could be grave, and help was far away. I was born into a privileged society where comfort and security were just handed to me, and it took only minimal effort to maintain them. This society taught me that time is best spent gaining more comfort and security, and only fools would throw away energy on a task that promised only struggle and pain.

I wiped mud from my knees and rotated my right arm. My shoulder was sore, but at least the joint was still attached. I continued pushing my bike up the trail, walking while I waited for involuntary shivering to subside. The clouds grew thick again and my head was foggier than ever, flickering between dreamy abstractions and anxious jolts of awareness. During these increasingly short periods of lucidity, I groped for bearings. "There's the A-frame." "This must be near the top of the pass, twenty-five more miles." "I don't remember these rocks. The mountains look different. Am I still on the right trail? Am I still in Alaska?" I couldn't be sure.

Dizziness returned as soon as I started pedaling again, and I nearly dumped the bike over another precipitous drop. I knew I had no choice but to sit on a rock and force down one of my sandwiches. I took slow bites amid waves of nausea and wondered how Geoff had fared in the Crow Pass Crossing. His race was twenty-four miles over a similarly rugged mountain pass, and he thought it would take him three hours and change to finish. I looked at my watch. It was six in the evening. What did that mean? How long had I been out here? It felt like years.

Memories collided with the present until time lost its elasticity. I imagined Geoff greeting me at the finish line in a far-away future. He'd look mostly the same, but with wrinkles carved into his face and a wild gray beard. The Seaview Cafe would be boarded up, the sky would have a red tint, and the whole marsh would be flooded with murky sea water from the oceans rising. "What happened?" I would ask, and Geoff would say, "You've been missing for forty years." We'd share a bewildered gaze, and I wouldn't know what to say, because what do you say after forty years?

I glanced down at my hands, which were smeared with dirt that made them look gnarled and aged. My grasp on reality was slipping, and I could almost convince myself that maybe, just maybe, time could dissolve. I looked up and remembered myself as a six-year-old child, tucking my head between my knees and tumbling down the grass of the hill behind my elementary school. Land and sky spun together in a dizzying kaleidoscope then, just as it did now. Dew would soak through my shirt as blood filled my head, carrying the sensation I was seeking — a feeling I still couldn't describe. It transcended the definition of fun to something deeper, and more lasting. When I rolled through the grass as a child, the world wrapped itself around my body and filled me with the vitality of life.

Finding that energy was so simple then, but the decades have a fatiguing effect. Our hearts become worn, and we can no longer feel the raw exuberance that we experienced as children. Or could we? Is it just that we forgot how simple it is? Adults tend to reject the notion of limitless possibilities, and instead cling to assumptions that offer comfort and security. Those who would throw themselves down a hill would be labeled as crazy, and those who choose to ride a mountain bike a hundred miles through Alaska wilderness are not far behind.

But I wasn't crazy, not quite — nor was I the brave athlete I wanted to be. I was a child again — a child and an old woman, straddling the great gap between consciousness and dreams. Images of Juneau flickered into my disconnected thoughts, with curtains of rain draped over drab and weathered buildings. For a place in my near future, it seemed impossibly far away. The finish of the Soggy Bottom 100 was just as distant. My mind and body were stalled in this present — a loop of pedal strokes, driven by shivering and exhaustion, as I traced a ribbon of trail that might have no end.

I shook my head, fighting a sleepiness that threatened to fully unravel my mind. I fixated on thoughts of Juneau and wondered what new adventures the city would bring. Would I enjoy my job? Would Geoff and I find an equally nice place to live? Would we meet good friends? What adventures would we find? Would we pursue all the same hobbies? Would I continue to ride my bike over the mountains, searching for new sources of raw exuberance? Is this all there was?

The sky darkened. I looked up from my trail of thoughts and felt anxiety. I wondered whether this was a storm, or simply the coming of night. Light rain began to fall, but I continued to fear night. The forest grew thick with wet hemlock branches, and the trail turned rockier. My bike bucked and shimmied, injecting hot pain into my shoulders.

There were so many rocks. Each one required gentle finessing to minimize pain, which motivated me to re-focus all of my fractured attention on the present. In this state of mind, immediate obstacles were all that existed. Boulders and branches materialized from the void, and then disappeared just as quickly into the past. I feathered the handlebars, pulled the brakes and settled back. Each moment brought new awareness, as though a second were all of time. My wheels crossed the splintered wood planks of a bridge, and then rolled onto a wide strip of gravel. The road's downward grade was barely discernible, and I continued to turn pedals mindlessly until the Seaview Cafe came into view.

Carlos was standing outside his camper holding a clipboard. Various mud-caked racers were sitting in lawn chairs, holding cans of beer and cheering. Carlos reached out to shake my gnarled hand and congratulated me for "winning" the women's race in thirteen hours and seventeen minutes.

"Am I the last one?" I asked.

"No, there's still three or four more guys out there," Carlos said. "You did well for your first Soggy. The women's record is twelve and a half hours."

I couldn't conceptualize how there were any riders behind me. I hadn't seen or spoken with anyone on the trail since shortly after I left Cooper Landing at mile thirty-eight. The cloud-saturated sky was becoming an even darker shade of gray; it was 10:30 at night. Time continued to roll forward at the same rate it always had, but the experience felt as though it spanned weeks or months. Why was that? There was this driver, this spark of determination that was so small, and yet capable of moving forward even when my body languished and my mind all but shut down in protest. It was through this tiny driver that I experienced the world in the largest of ways — an expanse of perceptions and emotions drawn in through the beating of my heart.

✳ ✳ ✳ ✳ ✳

Geoff's fifth-place finish in Crow Pass Crossing put him solidly in the top ten of the Alaska Mountain Running Grand Prix. He intended to improve his standing further with the most difficult race of the season — the Matanuska Peak Challenge. The course ascended and descended two technical mountains, and featured nine thousand feet of climbing in just thirteen miles. This race took place only two days before I was scheduled to start work at the Juneau Empire. There was one more race after that, and we agreed that Geoff would finish out the series along with our year-long lease in Homer, then travel to Juneau with our cats once I secured an apartment. Matanuska Peak would be the last I'd see of Geoff for three weeks, and I planned my move so I could be there for him at the finish.

However, thanks to banal delays during my last shift at the Tribune, I arrived at the trailhead in Palmer several minutes after Geoff finished the race. Craig greeted me first and exclaimed that Geoff took second, surprising everybody in the crowd. Behind him, Geoff was sitting on the pavement with his legs splayed and a drunken smile.

"How do you do it?" I stooped down to wrap my arms around him.

"I finished almost twelve minutes behind Harlow," Geoff said. "But I had fun. This course is crazy. It's steeper than anything I've seen, just straight up and straight down the rocks. You'd think there's no way the race goes this way, if it weren't for the course markings."

"It sounds crazy," I said. "You're amazing." I could feel Geoff's heart racing against my chest as I hugged him tighter. It was an electric feeling, like passion coursing through our bodies — shared passion. Even if this was all we had to bind us together, it was enough. Raw and powerful passion emanated from everything around us, and it was more than enough.

Rushing to meet Geoff in time for his afternoon finish meant I was still getting a ridiculously late start for my road trip. I was scheduled to catch a ferry to Juneau at seven the following morning. The ferry departed from Haines, which was seven hundred miles — at best, a fourteen-hour drive — from Palmer. It was after three. Even if I drove through the night, I'd still be cutting my schedule tight to catch my ferry in time.

I gave Geoff one last sweaty hug goodbye and drove my Geo to a gas station on the outskirts of town, where I stocked up on Pepsi to complement the two-pound bag of generic Fruit Loops cereal I'd purchased for sustenance. Only sugar and caffeine were going to get me through this endurance race. I pointed the car up the Glenn Highway, winding through a narrow canyon dominated by the Matanuska Glacier.

The long evening faded into blue twilight as I crossed the border into Canada. Driving to the mountain-guarded panhandle of Southeast Alaska necessitated a roundabout trip through the Yukon and northern British Columbia provinces before I could re-enter the state I left hundreds of miles earlier. In between was a veritable no-man's land, with only one incorporated town — Haines Junction, where I hoped I could find a twenty-four-hour gas pump at three in the morning — and thousands of square miles of boreal forest, craggy mountains, and glacier-fed rivers. I'd thought so of places before, but this was truly the far edge of the world.

Midnight passed under a sky that was deep violet, almost gray. It was August now, and it wouldn't be long before darkness returned, and then even daytime sunlight would sink into the southern horizon, and ice would return. As I looked out over green meadows bursting with fireweed, it was difficult to imagine winter in this place. Life is short but it's also long, at least the way we perceive it sometimes.

Amid the near-night, my headlight beam caught a gleam of something bright, shimmering just above the yellow line on the road. As the car approached, the light focused into two yellow circles — eyes. The owner of the eyes didn't even budge, so I took my foot off the accelerator. As the car rolled to a stop, the animal came into focus — rippling gray fur, triangular ears, bushy tail. It was a wolf. I took my hands off the steering wheel and let the car idle. The wolf continued to stand in the middle of the road, just looking at me. It didn't appear to be the least bit afraid.

After several seconds, the wolf moved to the side of the road and trotted toward my car.

"What's wrong with him?" I wondered. "Is he injured? Do people feed him? Is he looking for a handout?"

The wolf came within ten feet of the passenger's side of the car and approached no further. Instead, it turned around and loped along the highway shoulder. As I inched the car forward, the wolf broke into a run but still didn't leave the road.

For several seconds that seemingly stretched into hours, I kept pace a few dozen feet behind the wolf. Its long legs moved with astonishing grace, and I marveled as my car's speedometer crept up to twenty miles per hour, and then twenty-five. What was this wolf doing? It was such a strange mystery, and yet it also felt like a usual occurrence. "I'm in the Yukon after midnight. Of course there's a wolf running down the road."

The wolf stopped so I did, too. It turned and regarded the car once more, then turned abruptly and darted into the forest. There was no evidence to reveal its reason for departure, so the mystery would never be solved.

"Amazing," I thought. "A lone wolf." Next to my sighting of a phantom that I thought was a wolf during the Susitna 100, it was the first wolf I'd seen in the wild.

I reached for my cell phone to call Geoff, but there was no reception on this highway. Out here I was even more alone than the wolf, because this was his kingdom, not mine.

"Thank you wolf," I said out loud, as though this wolf had been some spirit animal descending on my journey to bestow sage wisdom. I smirked as I said this, because who was I to pretend a lowly human and her superstitions meant anything in the northern wilderness? But even if its meaning was only my own metaphysical yearning, the message was clear: Peace and freedom. The wolf was moving in the direction of Juneau, somewhere south of the snow-capped mountains, where strips of red sunlight still hovered over the horizon, and the future was bright.

About the author

Jill Homer grew up in Salt Lake City, Utah, and graduated from the University of Utah in 2000. She began her career working in community weekly and daily newspapers before moving to Homer, Alaska, in 2005. She never viewed herself as an athlete, but she was looking for a unique challenge, and the esoteric sport of snow biking fit that description. A couple of years worth of (mainly mis-)adventures landed her in the Iditarod Trail Invitational, a 350-mile bicycle race across the frozen wilderness of Alaska, in 2008. The unforgettable experience was the genesis of her first book, *Ghost Trails: Journeys Through A Lifetime*. She continues to balance an unquenchable thirst for adventure with a freelance career in writing and editing at her current location in Los Altos, California.

Other Books by Jill Homer

Jill Homer has an outlandish ambition: a 2,740-mile mountain bike race from Canada to Mexico along the rugged Continental Divide. *Be Brave, Be Strong: A Journey Across the Great Divide* is the story of an adventure driven relentlessly forward as foundations crumble. During her record-breaking ride in the 2009 Tour Divide, Jill battles a torrent of self-doubt, anger, fatigue, bicycle failures, crashes, violent storms, and hopelessness. Each night, she collapses under the effort of this savage way of life. And every morning, she picks up the pieces and strikes out anew in an ongoing journey to discover what lies on the other side of the Divide: astonishing beauty, unconditional kindness, and boundless strength.

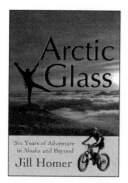

Arctic Glass: Six Years of Adventure in Alaska and Beyond compiles the best essays of "Jill Outside" from the thousands of posts that have appeared on the Web site. The essays chronicle the adventures of an unlikely athlete who takes on harsh challenges in the frozen wilderness of Alaska, the Utah desert, and the Himalayas of Nepal. Endurance racing, overcoming challenges, and self-actualization amid stunning outdoor landscapes are common themes in these vignettes about "The Adventure of Life."

Ghost Trails: Journeys Through a Lifetime is the inspirational journey of an unlikely endurance athlete locked in one of the most difficult wilderness races in the world, the Iditarod Trail Invitational. Through her struggles and discoveries in Alaska's beautiful, forbidding landscape, Jill begins to understand the ultimate destination of her life's trails.

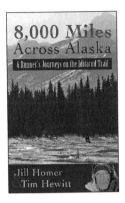

What compels a man to run, walk, and trudge a thousand miles across Alaska? "Because it's there" isn't an adequate explanation. "As a challenge" or "for the adventure of it" are closer, but still too vague. The thousand-mile dog sled race on the Iditarod Trail is often called "The Last Great Race" — but there's another, more obscure race, where participants don't even have the help of dogs. The Iditarod Trail Invitational challenges cyclists, skiers, and runners to complete the distance under their own power and without much outside support. Tim Hewitt is the only person to have completed it more than three times. His actual number? An astonishing eight. Six of those, he won or tied.

"8,000 Miles Across Alaska: A Runner's Journeys on the Iditarod Trail" chronicles Tim Hewitt's adventures across Alaska — the harrowing weather conditions, breathtaking scenery, kindness of strangers, humorous misadventures, humbling setbacks and heroic victories. From fierce competition with his fellow racers, to traveling backward on the trail to ensure the safety of his wife, to battling for his own survival, Tim Hewitt has amassed a lifetime of experiences amid the harsh miles of the Iditarod Trail. This is his story.

Avaiable from Amazon, Barnes & Noble, iTunes and other online retailers.

45615954R00124

Made in the USA
Middletown, DE
09 July 2017